Comfort ye, my people!

MY JOURNEY IN SCIENCE AND LIFE

T. C. Tso

-A Memoir-

Am I remembered in Erin?
I charge you, speak me true
Has my name a sound, a
Meaning
In the scenes my boyhood
Knew?

-Thomas D'Arcy McGee-

左天覺回憶錄

Comfort Ye, My People
My Journey In Science And Life

Contents

Prologue

Comfort Ye, My People
My Journey In Science And Life

My father sent me, a naive boy of 11 without benefit of preparatory schooling, to a Christian elementary school named Trinity. I was in the fifth grade. The schoolmasters issued strict instructions to attend daily morning worship services without fail. Though I understood little of the services, at Christmas I came to love the music of the Messiah. It gave me a sense of peace and security. It does today, almost eight decades later. One morning in sixth grade, I skipped the morning service for last minute study for a final examination scheduled for later in the day. Unfortunately, my absence was duly noted. A teacher discovered me hiding in the washroom, and proceeded to deliver three strikes on my right hand with a ruler before my fellow students. Though the punishment did not hurt a lot, my young pride and soul were badly bruised. At graduation, when that teacher handed my diploma to me, I gathered the courage to tell him that I would never again attend church for the rest of my life. I was so upset that I changed from Christian-sponsored schools to public Chinese schools for my middle school years.

Nevertheless, six years later I enrolled in the University of Nanking, a university with an excellent reputation in agricultural sciences, and sponsorship by the United Christian Board of the United States. The University of Nanking also is a sister university of Cornell University. I was fortunate to share a dormitory room with two students who came from a Christian middle school. One played violin and the other sang beautifully. It was November 1936. Both roommates, members of the university choir, were engaged in intensive choir practices for the Christmas performance of

Handel's Messiah. When they practiced "Comfort Ye, My People" memories of first hearing the stirring music at Trinity School flooded my mind. Suddenly I was inspired with love and forgiveness. From then on I gradually began to attend the worship service at the university chapel.

Another year passed. After narrowly escaping the invading Japanese army in Nanking and suffering hardship during the early part of the war, I arrived with many other refugee students at our wartime campus at the Western Union University in Chengdu. There were five Christian universities on the same campus. The university housed newly arriving students in a big gymnasium. While we awaited the construction of our own dormitory, we refugee students slept, ate, studied, and practiced our music in the gymnasium. At Christmas there was a formal performance of the Messiah with more than a hundred musicians on the stage in tuxedos or long gowns. It was wartime! When the performance opened with "Comfort Ye, My People" I felt tears of joy.

Another eight years passed. I came to Pennsylvania State University as a graduate student, having only a few dollars in his pocket. It was December 1947. In my rented room there was a small radio. When I turned it on, the little radio boomed out the Messiah! Without hesitation, I rushed out and bought a huge, standing RCA radio with record player, and a complete set of the Messiah recording of the London Symphony Orchestra. To this day, whenever I need solace, I listen to "Comfort Ye, My People" to regain peace and inner love.

During my lifetime, most of my contemporaries and I experienced war, peace, hunger, pain, success, defeat, blood, tears, joy, and sorrow in several ways, places, and times. The Chinese people suffered time and again from natural and human-made disasters. My personal story equals only one tiny grain of sand on this great earth. As we look into the world, there is much remaining suffering and need.

Still, I have great faith for the human race that crooked roads will be made straight; that pain will be relieved. There will be no more warfare or inequity. Yes, there will be great comfort for all.

Acknowledgement

Over the past five years, I devoted much time to writing and rewriting this Memoir. The process has been frequently interrupted by other projects; and thus there may be a certain lack of continuity among earlier and later chapters. At times, I was tempted to take the easy way out by giving up this Memoir project. Yet, because of my unusual background, my special experiences, and my long journey, I feel a strong obligation to tell this story. I sense an overriding responsibility to complete this work, to express my feelings and faith in total honesty and frankness. In the end, I hope it may represent a reference to the history of my life and times.

This Memoir covers a period of almost 90 years, and I know that memory and writing ability may at times fail. It is in large measure the continued support and encouragement of my family and friends that brings this Memoir into being.

Words of thanks are far from sufficient to express my deep gratitude toward many friends and experts who guide me, literately hand in hand, through out the whole period of writing, editing, and printing of this Memoir. Two dear friends, Jim Butcher of Maryland and Lin Yu of Florida were of great help in many ways. They did far more than one might expect of good friends, working tirelessly on this Memoir with great patience and expertise and in various ways and in different areas.

Thanks are due to Elizabeth Pennisi, Science writer of AAAS, for her professional guidance; and to Matt Butcher of SiteSafe for technical help.

I wish to express my deep appreciation to Michelle Luijben of the Netherlands for the trying and difficult task of reading the first part of this Memoir and to Beth Adle for expert proof reading and preparation of the final copy.

Finally, I wish to emphasize that this Memoir expresses only my personal feelings at various times and locations during my blessed journey, *including love, hate, fear, anger, tears, hope, and faith, with Comfort and peace.*

Partial funding for this book come from the Institute of International Development and Education in Agricultural and Life Sciences (IDEALS), a philanthropic, nonprofit, organization located in Beltsville, Maryland. The author dedicates this book to IDEALS and directs any donation that may arise from this book to IDEALS and to the Berwyn Baptist Church at College Park, Maryland.

Preface

History—Drop by Drop

History is made by people recording what they have experienced, what happened during a particular period. Scholars encourage people to write about their lives and interpretations. Such chronicles may be worthless at the time of writing, but they accumulate, drop by drop, to shape history.

Many events happened during my lifetime. Some of those drops are fresh in my memory. Big and small, these appear as reflections in my mind's eye:

—The moment a local "guard" using a long sword cut into my lunch bag without saying a word to my grandmother as we walked from one village to another. I was about seven years old.

—The moment as a ten-year-old when I stood in front of my house waving a flag at a passing KMT victory parade celebrating the defeat of warlords.

—My active participation in student demonstrations for two days and two nights against the Japanese occupation of the Custom House in Hankou, and the moment I crossed the Yangtze River to Hankou by ferry in the face of the enemy.

—My joy of hearing the war against Japan had finally begun, the first downing of a Japanese fighter plane.

—My narrow escape from Nanking in the dark of night when the Japanese invaders attacked Nanking.

—The first time I attended a performance of the Messiah. A soloist in coat and tails, accompanied by a five-university symphony orchestra, sang "Comfort Ye, My People" while war raged beyond the campus.

—The first time I saw a B-29 Superfortress bomber and U.S. pilots at an airbase in the mountains of western China.

—The frightful experience of being jobless with little money and no sign of support or affiliation with any school or organization. The war was at a critical stage.

—My total wild joy when hearing from a street loudspeaker that Japan had surrendered and almost being crushed by thousands of celebrating people.

—The moment my ship arrived at San Francisco, and I learned from an announcement that someone was waiting for me on shore.

—The moment when Prof. Richer asked me, "Is here better than home?"

—The moment when I stood 15-feet from a car bearing the expressionless, side-by-side Truman and Eisenhower riding to the Eisenhower presidential inauguration.

—The moment when Kennedy was shot, and running to listen on my car radio with colleague Tom Theis.

—A snowy Saturday afternoon when Ken Keller asked me to drop him on a main street near his College Park home. The road was slippery and I was a new driver, but I insisted on taking him to his door, telling him "this is the Chinese way".

—The moment when Challenger explored. I was in a local bank.

—The moment in Japan when I delivered a keynote address on tobacco as a food source.

—The moment I stepped on Chinese soil after 30 years.

—The fleeting shadow of a person running from my sight after delivering peanuts and millet to my door. This happened during my first trip back to China after 30 years.

—The moment when my aunt, whose husband had been "liquidated", walked into my hotel announcing how good the government was to her and her family, telling me to be thankful.

—The moment when my ship was prepared to depart from Hankou and I saw an old man with bent back and a heavy bag struggle to catch the ship to say good-bye to me. He had been a handsome young Ph.D. from the University of Minnesota 30 years before.

—The early Sunday morning following the Tiananmen Square Massacre, our whole family jointed hands with others in protest at the front door of the Chinese Embassy in Washington.

—After the Tiananmen Square massacre, the moment of a private dinner with six close friends for the departing Chinese Ambassador and his wife.

—The moment when meeting a top leader in China, we greeted by touching fingers instead of shaking hands, furtively looking away rather than at each other.

—The moment I witnessed Xinjiang farmers moving to a new settlement with housing, water, and land.

—The moment when Chinese farmers counted the kinds of taxes and fees they had to pay.

—The moment I chatted with young college students sharing their dreams with me.

The First Thirty Years
1917-1947

at thirty years of age, learn to stand firm.
-Confucius-

Chapter 1

The Heritage

The Lost Generations

China has been in turmoil for the most part of the last one hundred and fifty years. The infamous Opium War with England in 1840 signaled the commencement of a period of foreign invasions that would last through the next hundred years. Throughout these years, the sleeping giant remained dormant while other countries strived for progress and modernization.

I was born in a small rural village in 1917, in the Rain Moon District of Hubei Province in Central China. My father named me Tien-chioh, which meant "heavenly knowledge" in Chinese. I have used the initials T.C. almost throughout my adult life. In my professional capacity, colleagues gave the letters various appropriate meanings. When I was in charge of the tobacco research program, it was for "Tobacco Chief ". Later when I conducted international consulting, they changed it to "Technical Consultant".

I was the first-born son of an eldest son of the Tso family. In the Chinese tradition, I automatically enjoyed many privileges of the first-born son and much love from my grandparents and the extended family on both parental sides. The Chinese are usually proud to have generations live together as one big extended family. The ultimate blessing that one could expect was five generations living together under one roof. To accommodate such a large family, the Chinese housing structure in the traditional manner of the aristocracy was to build compound units (called with many "si-he-yuan"), with each unit possessing four wings with a space of open sky in the center called a "heavenly well". The center space served as either a flower garden or a family gathering and playing area. The master of the family lived in the

18

most prominent unit of the compound, followed in order of rank within the family by relatives domiciled in the side or branched wings. These could be extended indefinitely. Servants lived in the side wings of the service quarters, except for perhaps wet-nurses who would live with their young masters. The wealth of a family could be judged by counting how many "heavenly wells" its compound consisted of.

My father was a victim of his generation and times. He was the eldest son among six brothers and sisters. He was endowed with all the privileges of the first-born son of a wealthy family and accepted all the responsibilities. However, my father was not satisfied with the status quo and struggled to gain a modern education. Shortly after the founding of the Republic in 1911, my father left his hometown and went to the provincial capital, Wuchang, where he enrolled and graduated from the Normal School. He then entered a foreign language college for English studies with the intention of broadening his contacts in the outside world. My father's dreams were shattered when suddenly my grandfather died, and of course, as the eldest son, it was his duty to return home and to take over all of the responsibilities that had rested on his father. My grandfather had been a prosperous landlord with many tenants. He was also the owner of two pawnshops and several other businesses, and was the head of a large extended family. My father's world now was to manage the family holdings and to deal fairly with everyone associated with the big family. Yet such a life was very different from his own dream and ambition. My father suggested to his mother, my grandmother, a devout Buddhist, that each member of the family must receive a modern education and the family responsibilities should be shared. Grandmother had no objection but only wished to be left alone with her worship of Buddha and her personal devotion to her good deeds of providing medicine and free meals to whoever was in need in the neighboring villages and in the small county where they lived.

Time passed slowly and my father became restless. He experimented with raising acres of mulberry trees for silkworms and also with raising thousands of chickens using "modern" methods. At that time, a family usually grew two or three trees and kept five to ten chickens. Few of my father's endeavors were successful, however, partly due to lack of modern technology and mostly due to lack of transportation, marketing and distribution systems. He was far ahead of his times. My father finally made the firm decision that his brothers and sisters should all be independent for their own immediate family but should share responsibility for the extended family. It was not difficult since the extended family continued to live together, mostly due to the fact that my grandmother was still living with them. After much debate among the three brothers (their sisters had no voice on the matter) they arrived at a workable solution. My father would care for the big pawnshops and be responsible for the overall management of the family enterprises; the second son would take care of the family farm and the tenants; and the youngest son would continue his modern education. Daily family affairs were the responsibility of the sisters-in-law under the guidance of my grandmother.

It was 1919 when my father made his move to Xiaogan District, a full day's journey from Rain Moon where our family lived, to manage the large family pawnshop. The business of pawnshops in those days was in fact the business of banking, that was, the banking system accepted in the rural society. The pawnshops served people from all walks of life. This sizeable business was located in a large city for those times. The business compound consisted of 48 "heavenly wells" and was surrounded by a walled lane for the night watchmen to patrol the entire compound every hour, day and night. My father's staff included managers, accountants, clerks, treasurers, bookkeepers, trainees, a chef and kitchen helpers, servants and others, ultimately amounting to more than 50 employees. Within the compound itself, there were guest quarters with beautiful, well-tended flowerbeds, vegetable gardens, and living quarters for all employees. My father soon became a social leader in the Xiaogan community and entertained often, although we in his immediate family remained in Rain Moon. Because he was a lavish host, people gathered in his quarters to play mahjong, which was a classic Chinese game, to celebrate birthdays or other business or social occasions, to attend banquets or small dinners, or perhaps for romantic liaisons. Opium, food, and tea were always available. My father had made his mark! He was extremely popular and in demand as guest as well as host. He was a trusted friend. A word from him could settle a dispute or calm a heated quarrel.

My father usually visited our rural Rain Moon home at least once a month. It was a full day's journey to enjoy a reunion with immediate family, to visit my grandmother, and to attend to the family business that always seemed to be waiting for him. All family resources and family members' monthly incomes were pooled together and had to be turned over, however symbolically, to my grandmother. She then gave the monthly household manager (sisters-in-law in rotation) her "family fund" for that month's food and routine expenditures. She also doled out pocket money to every family member. It was always an occasion when father came home, particularly for me. At that time I was six years old and had already begun schooling by a private tutor. I followed my father closely like a shadow at these times. Father and son had a favorite pastime, which was visiting a cousin next door who was called "Cousin 5". He was a first cousin of my father as they shared the same grandfather. Cousin 5 was in bed all the time, not because of any illness but his opium addiction.

Wealthy families in those days did not care much about their children's higher education. What they did care about was how they could keep their existing wealth in the family and accumulate more. Rich parents even encouraged their children to smoke opium. Smoking opium was a status symbol in that period of China, rich or poor, young or old, thanks to the British Opium War! Opium smokers usually reclined across a huge bed. The smokers usually consumed sweets, fruits, and other delicacies with their opium. Some people smoked opium for social purposes and most became addicted to it, literally unable to function without the drug every two to three hours.

When my father visited Cousin 5, the two of them rested on opposite sides of the huge opium bed facing each other, with the opium tray placed in the middle. This enabled them to recline and talk for hours, catching up on gossip, news and family matters. Meanwhile, I usually stood at the foot of the bed enjoying the sweets and the drone of talk from the elders. I did indeed welcome my father's homecoming, but also was somewhat afraid of him due to his sternness on the issue of my education. I remember having to recite from the assigned textbooks and to demonstrate my Chinese calligraphy. I recall that the consequence for failing to do the assigned homework was three strikes on my hand with a ruler. I was also deprived of visits to Cousin 5 if I was considered scholastically inadequate.

My father's younger brother, the number two son of the big family, was good natured, but it fell to his lot not to receive much modern education. What's more, he had a soft ear to people's suggestions. As he was responsible for the local businesses, on one of my father's visits this uncle requested that he be allowed to expand the smaller rural pawnshop, a venture that could be financed by selling some farmland. But, alas, my father saw this as an unprofitable move - the community was simply too small to support a large pawnshop. The uncle then requested that the big family be split and the family compound be divided up so that each of the three brothers could operate independently. This proposal was unheard of in those days, as my grandmother was still alive and well, and my youngest uncle was at that time at the air force academy. Contrary to the norm and upon much discussion, the three brothers reached a solution with my grandmother's consent. The three would split up! My youngest uncle did not care to have a rural residence, as he was then on active duty and enjoyed his career with the military. My father and uncle, the two older brothers, divided the old compound in two. My grandmother would now enjoy the privilege of being a "most respected guest" in each family's compound in alternate months. The split was a sad occasion for the elder generation, but held high excitement for the youngsters.

I was very fond of my youngest uncle, whom I called Yao-shu (the last uncle). Yaoshu had just completed the air force academy and enjoyed the status of a pioneer in the middle 1920s. It was a glamorous profession and Yaoshu was young and handsome. I followed my young uncle everywhere. Like my father, he would visit Cousin 5's opium den, and I would follow and listen to their stories of a different, exciting world. Yaoshu was single then and young girls in the big city were crazy about him. He described his escapades in some detail without any bashfulness. Yaoshu and Cousin 5 shared their laughter when Yaoshu described the many young students who followed him to his hotel and asked for souvenirs. One enamored young woman even stole his hat as a keepsake.

I was eight years old when the big family divided. There was no public school in the rural area where my family lived. My father was unhappy with the private tutor and decided to bring me to where his business was located to attend a public school. Even at that tender age, I was happy for the opportunity of a better school, but dearly missed my mother's constant attention. My father was busy in his own job and had little time for me. Only rarely did we enjoy a private moment together. Even sharing a fresh peach or washing tired feet together late in the evening were treasured moments to me and remains so even today.

Along the front of the pawnshop compound, there were many street peddlers and small businesses selling candies, fast foods, cigarettes, and other small items. I enjoyed hanging about these stands and watching the procedure of business and trade. Young and innocent, I felt a strong urge to do some good for the panhandlers and other unfortunate in purchasing some cigarettes or food for those who could not afford the little luxuries. But, I reasoned to the merchant, "I don't have any money with which to buy." The stand owner, of course, would counter with, "That's all right. You are the young master. I can wait 'til you have money to pay me, but be kind and give these poor people something." Once commenced, I was trapped into "advancing" more and more for the needy. It reached the point where I no longer dared walk by the stands. Upon this, the traders promptly reported to my father that I had been advancing cigarettes and other merchandise without payment. At first, my father did not believe the story, but finally accepted the truth. He was so angry that he not only punished me severely with ten strikes on my hand, but the paddlers were also banished from the front gate of his business establishment.

During this period in the mid-1920s, China was continuously in the turmoil of wars and social unrest--war amongst warlords, conflicts amongst local bandits and violent criminals--to name just a few. Any sorts of businesses were fair game for coerced "contributions", "donations", "offerings", or "protections", on top of the already heavy fees and taxes. Even daily necessities such as salt and matches were controlled by monopolies of local authorities, or perhaps by bandits armed with rifles and swords. Businesses lost money daily but were ordered to stay open so that authorities could continue to gouge payment for "protection" by armed soldiers.

Such lawless condition affected every business. The entire surrounding rural area was in deep trouble. My father's pawnshop was no different and was approaching bankruptcy. Father decided to temporarily relocate his family to the home of his in-laws in another county, "Wang-jia-Qiao", where it appeared to be safer at these bad times. I was delighted by this move as I was glad to be back in the bosom of my family and was happy to live with the Wangs, my mother's side of the family. I remembered them fondly. Two years before they had celebrated grandfather Wang's 50th birthday. On that occasion, my father as "half-son" (son-in-law) had presented his father-in-law with a huge "bian" to commemorate his birthday. A bian is a rather large wood-based plaque usually about 2.5x6.5 feet in size with golden characters plated on top of black or red lacquer background displaying a message of good wishes, blessing or praising. A plaque was usually hung in a conspicuous place in a front hall entrance. For his in-laws my father had inscribed on the bian, "May the Sun and Moon Shine Together".

The Wang family was large and had been wealthy, but as was the case of many other families of the region, their wealth was gradually diminishing. Grandpa Wang had married three times. His first wife had given him four sons and three daughters. My mother was the eldest child in the family. The elder Wang's first and second wife died of illness. The third wife gave birth to three sons who, of course, were much younger than the seven produced by the first wife.

Grandma Wang, whom I affectionately called "Jia Poo", was not much older than my own mother, and the young uncles were my age. Jia Poo was respected and loved by all of the family, and she, in turn, was totally devoted to the whole family. She was kind, firm, fair and showered love on all of her stepchildren and grandchildren. They were prosperous and respected by friends and neighbors.

Jia Poo treated me with special love and care. I shared with the young uncles all of the privileges they enjoyed and received perhaps even more latitude as a guest relative. The children were given private tutoring and learned the Chinese classics. During winter, on the coldest days, my uncles and I, together with the young cousins next door, enjoyed warm baths, which was a rare and delicious treat. Evening study sessions under the dim oil lamp with one of my uncles, Gippu (Gibbs), who was about my age, were frequently visited by Jia Poo offering goodies to eat or to keep. I was often nostalgic for this happy period of my childhood with my Wang relatives.

In 1926 my father became dissatisfied with the private tutoring the two boys were receiving and suggested they should receive formal educations. Uncle Gippu and I were sent to Wuchang to attend a Christian grade school called Trinity, where we had our first contact with the English language, religion and modern science. At the same time, we continued private tutoring in the Chinese classics on weekends from an old friend of my father. During the winter of 1927 Grandpa Wang passed away and both Uncle Gippu and I were called home. After attending the funeral, Uncle Gippu had to remain at home and I returned to school alone.

The return trip almost cost me my life. In order to avoid the unsafe, slippery roads in the severe winter weather, the Wangs arranged a special cargo boat, a sampan, to take me along the waterway from Wang-Jia-Qiao to Wuchang. The small wooden boat carried a full load of soybeans and white turnips as well. I was the only passenger aboard, sharing the space with one helper and the boat owner. It was supposed to be a three-day journey. At the end of the first day, the weather turned severely cold with heavy snow. For fear of ice damage to the wooden bottom the owner stopped the sampan in a deeper area in the middle of the river. The river soon froze solid, however, and the boat could not be moved an inch. It did not take long for us to start running out of food, fuel and warm dry clothes. We were surviving by eating raw turnips. The major worry was the boat. Should the wood crack, water would reach the soybeans, which would cause the beans to expand, become heavy and sink the whole boat. In the meantime, both sides of my family began a frantic search up and down the river when I failed to show up at school on time. I was too young to do much worrying about my plight, and did indeed turn up at school four days late. But, as all were in agreement, this was the last wooden boat I would be allowed to take.

Despite the tumult of those days, with the family's splitting, relocation and business trouble, the Tso and Wang families were full of life and full of hope. In fact, as we soon would learn, those days were the finest hours of our lost generations.

The Chinese Republic was established in 1911. Except for a very brief period, however, the country was in internal turmoil most of the time afterwards, particularly in the mid-1920s. The central government had no real authority. Warlords, big and small, ruled the divided country by force. They did nothing constructive for the people, though they collected onerous taxes and abundant fees from those obliged to live in the cities. In the countryside some small communities were "protected" by a few hired guns, which subsequently often robbed those who had hired them. Armed bandits, robbers and thieves were everywhere. During 1926 and 1927, tenant farmers joined the anarchy, refusing to pay the landlords, and many rural people moved to nearby towns seeking protection from crime.

Cousin 5, who was dependent on opium and reliant on tenant income, did not dare move because he had little knowledge beyond his rural residence. It was the only home he knew and the only place where he felt comfortable. Without the income from his tenants, however, and with no other means to buy his opium and food for the family, Cousin 5 used his only reserve, a five-ounce gold bar, to trade for the root of his life, opium. Rumors immediately spread that Cousin 5 had a huge reserve of gold bars buried under his opium bed and he soon became the target of local authorities, opium traders and, most unfortunately, armed bandits. One evening three bandits

26

broke into his house, drove the servants away and demanded the gold bars. Cousin 5 said that he had no more, whereupon the bandits threatened to kill him and did indeed bind his hands and feet and beat him. They searched the house for hours but failed to find gold anywhere. Cousin 5's wife gave up all of her jewels, gold, silver and jade to the bandits and knelt to beg for her husband's life.

By now, the bandits, beatings had rendered Cousin 5 half unconscious, but even as he was covered in blood and tears still he cried and begged for opium. The bandits cruelly teased him, letting him smell the opium by placing an opium tray near his nose and then tossing the whole tray to the floor. When Cousin 5 bent to lick the opium off the floor he was beaten to unconsciousness. With no further hope of finding gold bars in the house, the bandits dragged Cousin 5 and his chained wife outside. In his lucid moments Cousin 5 kept crying for opium, infuriating one bandit enough to dump his almost lifeless body head-down into a pit used to store field water and animal and human waste. His body was not found until two days later.

Chapter 2
Japanese Invasion and Scorched Earth

The Ugly Beginning

In 1894, Japan defeated China in naval battles in the Yellow Sea for domination over Korea. This unexpected victory re-enforced Japan's insatiable territorial desire and prompted her longing to conquer the sleeping giant that was China. War between China and Japan by then seemed inevitable, particularly at the conclusion of the Northern Expedition, or China's unification in 1927. Starting in 1931, Japan instigated numerous military skirmishes with the clear intention to provoke a full-scale war.

The Chinese had suffered years of conflict in various civil wars and were ill prepared to fight an external enemy. China wanted to delay the war as long as possible in order to better prepare. Japan wanted to start as soon as possible so as to more easily conquer its large adversary. Common people from both sides were impatient. The Chinese fervently wished to drive out the Japanese or, as they were called, the "little devils". The Japanese were set on beginning their "holy war" to occupy the whole of China, Southeast Asia, and change the Pacific into the "Sea of Japan".

On September 18, 1931, the Japanese armed forces invaded and took over Shenyang, the capital of Liaoning Province. Without an official declaration of war, Japanese soldiers marched through Manchuria (the northeast three provinces of China) killing, burning, raping, and robbing as if they were conquering lords. The massacre of "Lao-Hai-Gou" (the Old Black Ditch) shocked the world. Lao-Hai-Gou was located about 30 miles northeast of the city of Jilin. The ditch was 25 miles long, some two and a half miles wide and filled with water. For five days, the Japanese killed anyone in sight and dumped the bodies into the ditch-old and young, women and men. Sometimes three to five people were chained together with wires through their collarbones and then set on fire while being driven to the ditch. Other times, dozens of people were nailed through their hands to a pole and then pushed into the ditch. By the end of the fifth day, human bodies filled the blood-saturated ditch. The infamous thirty-eighth unit of the Japanese Imperial Kwan Tung Force conducted these crimes. This was the same unit that would conduct the massacre of more than 300,000 innocent Chinese in Nanking only six years later.

On September 30, 1931, Japan conducted its first air raid. It came only twelve days after the Japanese occupation of Shenyang. Twelve Japanese airplanes in a formation of four units raided Jinzhou, in Liaoning Province, bombing schools and killing unarmed people, even after the Chinese government had ordered nonresistance. On January 28, 1932, Japan invaded Shanghai and successfully engaged in a local battle with the Chinese garrison forces. It was designed to test the limits of tolerance of the Chinese government and the will of the Chinese people. It also focused the world's attention on the Japanese occupation of Manchuria. The whole population of China, regardless of provincial or regional affiliation, was awakened by the Japanese aggression. They suddenly realized that once they committed to war, it would be a long and difficult period of great sacrifice, a critical struggle for life or death. There was little doubt of the willingness of the Chinese people to fight and die for their motherland. Yet government proclamations warned the people to swallow their pride and bide their time, waiting until the country was better prepared to fight. Once war was fully upon them, there would be no turning back until final victory was won.

Hatred of Japan welled up in every Chinese heart, and a feeling of superiority swelled equally among the Japanese population. A human conflict of great magnitude was brewing. Sadly, there was not a single statesman at that time that had the clout and foresight to prevent the ensuing tragedy.

Investigations by the League of Nations accomplished little but mild condemnations of the Japanese attack and invasion.

All these and numerous other incidents occurring between 1931 and 1936 made it quite impossible for any red-blooded Chinese student to concentrate on studies. Student demonstrations boiled over onto the streets every few days. Teachers gave priority to lessons in history. Students became well informed about foreign invasions, unequal treaties and forced surrenders of rights dating back to the Opium War in 1840. In the past, England had held the distinction of being foreign enemy number one, followed by Russia then Japan. Once the Japanese invasion began, Japan became China's foremost enemy.

The student movement became furious in 1934 when Japan took over the customs building in Hankou, flying the Rising Sun flag on its tower. Thousands of ferryboat passengers commuting daily between Hankou and Wuchang viewed the invaders' ugly badge of conquest with great indignity. Students from Wuchang, the educational and cultural center of Central China, took to the streets, demonstrating against Japan for days, and actually taking over ferryboats. They wanted to cross the Yangtze River to Hankou to remove the offending flag.

The population in general sympathized and agreed with the students. But it was clear that any attempt to remove the Japanese flag would lead to Chinese bloodshed. The Japanese would certainly shoot to kill anyone involved in such an incident. The Chinese authorities became alarmed and ordered all ferry boats immobilized. But the students would not be denied, nor would they return to their classes. I was one of the group leaders, at that time a second-year student at the Twin Lake Academy high school. For two days and two nights we refused to go home or return to school, shouting anti-Japanese slogans as we paraded the busy streets. The shop owners were with the students, and they provided us food, water and blankets as the cold night approached. On the third day, when there was no sign of weakening among the demonstrators, Education Commissioner Cheng Q.B., who was trained in the United States, requested a conference with our student leaders. Cheng assured us that he too hated the Japanese invasion, but he wanted us to live to fight, not be slaughtered like animals which might well happen if the demonstrations persisted. He asked for our solemn promise that no one would enter the customs building or throw bricks or rocks at the Japanese holdings.

Cheng did extract this promise from us that day. He then proceeded to join the demonstration and led the group on four ferryboats to Hankou, singing patriotic songs and waving Chinese flags.

The customs building was the tallest structure on shore at the ferry dock, and the Rising Sun still flew atop it. When we disembarked in Hankou the students' emotions were suddenly out of control; we burst into sobs, tears and sad cries. Commissioner Cheng immediately took control, commanding the students to join ranks, six to a row, and march hand in hand, much as a military column. He led the parade with the older students carrying flags on either side of the column. We passed the customs building shouting anti-Japanese slogans and swallowing our tears and rage. The Japanese soldiers laughed and jeered at us from the windows of the building and waved more Japanese flags. The moment of this bitter defeat remains etched in my mind and in the minds of others who participated in these demonstrations. Many years later when I met Commissioner Cheng in the United States, we shared our memories of that day and even then could not hold back our tears.

Instead of excitement at my high school graduation in 1936, I felt a deep sense of loss. All of us students questioned what the future could hold-for us and for our motherland.

It was a restless summer. My family resided in Wuchang and my father came home on weekends from his Hankou office. We enjoyed a rare closeness. Mother prepared ginseng soup for father, simmering it over a low heat all night so it would be ready to drink in the early morning. In the evenings we chatted about school, family and national events. My elder sister, Tien Chiang, was more at ease with our father than the rest of us. Occasionally she sat on his lap and teased him with various requests and playfully searched father's pockets. Once she found a baby girl's picture in his wallet. Father told her that it was a picture of a friend's daughter. No one paid much attention to this explanation and the incident was soon forgotten. Father advised me to study agriculture, since the vast majority of the Chinese population were farmers, but I was uncertain. My interest was in literature and mathematics. When the time came for university entrance examinations, I found that the exams were so tightly scheduled that I could take no more than two trials. My choices thus narrowed to literature or agriculture. It was still difficult for me to concentrate on my studies, as the situation between China and Japan grew more intense by the day.

In 1936 I failed my entrance exam for literature, while the famed scholar Hu Shi was teaching, but I passed the test to study agriculture at the University of Nanking. Almost 22 years later, when I met Hu Shi in Taiwan, I told him that I had not qualified to be his student in literature. Hu in turn shared with me his academic jaunt as a horticulture major at Cornell University in the United States. During an examination on the apple, he failed to produce a drawing of the fruit to his complete satisfaction. He became frustrated, ate the apple, and then transferred to study literature at Cornell, in which he received his Ph.D. Returning to China, Hu initiated a new movement to modernize and simplify Chinese writing. His goal was to make written Chinese more like the spoken word, and thus easier to read.

It was November 1936 when I entered the agricultural college of the University of Nanking, commencing in the middle of the school year. Nanking was a stately city, the Chinese capital as early as 229 A.D. In 1936, it was the seat of the Chinese nationalist government. For a country boy like me, attending such a modern Christian college was a considerable transition and required quite a bit of adaptation. Because I arrived during a school year, dormitory space was unavailable. I stayed at a hotel for two weeks before finding a vacancy, which turned out to be in the west wing of the East Dormitory.

Most university textbooks were in English; and most students spoke the language fluently. Many teachers lectured in it. Fortunately, I had received adequate English training beginning at Trinity and had continued English study at the Twin Lakes Academy. Yet this was the first time I came into contact with western music because my two roommates were musically inclined. This was also the first time I felt myself touched and inspired by worship music. The Christmas holiday was nearing and the musicians were rehearsing for a performance of the Messiah. The notes of "Comfort Ye, My People" touched my heart and revived my early fondness for Christianity.

The university was much more expensive than high school. At Twin Lakes Academy, the government had paid for everything. In Nanking I had to pay for everything. One Yuan--about a third of a dollar in 1936--bought seven meal tickets. Nanking was a bustling metropolis and cultural center. The city opened my eyes and broadened my horizons in countless ways. Once I accepted an invitation to join two other students from our native province for a dinner party honoring the graduation of a third student. It was my first introduction to a western dinner and I was unprepared for the social etiquette. The dinner was in a classy restaurant called Fuchang. When a black-tie waiter approached me with the main courses, instead of letting him serve my portion I tried to take the whole serving plate from his hand. Fortunately, one of my friends smoothed over the incident. As time went by, friends taught me proper table manners. That formal dinner cost me five Yuan, almost two weeks worth of meal tickets, but I learned more than one valuable lesson.

Another time, an air force general who was a good friend of my uncle treated me to a premier showing of the film Camille with Greta Garbo and Robert Taylor. The film showed at the grand opening of the Xindu (New Capitol) Theatre-a glorious night to be remembered. The price for box seats was three Yuan, or one American dollar, a princely sum at that time.

The days passed quickly when school was in session. Gradually I became used to the pressure and started to enjoy the academic environment and the company of friends. I planned to have a nice summer vacation at Wuchang with my family. However, the Japanese changed my plans--and indeed all of our lives.

On July 7, 1937, Japan started the war at the Marco Polo Bridge near Peking. An all-out war had begun! The radio flashed the news like lightning through the country. Day after day, newspapers produced "Extras" almost by the hour. Some Chinese set off firecrackers to celebrate the announcement of the first Japanese war casualties. My family was no exception. We were as excited as everyone and welcomed the opportunity to get into real fighting against our archenemy, the Japanese. We mostly ignored government warnings that once war began, it would be a long and hard struggle. China had been buying time to better prepare to fight a war, but Japan had not allowed the build-up to go on indefinitely. In China's favor, the Japanese had apparently underestimated the will and determination of the Chinese people. We were prepared to make any sacrifice in the name of defeating the Japanese.

Well-equipped Japanese soldiers engaged the rag-tag Chinese army. Fighting on the frontlines, the Chinese army demonstrated heroic fighting spirit in several battles. Civilians showed strong support, contributing money, materials, time and services from the rear and sending visitation teams to the front line. Japan soon sensed that victory would not be easy, that it would not bring China quickly to her knees.

On August 13, Japan opened a second front in South China, attacking and landing in areas around Shanghai, Wu-Shoon and Chiabei. Chinese soldiers held firm, using human flesh and incredibly strong wills to stand off the Japanese offenses. The Japanese sent wave after wave of superior firepower to finally establish a beachhead. Large-scale air and navy forces engaged in battle. A young generation of Chinese airmen, trained in Jian-Chio Academy in Hangzhau, demonstrated superior ability when they engaged in the first dogfight with Japanese aircraft. News of their downing three or possibly four Japanese airplanes on August 14 brought every Chinese to ecstasy and tears. The moment had arrived!

My air force uncle was married then and had become a training officer at the air force academy. He was now attached to the command headquarters. Soon they were to move westward, near the inland area of Hankou, where we lived. At that time, my father decided to join the armed forces. Father's friend, General Ting, the garrison commander of Hubei Province, was ordered to deploy his forces as the 197th Division of the National Armed Forces.

General Ting asked my father to enlist with him to manage the division's supplies and logistics. The whole family would have to move to a remote area, well away from the fighting. The plan was that my elder sister and I would stay in our respective schools, and my younger brother would stay with our mother. No one could anticipate what fate the war would bring to each of us.

The war in Shanghai dragged on, month after month. The hope for international intervention faded. Japan's strategy was to attract the best Chinese units to Shanghai in order to destroy them with superior air, land and sea power. The Chinese defended themselves by standing their ground and resolve, eventually driving the Japanese back to the sea.

The fall semester of 1937 approached. Following our family's plan, I prepared to return to school in Nanking, which was not far from Shanghai. Everyone was deeply involved in providing war services to the fighting men and making material sacrifices to support the effort to defeat the Japanese. Soon we learned that the war would demand more.

When I arrived on campus in Nanking, I found it half empty. Most students had chosen to stay home because Nanking was close to the fighting front. Also, many professors as well as students had volunteered for military service or were engaged in war support activities. Japan made little gain after the fierce battles in Shanghai and surroundings. China was persistent, taking advantage of the solid buildings in the city. Our fighters resisted the Japanese inch-by-inch, but at a high cost in life and property. Civilians, particularly students, actually went to the front lines almost daily to visit with combat soldiers and bring them gifts. Their presence comforted the hard fighting men. Even a young Girl Scout managed to make her way to the frontlines carrying a huge Chinese flag. She raised the flag atop an isolated tall building, a little Chinese girl's stronghold in the face of the Japanese attack.

Narrow Escape

After an almost three-month stand off in Shanghai the Japanese realized that the proud Chinese would fight for every inch of their territory. Japan changed its tactics, landing more marines and ground forces around Shanghai and encircling the city in an iron grip. Shanghai became an island, isolated from supplies except those that could be dropped by air. Japan now began marching to the capital city, Nanking.

It was the Chinese government and the university's policy that China's higher education system and its intellectuals must be protected at any cost during the war. Though the fighting would be long and costly, the seed of culture must be preserved for the future. University life thus continued behind the lines of fighting. Universities in war zones began to move to central and southwestern China.

In September of 1937, the University of Nanking discussed, debated and finally decided to move inland, the first move being to Hankou and then on to Chengdu, the provincial capital of Sichuan in the inner southwest. Once the official decision had been made, all of us students and our teachers were left to decide for ourselves whether we would move with the university, stay in Nanking, or return to our respective homes. Most professors, staff and their families, plus more than 200 students joined the big move. A few remained on the campus at Nanking. They were asked to care for the facilities as best they could.

Moving a university proved a most complicated task, especially in wartime. Teaching facilities, delicate instruments and family needs were just a few of the numerous considerations. The university originally chartered a huge merchant ship with adequate capacity for the job, as the whole group would be on board for more than ten days sailing against the stream of the Yangtze River toward the west. However, as the fighting reached closer to Nanking, the government had to move inland. At the last minute, the national defense department conscripted the ship originally chartered for the university. Wounded soldiers and civilians and refugees from the war zone filled the streets. Food and supplies were put under emergency control. All persons not involved in direct combat were ordered to leave town, but we at the university were left without transportation.

The American Embassy in Nanking had also chartered a ship to move its office and personnel. Since Nanking University was a U.S.-sponsored Christian college, the Embassy offered to help, but it could carry only the minimum necessities. Haste was called for too, as the fighting was close. In October explosions and anti-aircraft fire could occasionally be heard. Our escape ship could not risk coming to shore. Thousands of people lined the shores, trying to get aboard any means of transport that could take them safely away from Nanking. The university decided to organize its people into small travel units; each led by a strong young person. I was assigned to handle and care for the luggage. These units boarded an Embassy truck and went to a designated point near but not directly at the Chung-Shan Port at Hsia-Kwan Station. They were then transported by a sampan in total darkness and extremely rough waters to the big ship anchored in the river.

Our movements soon caught the eyes of the refugees. One woman begged our student group to take only her son, "We must preserve our lineage!" Everywhere we tried to move, we were confronted with, "Help us, please!" No one dared accept that responsibility. We weren't even sure of what our own destiny would bring. Some refugees tried at all cost to get into the boats and we had to push them away. Otherwise, the boats would sink taking all of our lives. One professor and his family carried two pieces of luggage, but the boatman, afraid of overloading, said they must leave one piece behind. The professor's wife, carrying her little daughter, pointed to the one to be left. The discarded case held family treasures and clothes; the one she chose to keep contained books and notes belonging to the professor.

The scene of boarding the sampan and cutting through the waves to our ship long remained with us, as fateful moments do. Our group remained motionless and quiet. Not even a child cried. We were taking part in history, but the roles given to us could not be compared to those of our countrymen fighting and dying on the front lines. When the sampan finally reached the ship, we found refugees from other small boats trying to board the ship. A few did succeed by climbing a rope ladder to the bow; and at that juncture, no one aboard had the heart to push them back into the water. We were told that the space reserved for the University of Nanking was the cargo bay in the bottom of the ship. All regular entrances to the bay were blocked; the only access was through a small opening on the side. We finally located the "window" through which people who had arrived earlier were calling to us. We helped each other climb into the cramped compartment. Luggage became meaningless. Survival was uppermost in our minds. The sampan boatman, witnessing what was happening, at the last minute asked if he could board the larger ship. The same professor's wife who'd had to select only one piece of luggage asked him, "How can you come with us? What about your family?" The boatman shook his head sadly and disappeared into the darkness.

There were no lights, no drinking water, no toilet facilities, no air circulation and no food in the cargo bay. In preparation for the journey we crowded together, sharing only a few flashlights and sipping water from a single hot-water bottle. We used a pitcher to carry human waste. I never felt closer to my own family than I did at that moment to this group of hundreds of people. When one elderly gentleman, the father of a faculty member, and a baby fell ill due to the poor ventilation and generally poor conditions, we all reached out to care for them, providing just a little more space where it was desperately needed and sharing whatever meager possessions we had been able to get aboard the ship. After two to three hours of idleness, the ship began to move. Soon after that, two stairways were opened to provide more air circulation and a means of communication to the bay compartment.

The captain obviously understood the dismal situation in the cargo bay, but it was beyond his ability to help. Neither the captain nor the crew could clear the walkway on deck. It was too crowded with refugees to bring water or food to those in need. The captain called on the students to help his crew, and I was among the volunteers moving back and forth carrying supplies to others. One disturbed elderly lady on the walkway complained, "You students, you patriotic students, you are suppose to help others, why are you the only ones eating and drinking?" A passing crew member happened to hear these remarks and he explained to the lady and others, that the students were helping others-they were not eating and drinking they were carrying food and drink to more needy passengers. But the other students and I understood the distress on board, and no one raised a voice after that.

The Yangtze River was full of ships and boats of all sorts because of the war, and traffic on the water was excruciatingly slow. After two days and nights the ship reached the port of Joujiang in Jiangxi Province. The captain gave permission for the university people to buy supplies during the short stop. His order was to return in one hour. Two teams each with four persons were sent to do the shopping. I was on one of the teams. The two teams divided the mission and went out in two directions for quick pickups. Being in a strange area, we four stayed close together and secured a local young man as a guide. Running against time, we picked up fruits, breads, and some ready-made food and candies because there was no way to cook on board. We made it back to the ship with just a few minutes to spare. But the other team was nowhere to be found. Five minutes over the one-hour deadline, the captain ordered the ship's engines started and began to move away from the shore. Two or three minutes later, we spotted the group running toward the ship, but too late. The crew called for them to wait for the next ship and meet the university group in Hankou.

Six days after our nightmare in Nanking, we arrived safely in Hankou. Thankfully, three days after our arrival, the lost team did eventually arrive. Without a local guide they had lost their way in the strange city.

The entire Nanking University group was welcomed and offered shelter in a local Christian high school. We were provided with all necessities, which was indeed heaven after our narrow escape and difficult journey. The university was slated to be moved to Chengdu, in Sichuan Province, which was another 900 miles distance from where we were. Consequently, that semester was suspended to allow people to travel to the new site. The students were nonetheless asked to complete homework assignments. Since Wuchang-Hankou was my hometown, I chose to visit my parents for a few days before continuing to travel west. My family would find me much changed. I had matured almost overnight and my experiences during the harrowing voyage had given me considerably more understanding of human nature. I had learned to control my own feelings in deference to others. I had seen respected professors fight for a small space for survival. I had also seen the selflessness of a professor's wife giving up her own belongings to save her husband's academic books and papers. And I had seen people sharing precious water and giving a last morsel of biscuit to a young child who was feeling ill. All of these had opened my eyes to those around me. The struggle for life, the desire of families to preserve their lineage, complaints and kindliness--all reflected human nature at its worse and its best. But human nature, even at its very best, is not perfect. Only together could we have survived.

It wasn't until I reached my father's office that I found out what had been happening in the outside world while we were on the river. The Japanese had encircled Nanking two days after our departure. Father and the rest of my family had been unable to get news of me for days. They had despaired and almost given up hope of seeing me alive again. Only then did I realize the danger we had been in, and how narrowly we had escaped. Father and I immediately took the ferry to Wuchang to be with my mother and the rest of the family.

What a celebration we had when we arrived! The family could not believe their eyes and their good fortune. The elder son was alive! Mother tried desperately to contain her tears, but finally broke into a flood of joy. Everyone joined in the tears and then laughter of happiness. My father tried to be home at least part of each day for the family reunion. Mother supervised the kitchen maid in preparing each family member's favorite foods. She tried to be brave, but broke down each night. No one knew what would be the eventual outcome of the war or the future of our family.

After resting for a few days, each family member would have to go his or her own separate way. Father would move with the division headquarters; mother would take my younger brother and sister to Yuanxi in Hunan Province where all of the 197th Division families were to be quartered. My elder sister would join her school as it moved to western Hubei's mountainous area; and I would join the University of Nanking, then in Chungking, but eventually headed for Chengdu. We did know that long days of separation were near and inevitable. The uncertainty of the future weighed heavily on us all.

My mother decided to make a short visit to her stepmother Wang before the long journey, and I was to accompany her. We traveled to Wang Jia-chiao. I was looking forward to seeing my beloved grandma, Jia Poo, who had decided to stay behind. Jia Poo, always full of love and wisdom, tried to make our two-day visit a cheerful occasion, although she knew times were hard for everyone. The evening before we all dispersed, Jia Poo asked for my thermal underwear. Due to the lack of indoor heating, it was common in China for people to wear thermal undergarments in cold weather. Jia Poo searched through her jewelry case and took out a gold bracelet, two-to-three ounces in weight. Looking at me, she insisted I take it. "You will say you do not need it, but it is insurance for your good luck," she said, "When you are in need, do not hesitate to exchange it for cash. Remember that you are more important than gold." She then sewed it tightly inside my underwear and patched material over it so it would not show from the outside. My mother and I tearfully watched as Jia Poo did the needlework, stitch by stitch. Indeed the bracelet did in a way save my life, but not until some ten years later. My mother and I returned to Wuchang and joined the rest of the family in preparation for the big move.

As our departure drew near, I went to see Uncle Yaoshu to say goodbye. Yaoshu was now in the Air Force Command and had his office in Hankou on the top floor of a high-rise building overlooking the customs building, where ten years earlier the Japanese flag flew as my fellow students and I demonstrated in protest. When I met him, I told my uncle the story and Yaoshu replied, "We are standing up now, but we have a long and difficult road to travel."

Before we parted on our various ways, my father gathered the family members together and gave us final guidance. I had never seen my father in such a solemn mood, and yet he was also full of love and concern for everyone. Father said that he and our mother would be in Hunan Province if Wuhan fell, which appeared to be inevitable. The remote Yuanxi District in Hunan Province was assigned to the 197th Division personnel and their families. The newly appointed Yuanxi District Commissioner was the elder brother of General Ting, the 197th Division Commander. My mother and younger brother and sister were considered safe there. As for the 197th Division, it would fight the Japanese with guerrilla warfare when the Japanese army entered Wuchang or Hankou. My eldest sister and I would each be given cash to cover expenses for our schooling. Father would continue to provide funds whenever possible. However, if the situation deteriorated, he trusted that our government would take sufficient care of the students.

In the end, Father looked at my eldest sister and me and said, "You have tasted a little bit of war, but the worst is yet to come. I know you both can stand on your own two feet," he continued, and added, as an afterthought, "Yaoshu will move with the air command to the west, and if the situation demands, he will look after you." He further told us that my grandmother would go west with Uncle Yaoshu's family. As father finished plotting our courses, each one of the family tried to be brave and hold back sobs. We all knew it would be a long time before we meet again. Still, never did I imagine that this would be the last time I would see my mother.

The Massacre of Nanking

The massacre of Nanking by the Japanese Imperial 38th Division started on December 13, 1937. Yes, this was the same division that had murdered and burned the citizens of Liaoning in 1931. Enemy soldiers entered the capital city of Nanking as conquerors. The Japanese government gave their armed forces three days of complete freedom to do as they pleased. Those troops were without a measure of discipline. They were heartless and inhumane. The murder, torture, rape and crime of those three days were among the most sadistic and inhuman in the history of armed conflict.

According to published account, at least 369,366 Chinese were massacred in cruelty beyond imagination. This animal-like behavior exposed Japan as a barbaric nation at that time in history. Japan has yet failed to openly accept its full responsibility for the barbaric acts and war crimes committed by its soldiers in Nanking. To say they murdered innocent people does not begin to tell the whole story. They killed in heinous ways in the streets, in offices, in schools, in homes, in beds. They set living people afire; they stabbed wire through their bones and laced them together; they nailed people to wooden posts and drove them through the streets; they raped old and young, women and men, indiscriminately; they cut open pregnant women while the kneeling husband was forced to watch. They forced mothers and sons, fathers and daughters, to commit sexual acts for their perverse and sadistic pleasure. The bodies piled up, blood flooded the streets. This shameful and atrocious scene was witnessed and recorded by several westerners who were unfortunate enough to be in the wrong place at the wrong time. Japanese soldiers also recorded events for posterity and as "victory" memoirs.

This massacre was unknown to the outside world until a few survivors escaped to tell the story. Later, westerners who had stayed behind and witnessed with their own eyes confirmed the atrocities. Again, the world was shocked to learn the outrageous crimes perpetrated on the Chinese people, but little action was taken. There was not even any international condemnation from other countries, including the democracies.

For me, time froze when I heard the news of Nanking. My mind strained to understand what happened to the mother of the child who had begged the group to preserve her "lineage", to the boatman who had turned back to Nanking, to the millions of suffering Chinese inside and near the city.

Such barbaric actions from so-called Imperial Forces were indeed beyond human decency and dignity. How could any "civilized" nation allow such atrocity to happen? How could anyone blame the Chinese people for their hate toward Japan as a nation? Yet, after Japan surrendered at the end of World War II, the Chinese government and its leaders forgave all Japanese payments and debts resulting from the war. This may well demonstrate the meaning of "magnanimity and the spirit of righteousness" between nations. Nevertheless, the ugly scenes from Nanking remained carved deeply in the memories of most Chinese people, including mine.

Retreat West

The University of Nanking moved to Chengdu, the capital of Sichuan Province, in 1937. In November, I traveled from Hankou to Chungking by ship and from Chungking to Chengdu by bus. In Hankou, through the university's liaison office in Chungking, I was fortunate to get a seat on a university chartered bus shuttling faculty and students between Chungking and Chengdu. During the two-day journey we passed trucks with people piled in and hanging off, people lying on top of buses, and people clinging with their bare hands to the sides of moving vehicles. Many refugees lost their lives when they fell or were knocked from vehicles traveling at breakneck speed. Some were bumped off by tree branches or when the vehicle entered a tunnel; some became too weak to hold on any longer; and some were crushed by vehicles scraping one another. Life indeed had become cheap, and the massive retreat seemed endless.

Traveling that route by bus usually took two or three days because of poorly constructed highways zigzagging through the mountains. Making matters worse, the war had forced route changes and vehicle use. There was no longer a normal bus service and the government had taken most vehicles for military use. Trucks, carrying military personnel or on other government businesses, clogged the highways. A few vehicles left for civilian use were likely powered by charcoal because gasoline was next to unavailable for civilians. The Japanese had cut off the supply lines from Chinese coastal regions. "A drop of gasoline is as precious as a drop of blood" was the slogan of the day.

Beginning in November of 1937, students gradually arrived in Chengdu. We settled down on the beautiful campus of West China Union University, which was also a Christian school. Four other universities had taken refuge there as well. It was to become one of China's "centers of excellence" during the war. The war capital by then had also moved inland to Chungking, a city surrounded by mountains in Sichuan Province, on the banks of the Yangtze River. Refugees, government officials and workers, armed forces, all had moved as fast as possible, mostly to the war capital and into Sichuan Province or the provinces of Yunnan, Guizhou and Guangxi.

On the war front, Japan contrived to conquer China in the shortest time possible and positioned their best divisions on several fronts for an all-out attack by land, air and sea. China valiantly tried to preserve some well-equipped divisions to protect the southwestern bases, and fought inch-by-inch on the frontlines. In January of 1938, the Japanese landed at Qingdao in Shandong Province in northern China, and pushed inland while facing strong Chinese resistance. Chinese morale remained high despite heavy casualty. In April 1938, the Chinese won a brilliant battle at Tai-er-zhuang in southern Shandong Province, annihilated three Japanese divisions.

As the Chinese people celebrated that victory, Japan poured in better-equipped and mechanized troops, killing, maiming, burning and bombing indiscriminately along the way. To stop the advancing enemy and to buy time for an orderly withdrawal, the Chinese military broke open the bank of the Yellow River in June 1938. The result was a devastating flood, which nonetheless did slow the movement of the Japanese tanks, trucks, heavy equipment and marching soldiers. But the flood exacted an onerous sacrifice from my fellow Chinese.

In October 1938, Japan took Wuchang and Hankou. They had now reached the heartland of China. The 197th Division in which my father served withdrew to the Da-Bei-shan Mountains to carry on guerrilla warfare in Hubei and Hunan Provinces. As planned, all 197th families were moved to Yuanxi, a remote district in Hunan Province. Now the separation of my family members from each other was complete.

45

It was then that the Chinese government proclaimed the "scorched earth" policy, as the Russians had done in the face of Napoleon's invasion in 1812. This meant destroying everything in the face of advancing Japanese troops so that the enemy could not make use of Chinese resources. This policy resulted in great sacrifice from the common Chinese people who already possessed little beyond the meager lands on which they lived. Great tragedy resulted from this policy as well. In Changsha, the capital of Hunan Province, the whole city was burned to ashes in response to a false alarm that the Japanese were approaching. Hundreds of thousands of people became homeless. The Japanese did conquer Changsha in a matter of months.

As the Japanese tightened their grip on the occupied areas in the north, east and southeast, and pushed toward the remaining Chinese bases of resistance in the southwest, particularly around the war capital of Chungking, China showed no sign of weakening. The dangerous mountain trails now served to the advantage of our defense. The Chinese fighting spirits remained high, though supplies were limited due to the lack of production lines, rail links and air fleets. The Burma Road was yet to be completed.

During 1939, Japanese planes bombed Chungking and its surrounding areas day and night. The onslaught was part of psychological warfare intended to destroy Chinese morale and force us to surrender. Since the city of Chungking was built on rocky mountains, people constructed underground air shelters actually cradled inside the rocks. People ran to shelters on hearing air raid alarms, and immediately returned to work when the sirens sounded the all clear. Knowing this, the Japanese frequently sent in only one or two airplanes, knowing that thousands of people would run to shelters for protection. Tragedy occurred in early 1941 when a prolonged air attack caused people to remain in shelters longer than usual, and the ventilation system malfunctioned. Fighting for breath, frightened people stampeded and rushed for the inward opening shelter doors. The harder people pushed, the less likely were the doors to open. Huge numbers of human beings, estimated in excess of 30,000, died in that horrible incident. Days and weeks were required to identify bodies and clear the site. It was one of the darkest moments during the heroic war against Japan.

On December 7, 1941, Japan attacked Pearl Harbor. The United States consequently declared war against Japan, and the Chinese knew they were no longer fighting alone. We nonetheless did not expect a quick victory. There was still a long and difficult road ahead.

College Life in War and in Sorrow

Even during a bloody war, college experiences remained a memorable and treasured part of people's lives. I was no exception, even though those years were perhaps more poignant for me than for many others. I spent eight years (1937 to 1944) on campus in Chengdu, Sichuan Province. In my first five years, I completed a Bachelor of Science degree. I then spent two years working as a research assistant and devoted my last year to completing my Master of Science degree.

After I first arrived on the campus in November 1937, I joined other students housed in a temporarily converted dormitory that still served as the university gymnasium. Rows of wooden bunk beds served hundreds of refugee students. Often a flying ping-pong ball would awaken someone in bed or end up in someone's food. At first, students were irritable in their cramped quarters, but soon they calmed down and adapted with good spirit. New dormitories were being built and would be available by Christmas. The young men's dormitory compound was located a mile from campus. It consisted of a group of six buildings, each with two stories and each story with eight rooms. In each room, four wooden bunks of double-deck beds, two on either side, provided living quarters for eight students. In the center, a long table served as a desk with side benches. It was a far cry from the facilities we had left in Nanking, but no one complained. Some of the single male teachers lived in similar quarters. Women--both students and some teachers--moved in with their peers at the host university.

After the students moved out, the gymnasium was converted to a music hall just in time for the Christmas performance of the Messiah. There were plenty of musical talents due to five universities being cramped onto one campus. The faculty, both Chinese and Western teachers, tried their best to maintain a normal academic life in the midst of war. Among the vast student population, some were local from Sichuan Province and many others were from the other provinces far away from the combat zone. Most students' families were still in the war zone or enemy occupied territories.

In only a year's time, I had lost all contacts from my family. In cases like mine, the government assumed school and education expenses in the name of war relief so that the students could continue their studies. Some people criticized the government for placing the students in an isolated environment, or "greenhouse", away from the war. But the fact was that no student could ever be completely isolated from this terrible war.

In 1938, the air command moved to a remote area near Chengdu. Uncle Yaoshu and his family plus my grandmother, also moved into a newly constructed rural house. Yaoshu had apparently attained a high-ranking position and was seldom at home since the war was very intense. My old grandmother remained devoted to Buddhism and had become a total vegetarian. She prayed constantly for my father and our family and for her second son in Rain Moon. I often made a special effort to visit her and Yaoshu's family. She was always a loving grandma, concerned about my well-being and my schooling. Her fond wish was that I would convert to the Buddhist faith for the sake of my parents. However, religious faith at that time was far from my mind.

In the summer of 1939, the Chinese government granted six special tobacco scholarships that would provide total support for the students selected. Tobacco was an important source of tax revenue in China, yet most of the Chinese tobacco industry was in the hands of foreign companies. In urgent need of financial support, I applied and was granted one of the six scholarships. This would have a profound impact on my professional career later.

A young professor, Dr. Tang, had recently returned from Cornell University and was placed in charge of the tobacco research program. His wife, Mrs. Tang, was a beautiful young American lady. The newlyweds, having completed their education in the United States in 1938, joined hands to teach in war-torn China. Professor Tang taught genetics and Mrs. Tang taught English. They were well liked and respected. I visited their residence in the evenings to discuss my research plans with the professor while Mrs. Tang attended to their infant son in the soft glow of candlelight. At the time, I organized a vocal recital by Mrs. Louis Kwan, a famous Chinese soprano, for the benefit of families of air force war martyrs. Both the professor and Mrs. Tang were sponsors and whole-hearted supporters of the event.

In the summer of 1940, tragedy struck the young couple. Professor Tang was vacationing with a group of Western professors in the Xichang area and exploring virgin forests and wild rivers. On the Dadu River their log raft broke up. The Westerners were strong swimmers and survived. But Professor Tang was swallowed by the raging waves. When the sad news reached campus, Mrs. Tang was so shocked that she lost consciousness for days and then refused to see anyone or eat anything. Not long after, she took her infant son and returned to the United States. My heart broke for the young family.

Soon after that awful accident, I received word that my mother had died in Yuanxi in Hunan Province. Yuanxi was so far from the unoccupied territories and there had been no news on the whereabouts of the 197th Division or of my father for some time. My mother had carried the family burden alone at wartime in many respects. Worry over her husband, her younger children, her far-away daughter and son had been too much for her! She died with only a young son, two young daughters and a remote cousin by her side. A thousand miles separated Sichuan and Hunan, and it was more than a month before the news finally reached me. I cried for hours. My friends arranged to take me to my Uncle Yaoshu's house, where my grandmother lived. I stayed there for three days, nursing my feeling of loss and deep sorrow.

Not long after, my beloved grandmother also passed away. She left instructions that she should be cremated, as were all good Buddhists. Yaoshu decided to keep her ashes in a Buddhist temple and hoped to take them home to Rain Moon district for final burial after the war. Yaoshu always felt that my grandmother was a family blessing; that she brought good fortune wherever she went. She had been staying with Yaoshu in these past few years, and it happened that this period was the best for his career.

My eight years at the University of Nanking shaped my character and prepared me for my professional career. In my first year in Nanking and seven subsequent years in Chengdu, I earned my bachelor's and master's degrees, conducted research projects, and fulfilled my duties for my teaching assistantships. On campus, I was known for my organizational skills and leadership as I led various academic and social groups. However, separation, tragedy, death and the horrors of war overshadowed everything I did. I perhaps became a more serious and understanding person than I otherwise would have; I became a person well in control of feelings and emotions. But it was only with great difficulty that I could suppress my hatred of Japan as a nation. Time, however, is indeed the healer of all wounds. In later years, I had many good friends who were Japanese.

After University

My eldest sister had graduated from her school, which had relocated to the western mountainous area of Hubei Province. She then joined the National Energy Resources Commission at a factory that manufactured fuel alcohol in Janyang, in Sichuan Province. She served in an administrative capacity and worked with other university graduates, some of whom were chemists and engineers. There she fell in love with Chang, a bright chemical engineer. She asked Uncle Yaoshu's blessing for marriage, as our father was far away. Yaoshu was glad to grant his permission, but he was too busy to get away from the Air Command Headquarters to attend the wedding. So I represented the family at my eldest sister's wedding. Life moved on despite the war.

Two years later, my sister and her husband with their newborn son visited Uncle Yaoshu's family in Chengdu. That occasion was the only time that could be considered a family reunion during the entire war.

Under the constraints of war, university administrators and professors tried to make us refugee students feel at home; their charitable effort succeeded. Students drew close together, emulating brother and sister relationships. The student turnover rate was low, and there was a deep feeling of sharing among us. We students were in a sense war victims, needing each other more than fellow students would in peaceful times. More than five hundred of us lived in the University of Nanking's small dormitory compound, and we knew and understood each other as if we had lived together for a lifetime. We knew about each other's families and where everyone came from, and we cared for one another. A group of mice being found nesting in someone's bedcovers; a young man receiving a love letter from a girl friend; someone whose clothes had not been washed for weeks and the lucky chap who received a tin of candy from relatives--we shared these bits of information and gossip with interest and in good spirit. Whenever there was sorrowful news, we rushed to provide comfort and support. Although all of us were poor, it was common to find friends sharing whatever little cash was available.

Among my many friends, some had graduated earlier and stayed on as teaching aides or joined the research faculty. Others had entered the university later than I and were slightly younger than I was. The whole campus, being inhabited by five different universities from various regions and backgrounds, provided vast opportunities for broad contacts professionally and socially. In 1942, Yenching University reopened its doors in Chengdu, and its students joined the others attending classes, making life on campus even more active. For those who had time to participate, there was music, sports, cultural activities, religious services, academic and alumni meetings, native provincial associations and other gatherings, both within and between university boundaries.

Yet my university years would soon be over. As the spring of 1944 approached, I completed my required courses and master's degree thesis months before the official summer session. Due to the untimely death of

Professor Tang, the university had scrapped its tobacco research program. Thus my hopes for a research position at the university were dashed. I needed to earn some money and to find a way to support myself while looking for a professorial position. At the time, the Americans had gradually built up airbases in Sichuan for attacking Japanese occupied areas in China or even Japan's home islands. This offered me an opportunity to join the War Area Service Corps (WASC). I was assigned a six-month duty as a hostel chief, in charge of Air Base A5, which was located in Qion-Lai, a mountainous area southwest of Chengdu. Two of the six months I was assigned to the WASC headquarters which was near my campus. I held a rank comparable to a major in the Chinese army. My U.S. counterpart was a Major Carr, a North Carolina native who had come out of retirement to fight the Japanese. A span of about 30 years separated our ages, in addition to differences in background and culture. Yet we worked side by side in complete harmony. Our objectives were the same--to aid the air force in defeating and pushing Japan out of China.

Air Base A5 was essentially an intermediate stop for American B-29 Superfortress bombers. Planes came in from airbases in India over the Himalayas, "the hump", for refueling and crew rest. I will never forget the first time I saw a B-29 landing; it was a wow-inspiring moment. The aircraft was so enormous that large trucks could pass under its wings! I gradually grew accustomed to the planes and their overpowering size, to the noise and the bustle, and I became friends with many American airmen.

I recall meeting a pilot, a colonel, though he appeared to be only about 20 years of age. Fresh eggs were the main interest of this pilot and his fellow officers, and a request for eggs was what I most often heard from them. There was obviously a great shortage of fresh eggs in India, and the pilots and their crews were tired of dry egg powder. I made every effort to honor their requests, often supplying eggs for their return flight to India. Major Carr took a dim view of this because our base had become busier with each passing day and shortages of many supplies, including eggs, were beginning to become a problem.

There was no normal housing at the airbase hostel, only tents on ten-feet square concrete platforms. However, there were shower facilities and excellent kitchens and dining rooms. These were considered luxurious in wartime and were extremely rare. Chinese operators at the hostel felt that a good meal and a good night's rest was the least we could provide for the American pilots and fighters.

During my four-month service at the airbase, many bombers failed to return to the base. I learned to avoid saying goodbye and to put on a casual air when the crews were preparing to leave for a new mission. Occasionally, the men gave me trinkets or personal items to remember them by as they chatted over a meal or showed me photographs of their families. War was the cruelest equalizer of men, no matter where they came from. The announcement that the young colonel was missing in action was etched deeply in my memory and lingers on even today, after 50 odd years. A regret that I will carry on with me forever was that I failed to get his full name and home address so that I could visit his family.

By the end of summer of 1944, the air war had moved consistently farther into Japan's home bases. With the opening of airbases in Mariana Islands and Guam, which were closer to Japan, the Qion-Lai operation became less essential, and was eventually closed down. Upon completion of my assignment with WASC, I returned to the Chengdu campus, completed my official university obligations and attended the graduation commencement for my master's degree. I was eager to move on to a new stage of my life.

It was hard for me to say goodbye to many dear friends and teachers. They had been my family and an important part of my life. Together we shared joy and pain. I attended many small and some elaborate farewell gatherings in my honor similar to the ones I had sponsored in the past for others graduating before me. But this graduation was different. I could hardly fight back tears on several occasions before my departure from Chengdu. I was headed for Chungking, China's war capital.

Chapter 3
My Other Half—What Price Freedom?

*Yu Yi (Margaret's) Daring Journey from the
Mouth of the Yellow River to the Free West*

It was late July, 1944. Not in my wildest imagination did I dare dream that a young lady, Lu Yu Yi, with whom I would share my life and fate, had also been on Chengdu's campus since March. But it was our destiny that two years later our paths would eventually cross and never separate again.

Although Lu Yu Yi and I lived through the same war, we each had quite different experiences. To begin with, her grandfather was a government official with the responsibility of taming the Yellow River.

To Tame the Yellow River

The Yellow River was considered the Cradle of the Chinese Civilization in the same way the Nile was to the ancient Egyptians. It is second only to the Yangtze River, China's longest waterway. The Yangtze River originates on the Tibetan Plateau and travels 3,200 miles through central China to the Eastern China Sea. The Yellow River, or "Huang Ho", leaves the Qinghai-Tibetan Plateau and flows 2,700 miles in a great loop through the Ordos Desert (Mu Us Shamo) then eastward into the Bo Hai Gulf. The Qinling Mountains form the watershed between the Yellow and the Yangtze rivers.

The Yellow River has also been known historically as the Sorrow of

China. Throughout the Chinese history, there is a love and hate relationship between the Chinese people and the Yellow River. In the upstream, the river passes through a region known as the "Yellow Earth Plateau", where the soil is porous and easily eroded. More than five thousand years of deforestation has sped the erosion process. Upstream of this region, the water of the Yellow River is clear. Downstream of this region, the water is rough, yellow and muddy because it carries a great amount of eroded soil away from the Yellow Earth Plateau. The high rate of sedimentation in the riverbed builds a rising water level, resulting in the Chinese historical effort to re-enforce and raise dykes to contain the rising water. In many sections of the Yellow River, the riverbed became as much as 33 feet higher than the level of surrounding cities and towns. Every few years, great calamities occurred when dykes broke down, causing the river to flood and change course.

Throughout Chinese history, a few rulers looked for ways to tame the Yellow River, often meeting with considerable success. However, war and social unrest contributed to the deterioration of the River and led the general public to believe that fate had dictated it to remain the Sorrow of China. Old tales even suggested that the whims of the water are in the hands of the Dragon King. River management officials could only pray or present sacrifices to the Dragon to control and calm the raging waters.

Although taming the Yellow River requires primarily reforestation and soil conservation at the river's origin and the Yellow Earth Plateau upstream, each dynasty or government in China's long history stationed high officials at key dyke points along the river's course. Rulers held them responsible for controlling the water level in times of emergency. This approach helped to ease the symptoms somewhat, but it would not cure the root cause.

In the early 1910s, just after the founding of the Republic of China, Lu Gee Ting, my future wife's grandfather, became the Yellow River Commissioner, the highest official for the Yellow River. Although Lu Gee Ting was a native of Jiangsu, it was customary for high officers to take their whole family to their assigned official post, which for him was Kaifen, in Henan Province. Lu Gee Ting held this important position for many years.

He was fortunate that no major dyke outbreak occurred during his tenure, and his diligence and ability were respected and admired. However, fate was not as kind to his immediate family.

At that time, Chinese men who were high officials and wealthy usually had one "official wife" (da-tai-tai). She was in charge of the household and enjoyed all of the official privileges and honors. High officials at the same time had as many concubines (yi-tai-tai) as they desired. In Lu's case, his first wife died at a young age, and he remarried. His second wife also died young without bearing children, and he married a third wife. It was the third wife who in 1895 gave birth to a son, Lu Dai-sheng, who would become Yu Yi's father.

Soon after his birth, his mother also died. Lu Gee Ting (Yu Yi's grandfather) decided not to marry again, but instead took six or seven concubines. The youngest concubine was 20 years old when he was 60. It was considered fair of him that he asked the young girls' consent before taking them to be his concubines. Some did refuse because of his age and also because society looked down on concubines. However, most girls he asked did agree because of his position and wealth.

Wealthy families had many servants, men and women, old and young. Some were hired, but most were young girls purchased from poor parents. Thus, from a young age, the young girls belonged to the household and became, in effect, part of the extended family, keeping company and waiting on the young masters and mistresses. The fate of those maids was completely in the hands of the housemaster. Young servants could be selected and even forced to become concubines, or be given as a "gift" to friends or relatives. Or, the master might treat a maid as one of his own daughters and find a good young man to marry her to.

In one case, Mr. Lu was interested in a young maid to become his concubine but gave her the choice. When she agreed to stay instead of following a friend's example and marrying a poor rickshaw boy her own age, Mr. Lu gladly kept her as his concubine.

Lu Dai-sheng, Yu Yi's father, eldest son of Lu Gee Ting and his only son born to a wife, thus grew up without a mother. He was well cared for by his father materially and academically, but not spiritually. He was talented and studied law. At age 17, by family arrangement, Lu Dai-sheng married a 16-years old young lady named Jiang Lin Yi. She became Yu Yi's mother. Jiang, was beautiful and very intelligent, physically tiny, and mentally a giant. Even at her young age, she soon won her father-in-law's respect and became the mistress of the big family. She soon took charge of the entire household. Her duties thus not only included routine household management, but also the care of several other concubines and the children born to them. Such children held lower status in the big family, but shared the same father, that is, Lu Dai-sheng.

Yellow River Commissioner was a prominent and busy position. Lu Gee Ting had little time for his son. Dai-sheng was handsome, bright and understandably spoiled. True to the lifestyle of a prominent official family, Lu Dai-sheng, a playboy and excellent horseman, frequently visited prostitutes and gambled heavily despite having a nice family and a beautiful young wife at home.

Within six years, Jiang Lin Yi bore three children. Yu Yi was the youngest child. Sister Shao Yi was five years older and brother Jia Yu was 18 months older than Yu Yi. Their mother could do nothing but tolerate her husband's behavior, as it was the custom for a good wife to simply obey. She did try to limit his spending. He died of cholera in 1923 at the young age of 28. A 27-year-old wife and three children between the ages of three and nine, plus his father and other members of the extended family survived him.

The elder Lu Gee Ting outlived his son by four years, dying in 1927 at the age of 65. At the time of his death, the family had settled in Jinan, in Shandong Province. The physical location of the Yellow River Commission office shifted frequently, following the vagaries of the water's power. Lu Gee Ting's tenure began in Henan Province then moved to Hebei Province, finally settling in Shandong, the home province of the ancient Chinese philosopher and educator Confucius.

After the passing of Dai-sheng and Gee Ting, the difficult task of managing the large Lu family fell upon the slim shoulders of the young mistress Lin Yi. Her family now comprised three children of her own, two concubines and three stepbrothers born to the concubines. The eldest son of the concubines, Yu Yi's second uncle within the big family, became a good friend to her mother. She cared for him, helping him to treat his opium habit and his alcoholism. Yu Yi's mother had stepbrothers-in-law who were younger than her own children, one four years younger and another six years younger. Jiang Lin Yi never remarried and devoted her life and heart to her children and the extended family instead.

A Mother's Love and 100 Day Oasis

Old China was patriarchal, like most old societies. An old saying on women's talent went like this: "Woman without talent means good virtue." On obedience to men: "Obey before marriage your father; after marriage your husband; upon the death of husband your son." Educational opportunity was seldom available to women. Yet Jiang Lin Yi's intelligence was obvious. She was evidently educated and possessed rare and progressive qualities well ahead of her time. She dared liberate herself from the then fashionable bound feet, and treated concubines and their sons as her equals. "My mother showed love and care, intelligence, determination, courage and wisdom in everything she did," Yu Yi would write years later. Lin Yi insisted on an education for all family members, including girls, and not just for her children. Her only recreation was reading and writing. She often recited poetry at her young daughter's bedside.

Yu Yi was seven years old when her grandfather died. Soon after, instead of hiring a private tutor to teach only Chinese, her mother sent all of the children to a nearby school, which happened to be one sponsored by a Baptist Church. The children thus received a better, more balanced education at a considerable savings to the family budget. Foreign religious missions supported elementary schools, middle schools and universities. Most of the teachers were devout Christians. Missions established similar schools in all of the larger Chinese cities. In Jinan, the capital of Shandong Province, Chee-loo University was a well-known Christian school supported by the Baptist Mission of the United States. The Cong-Dai Elementary School in Jinan, where the Lu children attended, was a mission-sponsored school. Aside from teaching reading, writing and mathematics, the school introduced the children to Bible studies, church services and Christmas.

Yu Yi's mother's determination to send the Lu children to a missionary school was revolutionary at that time, or at best uncommon. It was against the Chinese tradition and angered the Lu clan. They felt strongly that the young girls, Shao Yi and Yu Yi, who were twelve and seven respectively, should not attend a school mixed with other children who were considered wild and "lowly" in status. However, their mother insisted on her own way and ignored cruel criticisms. Without her determination, the future for Yu Yi, her sister and her brother would certainly have been considerably different. As the youngest child and with poor health during her youth, Yu Yi received special attention from her mother, and their relationship was close indeed. At her bedside, the mother tirelessly taught Yu Yi delicate Chinese paper cutting and read her poems.

While other family members appeared to gradually lose interest in school, the three children attended school together. Shao Yi was fond of Chinese literature and did good writing. Jia Yu was talented in mathematics. Their homework was frequently displayed on the school display board. Yu Yi, naturally shy, always seemed to be the teacher's pet. Despite being younger than fellow students, Yu Yi did well in her grade. In fourth grade, she was blessed with a good teacher, Mr. Chen, who became a family friend and almost a guardian to Yu Yi in later years. When teacher Chen married, Yu Yi's older sister, Shao Yi, served as bridesmaid. In junior and senior high school, Yu Yi was voted to represent her class in public speaking competition. At high school graduation, she again was chosen to represent her class. She prepared carefully for these occasions, often seeking advice and coaching from upper classmates and teachers.

After taking a competitive entrance examination and with their mother's blessing, in 1936 all three children enrolled in the Shandong Provincial Medical School. Shao Yi, five years older than Yu Yi, was placed one class ahead of her. Brother Jai Yu was a year and half older, but he and Yu Yi were placed in the same class. Because of Yu Yi's good penmanship, the anatomy professor asked her to help with handwriting at the medical college. She wrote, not in English but in German, the name of every muscle, blood vessel and nerve for the professor's instruction to the class.

In those days, Yu Yi's mother frequently attended Chinese Bible class in Jinan led by an American woman from Memphis, Tennessee, whose husband, Dr. Randolph Shields, was the dean of the Medical College of Chee-loo University. Yu Yi's mother soon won Mrs. Shields' respect and they became good friends.

In 1937, when Japan invaded the heartland of China, Shandong citizens suffered greatly from random bombings by the Japanese. The big Lu family could no longer hold itself together. They decided to divide the family property into three parts, in accordance with the last will and testament of Lu Gee Ting: one part to the second son and his family of seven children; another part to Lu Gee Ting's living concubine and his third and fourth sons, and third part to Yu Yi's mother and her three children. From then on, each of the three family groups went their separate way in managing their own properties and educating their young. Yu Yi's mother was always available to provide a helping hand or advice when she was needed.

As the Japanese forces approached Jinan, the Shandong provincial government with all provincial institutions of higher education, including the Shandoing Provincial Medical School, decided to withdraw into inner China, Yu Yi's family faced a difficult decision. Yu Yi's mother had tuberculosis and was physically frail, but her will was strong, as were her mental capacities. "I have three children," she said, "Two of them I will contribute to my country and the little one (Yu Yi) I will keep at my side." When Shao Yi and Jia Yu jumped into a big army truck with other departing Shandong Medical School students, Yu Yi swallowed her tears and sorrow.

Each of the four members of the family said goodbye in total silence. Yu Yi had the sad feeling that it might be the last time that her mother would see her two elder children.

Shandong Medical School moved from northeast China to deep southwest Guizhou Province, finally uniting there with the Guiyang Medical College. Yu Yi was left behind with her mother. Because her school had left Shandong Province, Yu Yi entered the nursing school of Chee-loo University in Jinan. Japanese language was among the many courses she took there. Her teacher, Mr. Yu, was a graduate of the Imperial University of Tokyo.

In 1938, the Japanese occupied Jinan, and ruled Shandong through a puppet government, of which Yu became the number two man. Yu asked Yu Yi to be his six-year-old daughter's private tutor. Besides being a traitor, Yu did not fare favorably among his neighbors, including Mrs. Shields, who disapproved of his everyday behavior. For one thing, Mr. Yu was impatient and volatile. When returning home late at night, he would kick at the front door when his sleeping wife, tired from caring for their young daughter, was a bit slow in answering the door. The whereabouts of Yu after the Japanese defeat is not certain.

During the Japanese occupation, Yu Yi attended nursing school for almost three years. Unfortunately, her mother's health gradually deteriorated. She worried in silence about her other two children, while being cared for by her youngest daughter each day. Yu Yi often heard her mother calling out her brother's name in her sleep. She died of tuberculosis in 1941, longing for the two children who were far away. Although they shared a deep faith in God and were spiritually prepared for death, the loss nonetheless instilled a deep sadness in Yu Yi. Like many children during these difficult years of war, she grew stronger and became mature beyond her years.

Yu Yi managed her mother's funeral, bought the best coffin she could afford, and buried her with deep sorrow. Little did Yu Yi know that because of its high value, 50 years later the Lu clan would steal this "best coffin" and trade it for cash. Her mother's remains were thrown away. Although there was no inquiry or investigation into this ugly act of indecency, it did reflect the moral standard of the time. Yu Yi harbored no ill feelings over what happened. Upon hearing the news, she wrote to her sister, Shao Yi, "Mother was great, she is in heaven. She will be happy to see that her coffin can help others in need."

After her mother's passing, Yu Yi knew she must not be sorry for herself. Determined to move on, she studied day and night for two months for the college entrance examination. She reviewed her high school Chinese, English, chemistry, physics, mathematics, history and geography. She hired a teacher to tutor her in mathematics. It was a difficult and extremely tense period. Time was limited and she had to make the most of it. Yu Yi took the entrance examination in July 1941. In August she received her letter of admission from Yenching University in Peking. It was her happiest moment since her mother's death.

Yenching University was a Christian university supported by the United Christian Board of the United States. Despite the Japanese having occupied Peking since 1938, Yenching University had declared itself an U.S. property and managed to maintain itself as "free" from the Japanese intervention. The Americans had yet to enter the war. President Leighton Stuart of Yenching stood firm in defense of his "American" University. It was in the fall of 1941 when Yu Yi joined her classmates in Yenching.

Yu Yi began to enjoy her friendships at Yenching and studied hard. However, her respite from war came to a sudden end on the morning of December 7, 1941. Exactly 100 days had passed since her arrival at the school when the Japanese attacked Pearl Harbor and the Pacific war against the U.S. began. The following day, Japanese military police surrounded Yenching University. That afternoon the military police, with their Chinese agents and traitors, entered the university compound. They took out a black list and called students one by one. Students whose names were called were ordered to line up, seven to eight in a row, in front of the shining bayonets of the Japanese. Afterwards, the blacklisted students were ordered into several army trucks. Those students were never seen again--how many were taken, what happened to them, nobody knew.

The remaining students faced an uncertain fate. They waited with apprehension. The next afternoon, December 9, the remaining students were ordered to gather with all their belongings at the university entrance, the very spot where higher-class students had welcomed Yu Yi as a freshman only some three months earlier.

The atmosphere was tense, and the students seemed unable to breathe in the presence of the Japanese military police with guns and bayonets. An hour ticked slowly by. Finally, Japanese soldiers began to "inspect" each student's belongings. When they stopped in front of a student, the student was obliged to immediately and obediently open everything for inspection. The students were to wait humbly while their possessions were turned inside out. Finally, a soldier stopped before a student who was so frightened that he failed to open everything immediately. The angered soldier raised his right hand to strike the student, who instinctively raised his arm to prevent the blow. This made the soldier angrier, like a wild animal, he shouted loudly, reached for his pistol and was ready to shoot. Another Japanese police agent strode toward the twosome and they took turns repeatedly slapping the student's face, left and right, right and left until the student's legs could no longer support him. The group was stunned. Nobody dared to make a sound to protest. Clearly, human life meant nothing to the Imperial Army. They would shoot to kill, one or all, on any pretense. The "inspection" seemed to take years rather than hours.

Finally, the "inspection" was over and the students were ordered to leave the campus immediately. Yu Yi and her classmates, without any means of transportation, walked step by step from Hai-Dien toward downtown Peking, a distance of almost 20 kilometers. They carried their own luggage and books in the darkness of the night. When a young man helped Yu Yi to carry her suitcase, a Japanese soldier slapped him in the face without giving a reason.

No words were exchanged among the students during their long march to the city. They found lodgings for the night, and the next day they departed on their separate ways. Their hearts shared a common resolve: this debt will be paid!

Yu Yi returned to Jinan by train, and made up her mind to continue her studies. But where would she study? Jinan was under Japanese occupation. One day Yu Yi was walking down a street. Japanese soldiers called their dogs to knock her to the ground while Chinese bystanders watched helplessly. The soldiers soon grew tired of their fun and called off the dogs, whereupon Yu Yi fearfully stood up and walked to her lonely home. She knew she could not stay in Jinan. Her American friends and the missionaries from the medical school were all under house arrest. Yu Yi did manage to visit briefly with Mrs. Shields, her mother's dear friend whom Yu Yi called Auntie Ella.

Escape to Freedom

Knowing that Yu Yi had been a student at an American university, the Japanese in Jinan watched her closely, finally seeming to decide to arrest her. Her mother was dead, her brother and sister were far away, and the Shields were under house arrest. Her old teacher Mr. Chen was the one contact Yu Yi had left. She was sad with despair, depressed with fear, but she had to play cat and mouse games with the Japanese. Japanese soldiers, with loaded guns and bayonets, searched her house several times but failed to capture her. She hid at Mr. Chen's house for a few days, but feared for the Chens if she was found there. Even sunshine and fresh air were no longer hers. She had to leave Jinan to seek freedom and an education.

It was at that time that she learned that a university using Peking University's name, and using Yenching University's campus had been established under the Japanese controlled Northern China puppet government. Yu Yi decided to try returning to the university, as anywhere would be better than staying in Jinan. She arrived in Peking again in 1942. Now run by the Imperial Forces of Japan, the campus was a shadow of its former beauty and vitality. Japanese teachers taught classes through interpreters. Yu Yi sensed this was not the place for her either, and she knew in her heart that many students felt the same way, though nobody dared share feelings openly.

When news spread about the planned re-opening of the real Yenching University in the Free China of the southwest, Yu Yi's mind began to form a plan. Many of the former Yenching students were also attending "Peking University" in 1942. Among them was Sun Rong-zhen, who like Yu Yi was from Shangdong Province. They began to communicate. At last they found four trusted friends with a common desire, and they decided to escape together from the Japanese occupation, and to seek freedom and education in Free China. The women students were Lu Yu Yi and Liu Wong-rong; the two male students were Sun Rong-zhen and Liu Hon-shen. The next step was to decide how and when to start their journey to freedom. Once their minds were made up, they became calm and alert. No plan would be fail-safe. They had to rely on faith.

Several routes were known to lead to free areas--areas not occupied by the Japanese invaders. Each route posed its own risks and travel problems. Certainly the four of them had to prepare themselves physically and mentally. They would need great endurance to overcome the hardships. Many factors were unknown--there were no normal means of transportation; enemies were everywhere, including Japanese soldiers and their collaborators, the Chinese traitors. The foursome also lacked experience in long distance travel and they had little money. The only things they did have were firm determination and deep faith.

Yu Yi was blessed by her faith in God. "I had no time to be afraid of my enemy," she would write years later, "I recalled the Psalm:though I walk through the valley of the shadow of death, I will fear no evil for thou art with me." She brought with her an English Bible and an English dictionary, risky possessions in a time of war involving the Americans.

They knew two escape routes to Chengdu that were frequented by students. The northeast–to–southwest route crossed the dusty part of China. The other route, from southeast–to–southwest, crossed the mountains and hilly parts of China. They decided to take the northern route because they were already in Peking. They plotted their major stops, collected as many names as possible and carried only bare essentials. They began their long march in early December 1942. They tried to avoid being noticed in public by Japanese spies and Chinese traitors; they watched out for each other closely. Among the four, Liu Hon-shen was the most active and capable leader. Liu and Sun led the two women like big brothers protecting and watching over two young sisters. Liu was diplomatic and quick to respond when dealing with enemies and facing difficult situations.

Their first stop was Jinan in Shandong Province, Yu Yi's hometown. Yu Yi spared a few moments to visit her mother's grave. She stood silently at her mother's final resting place and prayed for her blessing. Yu Yi had no idea if she would be able to return again, but she was sure her mother would want her to seek freedom and a better future. At her childhood home, Yu Yi found most of the house empty. Furniture and clothes had been stolen. Anyway, it did not matter anymore. She visited Mr. Chen and asked him to care for her house and its remaining contents. On her departure, Mr. Chen saw her and her friends to the train station. He wished them well and presented Yu Yi with a box of fancy cookies to eat on the road. Though their hearts were heavy, there were no tears to shed as the train began to move.

Trains were the main means of public transportation within the Japanese occupied zone. When there was no military action, the trains occasionally carried passengers. Tickets, however, did not necessarily guarantee a place on the train, or even if you did get on, you might not have a place to sit. Buses were the secondary means of transportation. But there was no fixed bus schedule, vehicles were undependable, and travel conditions were even worse than the train. A third means of transportation was by "yellow fish". That meant paying a passing truck or bus driver a negotiated, usually extremely high price, for a lift and walking where no ride was available. Boats were also sometimes available, though they were usually quite crowded, overloaded and risky. On the smaller rural paths, hand-pushed or pulled wheelbarrow-type carts (gee-kwon-zai) could sometimes be hired. It took considerable skill and physical strength to maneuver these "vehicles". Balancing a passenger or load could certainly be considered an art. Travel by gee-kwon-zai was time-consuming, as the "driver"zigzagged to negotiate holes and sharp corners along the way. Though some travelers did ride animals, such as horses, mules or donkeys, such beasts were difficult to find. None of Yu Yi's group was experienced in riding, but animals could share the load of their belongings. Walking was most dependable. Move the feet one ahead of the other to carry the tired body. Yu Yi's small group experienced all of these transportation means, but for the most part, they traveled on foot.

Lodging also proved difficult along their journey, except when they were aboard a moving train. The group usually started moving before dawn and stopped long before sunset to be sure they had cover during the cold dark nights. There were no hotels or hostels. In remote rural areas, they would be to find a temporary shelter built of bamboo and mud, mostly just a simple roof of poles. In the farming areas, they often found cover in animal stables, pig pens and sheep compounds. If they were fortunate, they might share the animals' straw bedding. Yu Yi and her friends usually sat back−to−back in a group to keep warm and maintain constant watch. Yu Yi was a heavy sleeper. One night she was awakened by Miss Liu, who whispered to her, "Someone is taking our suitcases." Both were too frightened to yell for help. Finally, Yu Yi uttered some faint noises and Mr. Liu came to the rescue with a lighted candle and found all luggage was there. The next morning, they joked with Yu Yi, "How terrible you sounded last night!"

Within Japanese occupied areas, refugees were everywhere, and so were spies, traitors, Japanese Imperial Forces and sometimes thieves and robbers. By the end of December 1942, the four had traveled only about a quarter of the distance of their journey. They began to feel the pain, but kept high spirits. Money worries began to nag at them, as travel expenses were proving well above their estimates. They passed Shangqiu and approaching Bo-Xian walked toward Jieshou, a town on the dividing line between the Japanese occupied area and Free China. The previous day Liu Hon-shen had discovered that his brother, who was working as a nurse in the area, operated a clinic to treat patients that included Japanese soldiers. Liu had arranged for the group to stay at the clinic overnight.

To get to the clinic, however, they had to pass an inspection checkpoint. Many travelers crossed back and forth at the checkpoints. One young man, who looked like a student, was just ahead of them. The Japanese officer questioned him thoroughly. When the young man was too slow to open his bags, the officer cut through his cases with a bayonet, laughingly observing that his toothpaste tube was cut into halves. Finally, they allowed the student to pass. It was Yu Yi's turn. All went smoothly until they reached her belongings. When the officer found her English Bible and dictionary, his mood suddenly turned angry. He threw the books on the ground. Yu Yi was numb with fear. Yu Yi was clearly in trouble. Liu Rong-shen quickly moved to his brother's side and whispered into his ear. Brother Liu said loudly to the officer's superior, "She is only an innocent student." Yu Yi was allowed to keep her books, and her relief was palpable as she passed.

That evening, brother Liu generously treated everybody to a banquet. The four travelers were on one side of a partition, and some Japanese officers on the other side. Yu Yi couldn't help reciting the Psalm 23 "You prepare a table before me in front of my enemies." At the end of the banquet, Yu Yi served the fancy cookies that Mr. Chen had given her.

After that breathtaking escape, the group quickly moved across the "yin-yang-jia", the "dividing line between life and death". As they entered the free zone, the four were physically exhausted and mentally near collapse. They could not believe they were indeed beyond Japanese control. They caught their breath and moved forward, realizing at the same time that they were still in a war zone. Numerous refugees and disorganized armed soldiers ambled and loitered about. A few fortune hunters quickly approached them in hopes of making some fast money. The four had yet a long way to go. Their plan was to travel westward to Luoyang, Baoji, and then southward to Chengdu. Finding transportation and lodgings here was as difficult as before, if not worse. In addition, now they had to worry about air raids by Japanese warplanes. Yu Yi and her friends had to change their travel pattern. Instead of moving by day, as they had in the Japanese occupied zone, they now traveled by night to avoid air raids when using public transportation such as the train. They soon found that Henan Province was suffering from flooding, drought, field locust and rural unrest due to the drafting of young people. The flooding was from the strategic destruction of the dikes of the Yellow River to prevent Japanese tanks from advancing. Drought was due to the lack of rainfall, and the locusts made matters worse by consuming most of the fall harvest. The nationalist government's drafting of every able body made the shaky rural society even unstable. As a result, food supplies were short and prices extremely high. All this made the refugees' lives extremely difficult.

The four began their long journey to Luoyang on foot. They could find nothing green in the wide-open fields. The road was a bed of loose soil at least six inches deep. When a truck or animal cart passed by, dust was swept into the air, forming a thick cloud that obliterated all. Many dead animals, horses and mules, lay on the roadside. Nobody seemed to care. When the group came to a stop at the end of a day, each was covered with a layer of dirt so thick that it was difficult to distinguish one another. Overhearing their complaints, somebody quipped, "Be thankful for the dry weather; if it had rained you would all have been stuck in knee-deep mud."

Food prices were so high and many people were so poor that Yu Yi saw price tags hung on children's necks by parents trying to sell them or just give them away. She felt sad and too hurt to cry. A single dumpling, cold or warm, cost two Yuan, almost the cost of two weeks' rations only a couple of years earlier. Once a hungry child grabbed a hot dumpling from Yu Yi's hand and ran away. She watched and let it go. Adults, too, resorted to this type of thievery, only they spat saliva on the dumpling as soon as they grabbed it so that nobody would want it back. Actually, few people had the heart to insist on getting it back anyway.

After more than two days walking, they reached Luoyang. Exhausted, they decided to risk taking a train to travel from Luoyang to Baoji. The railroad was under constant bombardment by Japanese air raids. They arrived in Baoji safely but soon realized how severely the expensive food and transportation had drained their resources. They had to find some financial help to complete the journey. Liu Hon-shen volunteered to go eastward – the opposite direction to Xian – to seek help from a provincial refugee alliance, the Shandong Natives Association. So the four pooled what was left of their money to purchase a one – way train ticket for Liu, and hoped for the best. Indeed Liu did not disappoint them. He returned with sufficient funds for the four to move on.

The highway from Baoji to Hanzhong and Chengdu had been hastily constructed for wartime emergency use. It ran through high mountains and along narrow steep paths. Buses used alcohol or charcoal as fuel, because gasoline was unavailable or forbidden for use in buses, even for military transportation. As usual, tickets were hard to get and the schedule uncertain.

By now, they were experienced travelers. They knew how to save their energy and were stronger and wiser. Their feet were seasoned as well-full of thick calluses after blisters, bleeding, swelling and the pain of earlier days. They could now effortlessly sleep on stable haystacks to keep themselves warm without worrying about hygiene. They could tolerate hunger and thirst for many hours and they learned to share what they had with strangers weaker than they were. Yes, their characters had been shaped by the hardship and suffering of the war.

From Baoji southward towards Sichuan, they crossed the Qinling Mountains to Hanzhong and then to Jianmen. Those vast areas were almost uninhabited and the weather was cold and unpredictable. They dared not take any chances in the cold and spent some money to catch "yellow fish" rides on buses and open trucks. The road was rough, narrow and close to the edges of mountain cleaves. A slight misjudgment by the driver would mean the end of their lives. They sat on their luggage and held tightly to the shaky vehicle frame. On the highest mountain ridges, the vehicle moved in thick clouds. In most places, the road was carved out from steep mountainsides, and they swung back and forth, and back and forth. It took hours to pass over one mountain, which was followed by another, and another. In the depths of the valleys, the sky overhead was but a thin strip of light despite the brightness of daytime.

It was dangerous to ride on vehicle sides or tops, especially on poorly maintained mountain roads. In one of the buses in which Yu Yi and her friends were traveling, a passenger felt something sticky that smelled like blood drop from the roof. The next morning, they discovered that tree branches had gouged out the eyes of a rooftop passenger during the night.

The whole distance from Baoji to Hanzhong and from Hanzhong to Jianmen passed like this. The journey went on for days. It was breathtakingly dangerous, but at the same time vastly beautiful. Occasionally passengers pointed out fallen automobiles or trucks in the deep valley or to spots they described as historical locations of famous ancient battlegrounds during the 220 to 265 AD periods of the Three Kingdoms. Beyond Jianmen, the landscape became open plains. The next stop would be their final destination, Chengdu and the Yenching University campus!

In March 1943, after a four-month journey, the four students finally arrived in Chengdu. They were happy, but also numb from their travels. They could no longer shed tears. Upon arrival, they were directed to the housing manager, a Miss Lu Hui Ching. As they stepped inside her beautiful home, their eyes widened in astonishment at the clean white tablecloth and shining table settings as she served them their first real meal in ages! Only then did they comprehend that they had indeed reached safety. The boys began to wipe away tears, and the girls sobbed outright. "Go ahead, children, cry your hearts out," Miss Lu Hui Ching told them in her soft motherly tone, "You are home now."

At Chengdu

Though Yu Yi and her friends arrived on the Yenching University campus in the middle of a semester, they soon settled-in and adjusted to "normal" college life. There were seven Christian universities in and around Chengdu. Among the seven, five clustered on the Huaxiba campus of the host West China Union University. Chengdu was recognized as one of the two cultural centers of Free China, the other center was Kunming in Yunan Province, where many other universities had resettled. The presence of famous professors and scholars created an excellent education system. Students could elect almost any course and cross-register among universities for the best of academic training. Yenching students who lived in the city walked 30 minutes or more to attend classes at the Huaxiba campus. Students never really minded because they all had acquired callused feet. In fact, they appreciated the opportunity to walk together.

Between 1938 and 1944, I was a student at the Huaxiba campus of the University of Nanking, one of the original five Christian universities to move to inner China in the early phase of the war. Yu Yi and I did have one year overlapping at the same university compound, but we did not meet then. Yu Yi reconnected with her sister Shao Yi and her brother Jia Yu. They were attending medical school in Guiyang, the capital of Guizhou, another remote southwest China province that was beyond the reach of the Japanese.

Yu Yi majored in sociology at Yenching. She was fortunate to have excellent teachers who not only taught her in classrooms but also helped shape her character, and thus her future. Among them were Professor Wei Yong Qin, Professor Wu Chi-yu and Professor Hsu Ron Hsiun. Yu Yi remembered them well. Visiting Beijing in the 1980s, she introduced me to Professor Wu, one of the most respected scholars in China. He died in 1995. Unfortunately, Professor Hsu died during the Cultural Revolution, which stirred much grief in Yu Yi when she learned of his death.

Professor Wei Yong Qin had earned my respect and everlasting gratitude as a co-worker. In 1946, Professor Wei moved from Chengdu to South Bank, near Chungking, to become president of the Experimental Academy for Relief and Rehabilitation in the Ministry of Social Affairs. He took a team of young associates together to assist him. Among them was a new graduate social worker named Lu Yu Yi.

Chapter 4
Struggle for Survival—One War
after the Other

Jia Poo's Gold Bracelet

Chungking, the Wartime capital of China, is built on steep rocky hills.
Steps and slopes are everywhere. Being the wartime political and economic
center, the city was always bustling and crowded. Armed with several
recommendation letters and good credentials, I arrived in Chungking full of
confidence and hope. I had little doubt that I would land a good job. During
my eight years at the University of Nanking, I had received a two-year research
assistantship plus a three-year full scholarship for tobacco research. This
five-year support was financed through the Ministry of Finance. I had always
assumed that the government would employ me to work on tobacco
improvement.

However, when I was interviewed by Mr. Lu, the Director General of
the State Treasury, who happened to be a Nanking University alumnus, he
could offer me only a desk job in the tobacco tax office. Stunned, I
immediately turned down the offer. In fact, I felt insulted as I walked out of
the director's office. It was the summer of 1944. I had relatives and knew
many Nanking alumni in the Chungking metropolitan area. I wasn't looking
for just any job. I wanted to place myself in a good starting position
commensurate with my training.

Discouraged by what happened at the Ministry of Finance, I moved
out of the hotel where I was staying and went to visit an aunt, who was my
father's youngest sister. She lived in downtown Chungking. She and her

husband, Mr. Hsu, had escaped from Wuchang to Chungking at about the time that the Japanese invaded Hankou. When I reached their address, I was surprised to find it was a small store with a narrow street entrance. It sold clothing materials and other fabrics. I entered and found Mr. Hsu at the counter apparently waiting for business. Hsu originally came from a rich family and naturally had smoked opium in his early days. He had never before had a trade. Hsu was surprised to see me arriving unrepentantly with luggage in hand. He explained that because of frequent air raids my aunt had moved to a distant rural village. He stayed in the city to attend to the shop and make a living as best he could.

I sensed some uneasiness in Hsu when a young woman carrying an infant appeared. He introduced her as "Lian". Later Hsu explained that Lian lived with him to help with the store and she had also born him a son in order to continue the family lineage, as my aunt had no children. This fact, of course, was kept secret from my aunt. Knowing that I was seeking a job in Chungking and had no place to stay, Hsu offered me a corner of the floor in his store to sleep in. He also offered to share their meals with me for as long as I stayed with them. Over the weekend, I joined Hsu in a long bus ride to visit my aunt. The situation was awkward. My aunt welcomed me warmly and lovingly, as her husband had. It was difficult for me to conceal from my aunt the truth that Hsu had a second family in town. I decided to find another place to stay once I returned to the city.

Tseng-Jia-Yai was a downtown neighborhood in Chungking where many government offices and schools were located. A Nanking University alumnus, Mr. Kung, worked in the War Area Relief Commission located there. Kung's wife was a librarian at the neighborhood school. The couple lived in the office building that housed the War Relief Commission office. Their bedroom was upstairs and the meeting rooms were below. The office had become a gathering place and information center for Nanking alumni living in the city, as it was centrally located, with a large bus terminal nearby. The Kungs treated each Nanking alumnus as a brother or sister, sharing their food and converting the meeting areas to serve as makeshift overnight bedrooms.

Friends, coming and going, brought food and supplies and contributed necessary items and money for the common good. Mrs. Kung occasionally used contributed cash to purchase supplies for unexpected guests and travelers. No one really kept track of who contributed what--there always seemed to be just enough to go around.

At first, I stowed only my luggage for safekeeping at the Kungs. I traveled outside the city to apply for a position at the Central Agricultural Experiment Institute, which was the most prominent agricultural research institute in Free China during the war time. There were many well-known agricultural scientists at the institute. Many were Nanking alumni. Again, to my great disappointment, there was no position in tobacco. But I learned that the government did indeed plan to establish a special bureau for tobacco research. However, no definitive date had been set to begin this project. Dr. Shen, the institute director, knew of my training and asked me to wait a few more months for a possible opening.

Upon my return to Chungking, the Kungs invited me to stay at their compound while I continued my search for an intermediate position. It was late August, almost six weeks since I had left Chengdu. I had no income during this period, and much of my meager resources had been spent on travel and hotel expenses. It was wartime, and no one had cash reserves. I could not in good conscience continue drawing on the Kungs' common fund, although no one seemed to notice or complain. After much struggle with my own conscience, I finally decided to sell the gold bracelet which Jia Poo (my grandmother) had given me ten years earlier.

When I sold the bracelet, I did not even know if my beloved Jia Poo would be pleased or disappointed if she knew I had to put her bracelet to such use. It was indeed a sad moment in my life. I never had the opportunity to tell the story and explain to her in person what happened to the bracelet she gave me. However, one thing I was certain: Jai Poo would never blame me for what I did.

Opportunities and Missed Opportunities

The war raged on and on, and refugees poured into Sichuan and the other rear provinces, compelling the government to provide for the needs of the displaced. The Ministry of Social Affairs therefore established the Experimental Academy for Relief and Rehabilitation (EARR) in South Bank, in the Chungking suburbs. Seven institutes were set up under the Academy: pediatrics, nursery, health, handicapped, education and correction, industrial training and agricultural training. The Academy was located in a beautiful setting and was encircled by a deep running stream. In fact, it was an island set apart from the city of Chungking. Though not very large, the experimental farm had orchards, vegetable farms, ornamentals, field crops and fisheries.

In September 1944, I was offered the directorship of the agriculture institute of the EARR. At first I was hesitant, but after almost ten weeks of unemployment, I had little choice but to accept the challenge.

I soon realized that most people who worked there were originally from the war zones, and almost everyone had received a higher education with good credentials. Consequently, many were overqualified for their positions.

Soon after my arrival, I hired three Nanking alumni to assist me. We began the rewarding task of working with young refugees, training them to be productive and responsible citizens despite the war.

During my tenure, 1944 to 1946, we gradually gave the rural location of the institute a new face, turning its surroundings into a pleasant, modern environment. Trees were trimmed, their lower trunks cleaned and painted with lime. Weeds in the gardens and along the roads were torn out and replaced with neat flowers and grass. Our new varieties of "war garden" vegetables won prizes in city-wide competitions. Fish-stocked streams became a source of income. Trainees, in their smart new uniforms, were happy and eager to work in the flower gardens or fields. In fact, the farm income was almost sufficient to support the institute, but I insisted that all earnings from production be reinvested in new projects.

In my new position at South Bank, I was rather isolated from the center of Chungking, where many important things happened. The war was still fiercely fought on all fronts. Japan tried a final push into inland southwest China toward Guizhou Province in hopes of cutting off the Burma Road, Free China's supply line. They almost succeeded, but by then Japanese air power was no longer a decisive or dominating factor. In addition, the tide had begun to turn in favor of the Allied Forces in the Pacific.

In late 1944, the WASC passed word to me requesting that I re-enlist because the U.S. was intensifying its activities in the China Theatre. Waves of new Chinese graduates were joining the service as interpreters. In 1945, the U.S. established the Office of Special Services (OSS) which also needed interpreters to join paratroopers for airdrops behind enemy lines. Those opportunities were indeed tempting. However, President Bien of the Experimental Academy and Minister Goo convinced me that I was doing an equally important service at the Academy, and they did not want to lose me. I felt duty bound to remain on the job that I had started. It was wartime! In those days, it was anyone's guess which of these seemingly small daily decisions would prove decisive to our course in life, as indeed this one proved to be!

I had long lost contact from my father and the rest of my family. Occasionally I heard news indirectly via Uncle Yaoshu, who was still in Chengdu with the Air Command. In mid-July 1945, Yaoshu briefly informed me that something had happened to the 197th Division in which my father, Yafu, was serving. The 197th, together with two other friendly divisions, had been ordered to do a surprise hit-and-run on the Japanese occupying forces in Wuchang and Hankou. Two days prior to the attack, the 197th was instead attacked at night by an unknown enemy, and the whole division was disarmed and considered lost. Yaoshu assured me that Father was safe, but he did not know his whereabouts. Neither did I know anything about the rest of my family who were in a remote area of Hunan Province.

I was angered to hear what happened. I was concerned about my father's whereabouts, and, of course, worried about my whole family's safety.

Throughout July and August, I visited Chungking often to see my aunt and friends in an attempt to get news of my family, but to no avail. I walked the streets of Tsen-Jia-Yia aimlessly for hours. The U.S. had dropped the atomic bomb by that time and by all indications the end of the war was near. But what had happened to my family?

It was at that time that the nationalist government started a movement to enlist 100,000 students for military training. The idea was that students would help modernize the armed services as advanced equipment was introduced. Also, students would revive the fighting spirit as the war was near its end. Refugee students in particular were encouraged to join. Their return to their respective native areas would help to stabilize the area after the war. I was wondering whether my younger brother was among the enlistees.

The Hollow Victory

On August 15, 1945, I was in Chungking when a sudden news announcement broke: Japan had surrendered! Shouts of joy, newspaper extras, firecrackers and joyous noises of all sort welled up. People poured out of offices, shops and schools into the streets. Traffic became so crowded that it halted altogether. People cried, laughed and yelled happily. Strangers hugged, flags waved in every window and on every store front in celebration of the end of the long, long war. I felt trapped as I moved to the foot of a statue in a city square near Tsen-Jia-Yia. My fear of being stampeded by the enormous crowd was very real. Crowds in a few locations were out of control. Fire engines rolled out. Police called for people to listen for further important news following the first victory announcement.

Taking advantage of a lull in the crowd, I eased my way out of the mass and walked to the Kung's. Nobody was home as I had expected. I felt extremely lonely, empty and lost. I sat on the steps, buried my head in my hands and let out an anguished cry. Yes! Japan had surrendered, but China had paid a dear price. And, what price had my immediate family paid? The cost to me had been a large part of my youth. Where was China going now, and for that matter, where was I going?

The victory celebration continued day and night in Chungking, making me uneasy and restless. Despite the Kungs' request that I stay with them in downtown for a few more days, I insisted on returning to South Bank.

After the Japanese surrender, the United States announced passage of the U.S. Lend-Lease Act. The Lend-Lease Program enabled China to send university and institute teachers, researchers, and technical persons to the U.S. for short-term advanced training. The goal was to help China prepare for a speedy postwar reconstruction and recovery. Almost everyone I knew at the university or in the agricultural institutes went for six-to-ten months of advanced training or refresher courses. They journeyed "over the hump" by air to India and on to the United States. My institute, under the Ministry of Social Affairs, was not awarded a training quota. I was therefore left out. I felt so frustrated and disappointed at missing the opportunity. I was simply at the wrong place at the wrong time. I made up my mind then and there that I would go to the U.S. through my own efforts to continue my advanced study. But how would I get there?

Soon everybody was returning to hometowns or planning to move somewhere. Some had good jobs lined up; others just wanted to return home. Travel was extremely difficult. Airfare was well beyond the means of average people. At the Experimental Academy, President Bien was the first to leave his post, taking an appointment as director of Liaoning Province's Education Department. I knew of others who were planning to return to Jiangsu, Zhejiang and Hebei provinces. My uncle Yaoshu would return to Nanking, the capital, as soon as the Nationalist Government officially accepted the Japanese surrender. This formality took place in Nanking on September 9, 1945. The Allied Forces under General McArthur had accepted the Japanese surrender on September 2, on the USS Missouri. Yaoshu informed me that my father, Yafu, had safely escaped and would join my brother and sisters in Wuchang. We would have to begin our lives over again. Our former lives were in ruins and our old houses in ashes.

Union of the Sky

In South Bank, a new administrator arrived at the Academy to replace the departing President Bien. Our new President Dr. Wei, a former university professor, brought a new team, most of them from Yenjing University, a sister Christian college of Nanking. I did not understand why Dr. Wei accepted this position, as most people were eager to get out. In any event, I welcomed the change and we worked in harmony as our backgrounds were similar. At my first official meeting with Dr. Wei and his party I noticed a somewhat shy, attractive, smiling-faced young lady--Lu Yu Yi, my future wife--though at the time romance was far from my mind.

Yu Yi possesses many rare characters in addition to her natural beauty. She is gentle, considerate, and has deep concern for the well being of others, and is a model Christian. We felt immediately close to each other, visited each other often, cared for each other, and soon fell in love. Others in the Academy blessed us with respect and understanding.

One day I did not feel well and was confined in my room. Yu Yi brought a hot noodle lunch for me with great comfort and care. It is rather rare to enjoy such close attention. She also treated other co-workers, especially those from University of Nanking, with kind friendship and gentle love.

As time went by, Yu Yi and I saw one another frequently. My office and living quarters originally occupied an independent building on a hill of the Academy compound. Dr. Wei soon asked if I would mind trading lodgings with him so as to give him and his wife some privacy. I, of course, had no objection, as the move would put me closer to the Yenching group, of whom I was fast becoming a friend. Occasionally, Yu Yi and I joined Dr. and Mrs. Wei to make Chinese dumplings and chat in English and Chinese, which recalled my "family" days on the Nanking campus. We occasionally went to Chungking together for business, shopping, or recreation. In fact, she helped me select the material and color for my very first suit. It was a rare joy when we shared the short bus ride between Tou Chaio and the Chungking city, to a movie, or a meal together with an extra additional egg in the noodles or on the top of an onion cake at the only small food stand near our Academy.

Neither Yu Yi nor I had marriage on our minds, but the joy we felt in each other's presence and the care for each other's needs and concerns soon developed into love. We had both experienced pain during the war and uncertainty regarding our careers. We both understood well the struggle that could be involved in securing a happier future.

At that time, Yu Yi's sister and brother, both medical doctors, relocated to a hospital in Chungking. We sometimes got together with them, and they occasionally visited us at the Academy. Those trips across the Yangtze River to Chungking by bus, boat or "hua-gair" (a chair made of bamboo and carried by two laborers on their shoulders) were always pleasant and memorable. Movies in downtown Chungking or meals at restaurants were rare treats. Returning to the Academy, we usually enjoyed noodles together or shared fried onion cake with an added egg. It was beautiful. People at the Academy, of course, noticed our growing affection for each other, and were happy for us. Yu Yi supported my effort to seek advanced study and a permanent career as I did hers.

By the summer of 1946, Nanking University had completed the task of returning to its original campus in Nanking, the capital city. The Central Agricultural Experimental Institutes had also moved back to Shaoningwei, a suburb of Nanking. Most scientists involved in the refresher training in the United States had by then completed their work under the Lend-Lease program and had gradually returned to their posts. Only a few extended their stay in the United States to complete advanced degrees. I became even more anxious and restless in South Bank. Of my three assistants, Tong, Chen and Wei, Tong had left for Nanking. Chen, a native of Sichuan, died in a swimming accident in the stream surrounding the Academy. When Chen disappeared in the deep water, Wei dove in after him but could not find him. The campus police had to stop Wei by force for fear that he too might be drowned. Finally, the police fired a rifle bullet into a rock in the deep water. The sound waves brought Chen's body to the surface. Yu Yi was the only women present and she insisted on accompanying Chen's body to the hospital despite my imploring her not to. Her act of courage and affection for a friend touched my heart deeply. After that tragedy, only Wei remained to help me at the agricultural institute.

Spoiled by Spoils

Both Yu Yi and I were educated at Christian universities, and we both were war refugees and devoted workers in our respective fields. Indeed, since we had much in common, it seemed that our falling in love was predestined.

In September 1946, a year after the victory, I finally received a letter from Dr. Shen, the Director of the Central Agricultural Experimental Institute, stating that the government had approved the establishment of a national bureau for tobacco improvement. Shen requested that I join the team for planning work for the bureau. Yu Yi and I were overjoyed, and I took the next available flight to Nanking. Yu Yi would follow later. I thus returned to Nanking ten years after I had fled the city in the face of the advancing Japanese.

In Nanking, Yaoshu's family lived in a nice western-style house. He told me that my father, Yafu, had already returned to Hankou, and also that Yafu was combining his two families into one. The latter came as no surprise to me since I had long suspected that my father had a second family in Hankou during the week. The picture that my sister had found in father's pocket so long ago was indeed our own halfsister, the daughter of "the other woman". It seemed almost normal at that time, and it was socially acceptable, especially my father's generation. No apologies need be offered.

Without wasting one minute, I arrived at the Central Agricultural Institute in Nanking. Dr. Shen and the others were surprised to see me so early because the bureau would not be officially in business until January 1947, and that was three months away. However, I would not be put off any longer. I asked only for a desk and a place to sleep. I knew there was much I could do to assist in the planning. The director understood my determination and eagerness and provided me with a temporary position in the existing "special crops" group so that I could help in the planning for the tobacco improvement bureau.

By now, the civil skirmishes between the Nationalist and Communist factions had intensified and escalated into the open. Before the end of the war, the U.S. and Chinese governments had decided to establish a Joint Commission on Rural Reconstruction (JCRR). However, because of escalating military conflicts, the JCRR planning team ran into difficulty traveling through rural China to survey and map out an overall plan. Shen and an American colleague were preoccupied with the JCRR mission, meaning that the planning for the tobacco bureau and its operation fell mostly on the shoulders of Dr. Chang, the Bureau Deputy Director, and me.

I was involved in drawing up an operations plan, a budget, and even in organizing the construction of the facilities. None of this was related to what I had learned in the classrooms. My dedication to the job, however, more than made up for my lack of book knowledge. When the bureau was officially established, I was appointed senior scientist and acting secretary-general. The government was so eager to get things moving on the tobacco improvement program that they requested a weekly one-page progress report in English and in Chinese. It was to be hand delivered each Saturday to the office of President Soong of the State Council, the position equivalent to a premier.

Composing the reports was the responsibility of the director, the deputy director and me. There was no escaping the Friday-night ritual when the report had to be produced. I loved the challenge and appreciated the confidence placed in me. Within six months under Directors Shen and Chang, the staff members and workers grew to more than 300, distributed in three tobacco-producing provinces.

In early 1947, Yu Yi also came to Nanking through the encouragement and help of her many teaching professors and friends. She is a Christian of deep faith. In school or in work, professors, follow students, co-workers and friends all liked her. In Nanking, she was friends with many people from the Ministries of Social Affairs, Foreign Affairs, Agriculture, the Central Medical Center, and others. Together, we knew many people in Nanking, including my uncle and his family. He was serving in the Air Force Command headquarters. We enjoyed a circle of hard working, socially active friends. However, we were not satisfied with the status quo, and we sought opportunities to receive advanced education in the States. I was as determined as ever to apply for advanced study scholarships at Cornell University and Pennsylvania State University.

While matters moved smoothly within the bureau in Nanking, the major tobacco station in Henan was having personality clash problems between the senior tobacco experts and the regional administrator. Moreover, the civil war was worsening, and fighting was nearing the Henan station. Inflation was out of control. The Nationalist government had begun to collect gold reserves and issue "gold certificates" as currency. Many high-level Kuomintang (KMT) and other government officials turned to graft and profited handsomely. The government printed and exchanged useless paper money for real gold. Vast numbers of Chinese people were cheated out of their gold. In the face of such difficulties, Bureau Director Shen requested that I, on behalf of the director, visit the main tobacco station at Hsuchang, in Henan Province, to resolve personnel problems.

I obtained permission to travel by ship from Nanking to Hankou–the same route by which I had escaped from Nanking ten years earlier. I wanted to travel this way to visit my father and family, and then go by rail from Hankou to the Henan station. Total destruction greeted me all the way along my journey over the Yangtze River. The river was dotted with sunken ships; the shoreline was a pathetic scene of burned houses and buildings; and the war-leveled land was littered with disabled war machinery spread out over large areas. The tragic fact was that China had not even begun to recover from the war against Japan, and the civil war had already begun brewing and spreading widely. Why had this tragic series of events besieged China?

Civil War Renewed—Have Chinese People Suffered Enough?

Throughout China's long history, each dynasty change was usually the result of a civil war. The old Chinese culture appeared to accept the old adage "division will follow long time unification, and unification will follow long time division". During the Yuan and Qing dynasties, for instance, the Han people were conquered by ethnic minority nationals. Because of the breadth and depth of the traditional Chinese culture, it had absorbed and assimilated ethnic minority cultures resulting in an overall richer Chinese culture. Consequently, breadth, depth and richness are the essence of the Chinese culture today.

In recent history, the Qing dynasty fell in 1911, and Dr. Sun Yat-sen formally established the Republic of China. The following year, Sun founded the Kuomintang Party (KMT - the Nationalist Party in English). In 1921, the Communist Party of China (CPC) was born. From 1911 to 1921, the Republic of China existed mostly in name only. In reality, local warlords ruled each of the regions and provinces. Those warlords had little interest in a central government. They were kings in their own spheres of influence. The warlords fought each other for greater control and more territories. Foreign powers also got involved, took advantage of the situation and carved out territories called "foreign concessions", whereupon the effective rule of law in these territories was based not on Chinese law but on the law of foreigh powers-- the so-called "extraterritoriality".

As the result of all this, millions of innocent people were killed during this Warlord Period. Houses and properties were destroyed, families broken, farms were left unattended and wasted, and poverty was everywhere. Though Sun Yat-sen declared his "Three Principles for the People" and strived to build a modern China, in practice he had little influence and failed miserably.

Leaders from the KMT and CPC soon realized the necessity to take China from the warlords and unify the country. They formed the first united front in 1923, twelve years after Sun's revolution.

During the Warlord Period, I was too young to comprehend politics. However, one incident remained carved into my memory. I was walking with my grandmother to visit another village. My left hand was holding hers. My right hand carried a small bag containing my lunch. Suddenly a man dressed in uniform, which we could not tell was a soldier or a bandit, appeared in front of us. Without uttering any words, he raised his sword and cut my bag open while I was still holding it. My grandmother eyed me to be silent and I dared not to cry. At that time, all food and necessities, including salt, matches, and tobacco, were "regulated" by monopolies, to which citizens had to pay "taxes". "Smugglers" were punished or even executed. Control of these "taxes" was one reason why the warlords fought to expand territories under their control.

Any warlord, strong or weak, big or small, who showed even the slightest kindness to the people quickly become a beacon of hope. One name I recall is General Wu Peifu, who occupied Henan Province. Wu was known in China for his scholarship of the Qing Dynasty. People respected his character, for he did not smoke opium, a rarity among warlords. In addition, during the Japanese occupation, he was one of the few warlords to refuse Japanese summonses to serve as the figurehead of a puppet government propped up by the Japanese.

To wipe out the warlords and truly unify China, the first united front of the KMT and the CPC, under the leadership of Generalissimo Chiang Kia-shek, began its war of Northern Expedition in 1927 with great success. The Chinese people supported them, dreaming of peace and stability. I was then a ten-year-old student and stood on the street happily with the others waving our welcome. All of us hoped for better days.

However, further and more severe suffering awaited the Chinese people in the coming months and years. In April of 1927, the year of the Great Victory, Chiang ordered the bloody suppression of strikes and a coup against the CPC. Thousands of communists and those suspected to be their sympathizers were arrested and massacred. Thus the "white terror" began. In 1928, the KMT established the Nationalist government in Nanking, and soon the civil war between the KMT and CPC was brought into the open.

The civil war began with arrests, murders, strikes, labor unrest, rural unrest and student unrest. In a young boy's fearful memory, there were daily headlines on how many "enemies" were killed and how many "towns" were overtaken, with pictures of dead bodies on the front pages of newspapers. No doubt there were similar reports from the opposite side. The cruel fact was that things were not getting any better than they had been in the warlord days, only now the atrocities were committed in the name of national security and stability. The fighting forced the CPC on its famous "Long March" to Yen'an, through 1934 and 1935, to escape from the KMT's encirclement and annihilation. The CPC's army finally reached poor, rural Yen'an in Shan'xi Province on the Yellow Earth Plateau and established its base there. Yen'an became a holy place to the Chinese communists.

The KMT and CPC missed an opportunity to establish a modern China following their success in defeating the warlords under the united front. History attests that, after 1927, the Chinese masses, including farmers and labors, were as poor as before. Government was divided and there was no established education system. Military forces were weak, perhaps even weaker than in the warlord period. All those factors encouraged Japan to broaden its plan to conquer China.

The questions before the KMT leaders were clear: Should China fight Japan before the CPC was completely destroyed, thus embarking on multiple frontlines? Should the KMT and CPC unite to fight Japan? Chiang decided to first destroy the communists before fighting the Japanese, hence committing great resources to fighting the communists. His reasoning was, "To fight external enemies, one has to first cleanse his own backyard."

China's armed forces were ill prepared for a modern war. How could it fight against an adversary as strong as Japan? Japan seized the opportunity to force China into war as quickly as possible. First, it occupied China's vast and natural resource-rich three Northeastern provinces without firing a single shot. Japan then advanced into northern China. At the same time they instigated numerous skirmishes throughout the country, in the hopes of starting a "holy" war aimed at forcing China into becoming a part of a Greater Japanese Empire.

While all of this was happening, the KMT government asked the Chinese people for patience. We were to wait for the army to become better prepared and for the international climate to become more conducive to fighting a war. The people knew that once the war between China and Japan started, every Chinese would face long, exacting suffering, struggle and sacrifice. Nonetheless, we were prepared to accept all and give our lives to defeat Japan. The CPC, in the meantime, had grown stronger after rest and regrouping. It, too, expressed its desire to join in the fight against Japan. Thus, in 1937 the KMT and CPC united on a second front.

The war against Japan lasted eight years, from 1937 to 1945. When Japan surrendered in 1945, China had almost nothing left--tens of millions of lives lost, properties gone, families broken, industries almost non-existent, transportation destroyed, and daily supplies of food and cloth disrupted. When most KMT high-ranking officials had revealed themselves as spoiled by spoils, corrupted and out of touch with the people, the CPC took the opportunity to strengthen itself.

Early on, there were sparks between the KMT and the CPC. Big or small skirmishes followed. At this point, the Chinese people wanted nothing but peace, time to heal their wounds, to construct a roof over their heads, to get a job, to plant seeds and be left in peace after eight long years of bloodshed and tears. However, the specter of a full-scale civil war was already imminent. Who could comfort them? By the fall of 1947, few people had the heart or strength to move and become refugees again, so they fatalistically accepted what that would soon come. Many of my friends had narrowly escaped death and told me their horror stories in that period. A dear friend with his family of four got caught in the middle of the fighting. They had no place to go or hide but stayed in a field with only some scant growth to cover them when lying down flat. Armed forces surrounded them. A gust of wind could reveal them in their hiding place. At one point both sides shot at anything that moved. There they remained for three days and nights without water or food, but they did survive.

A series of big battles of this civil war took place in 1948, and became well-known to the world. In those decisive battles, the CPC annihilated millions of the Nationalist's core army and defeated the KMT in northeast, central and eastern China. After these battles, the KMT could hardly put up any effective defense at all, let alone any offense. The game was essentially over. The KMT was finished on the mainland.

It was told that in this civil war 20 million lives were sacrificed to establish a new order. The bare and cruel truth is that the Chinese people wanted only peace and rest. They were tired from the war against Japan and against each other, and tired of corruption. They would accept any change that promised to bring peace and stability. The CPC filled this promise.

In 1949, the People's Republic of China was established in mainland China. And Chiang Kai-shek and the KMT fled to Taiwan to regroup.

The Second Thirty Years

1948-1977

at forty, exercise judgment;
at fifty, know own destiny;
at sixty, tolerate the intolerable.

-Confucius-

Chapter 5

Struggle for Advanced Education in the States

Long Journey to the States

In my college years, I fully understood that America was the land of opportunity if one was intelligent and diligent enough to take advantage of it. The free spirit, the abundant support in education and opportunities, together with the stable system made failure impossible for those who kept trying.

In my freshman year at the University of Nanking, I enjoyed the luxury of financial support from my father. After the university was forced to move to inner China, I was completely cut off from my family and relied on government relief funds for tuition as well as daily rations. Most students from the war zone accepted the difficulties without complaint. Perhaps it was partly my poverty and struggle that encouraged me to take a leading role in organizing concerts, performances and professional or amateur plays on the campus. I wanted students to have an opportunity for joy and inspiration. Artists included the famous Louis Kwan, Shi I-Gui, Ma Shi-Zhun and others. They performed partly for charity. Students who helped could earn free tickets.

I was in my junior year when the Dean's Office offered me a tobacco scholarship, which I accepted and used to earn my bachelor's and master's degrees in tobacco. Though I did not do tobacco research from 1944 to 1946, my expertise became tobacco science.

In 1947, two American universities granted me tobacco fellowships.

91

Cornell University offered me an opportunity to study plant breeding with Prof. H. H. Love, and Pennsylvania State University invited me to study biochemistry. I did not decide which university to attend before leaving China. I simply headed to the United States via San Francisco on the first available ship.

On this trip, I knew that an old chapter of my life had been closed, a new chapter opened, and a new life was ahead of me. I was full of anxiety, ambition and expectations. However, I did not realize that I would not see my motherland or my family for the next 30 years, and I would never see my father again.

First Impression about America

It took me 25 days to travel from Shanghai to San Francisco on the ocean liner General Gordon of the President Lines. A great number of passengers were students. I occupied one of the triple-deck beds in the general compartments. Here, thirty to forty passengers shared a single open room. Some fared well on the rough seas, but unfortunately I was not one of them. I lost five pounds during the voyage. Many passengers became good friends and accomplished scholars--one became a medical doctor. He is now Dr. Wu and a national leader in public affairs, an educator and a top physician in China. Years later, many of us had remained in contact, and we enjoyed sharing and re-telling experiences and stories from that trip.

The Golden Gate Bridge was beautiful and inspiring to us coming from the other side of the Pacific. It was and is the symbol of freedom to those traveling to opportunity from across the Pacific. When I first arrived, I had $200 in my pocket and an old leather suitcase that my father had given me. As the General Gordon anchored in San Francisco, I heard my name called through the loudspeakers. It was George Hsu, a Nanking University alumnus whom I had never met before. He came aboard to welcome me at the request of our mutual friend, Lu K.C. George was a kind and helpful gentleman. It would be he who would assist Yu Yi, my future wife, when she landed at the same port the following year.

As it was two months before the beginning of the new semester, and also in the interest of saving money, George suggested that I travel by Greyhound bus from the West Coast to the East Coast through Oregon to Iowa, then to Chicago, and continue on to Pennsylvania, along the way visiting friends and commencing my initiation into the American way of life. Taking his advice, I took a Greyhound bus to travel eastward. I rode by night to save on hotel bills, stopping by day to visit friends and sightsee. It was easy because I had only one suitcase with me, and I did not care where I sat on the bus, or where I ate at the bus stop. I was indeed a free soul!

I arrived at Corvallis, Oregon, on Christmas Eve to visit my friend Lu K. C. He was out for a party. With the landlady's permission, I waited alone in his rented room, and eventually went back to the Greyhound station for a sandwich. When K.C. finally returned to his room he learned to his deep disappointment that his wife, Lan, had not come to the States with me as he had hoped.

My next stop was in Iowa City, where I visited Fred and Alice Yu, another dear friend and his family. They proudly showed me their newborn son who lay asleep in bed. This infant was the first American-born Chinese among all of my friends. At that time, the family was staying in a hotel room with cooking facilities.

In Chicago, I saw Dr. Wu again. He told me that Pennsylvania and New York were even colder than Chicago. He helped me to buy a heavy coat that lasted me for the next 15 years. Indeed, continuing my journey eastward, I ran into a heavy snowstorm.

I still faced the choice of studying both genetics and breeding at Cornell or tobacco biochemistry at Penn State. As I had been offered full scholarships at both universities, I discussed my possibilities with Professor Cliff O. Jensen, a well-known tobacco scholar at Pennsylvania State University. An immigrant from Norway, who was experienced in tobacco industry research, Jensen convinced me to stay at Penn State.

This was my first lucky break, but I did not know it. It all came too easily. I was so innocently ignorant of American scholastic protocol that I totally forgot even to inform Professor Love at Cornell University, who held another scholarship for me and was expecting me in Ithaca. A sincere apology later did nothing to allay Prof. Love's anger, as other students were eagerly waiting for the rare opportunity.

The Pennsylvania State University

American university life was not too different from that at the University of Nanking. After all, Nanking was modeled after Cornell. I quickly adapted to the routine at Penn State.

At Penn State, I lived in a rented bedroom of an engineer's family about a mile from campus and worked in my professor's private laboratory.

Generally, I worked in my laboratory until midnight or early morning and studied very hard. I was told that almost one-third of my academic credits from the University of Nanking Graduate School were acceptable toward my Ph.D. degree requirements. As a result, I only needed to take some essential courses, and devoted most of my time conducting research on my thesis. What other good conditions can one expect?

I had an advantage at Penn State. At that time, I also represented my institute in China, the National Tobacco Improvement Bureau (NTIB). In that capacity, I frequently contacted major tobacco research laboratories and visited tobacco fields in other producing states. I met and talked with leading scholars, and occasionally visited them in person. Those contacts made me aware of how little I knew and how weak the base of tobacco programs was in China.

The tobacco experimental field was located near Lancaster, and laboratory research was conducted at the State College campus. I shared Prof. Jensen's private laboratory with another graduate student who was completing his Ph.D.

There was a big Chinese student community in Penn State, about 50 on the campus. Considering the total student body was only seven thousand, I did not feel any special treatment toward Chinese, positive or negative. Most Chinese students were close. I joined with two other Chinese students, Hou

Xue Yu and Stella Yang, and we soon became known as "The Trio" in our social circles. We cooked Chinese food together each evening in Hou's Soil laboratory. Hou later became a distinguished ecologist and Stella a chemist.

My studies and research formed the center of my existence during these years. I spent evenings quietly and worked and studied alone early nights in my laboratory. This was particularly true in my second year, when I fulfilled most of my degree requirements. I slept in my room. The landlady arranged for the milkman to deliver a pint of fresh milk each day, which I drank when I returned "home" in the early morning. I spent the rest of my time on campus pursuing my studies and visiting friends. During my three years at Penn State, I was so absorbed in my study and research that I never attended one football game even though Penn State had already become famous for her football team.

In my undergraduate and master's degree training, I had majored in agricultural chemistry in the agronomy department at Nanking University. At Nanking University, the Agronomy Department centered on plant and soil sciences. Yet at Pennsylvania State University, where I hoped to complete a Ph.D. under Prof. Jensen in the department of agricultural biochemistry, the basic prerequisites for acquiring a Ph.D. were quite different. I would need a full additional year of study to satisfy the general requirements at Penn State. Moreover, those general requirement courses would be of little practical value to me in my work.

A compromise was worked out between Prof. Merkel at the Agronomy department and Prof. Jensen at the Agricultural Biochemistry department of Penn State. It required that I conduct my studies under Prof. Jensen but receive my degree from the agronomy department, with agricultural biochemistry as my minor. In doing so, most of my credits from the University of Nanking were accepted. It would take only two years' full-time study to complete my doctorate, but with a heavy academic load and summer sessions as well. A scholarship provided me sufficient funds for tuition and a stipend for living expenses.

My classroom and laboratory work were at the State College campus, and field experiments were on farms in Lancaster, Pennsylvania, under the supervision of Dr. Orman E. Street, who at that time was employed by the U.S. Department of Agriculture at the Lancaster Station. Dr. Street later became a professor at the University of Maryland. Our association lasted for many years.

Prof. Jensen had at one time supervised the research department at the Lorillard Tobacco Company. He was well respected, and had an excellent academic and industrial background. His teaching philosophy was to first help his students build a solid academic base and then give them plenty of freedom to explore research topics and reason out solutions. This was the typical American style of advanced training. Even under the tremendous pressure of my studies, I enjoyed the freedom.

In those days, Ph.D. candidates were required to take two "foreign languages". Reading level in two languages other than English and Chinese was required for a Ph.D. I passed French at my first try, but struggled with German for several months. Fearing failure, I avoided taking the German exam. My upbringing in China had engrained in me never to take a risk. When Prof. Jensen learned of my caution, he called me to his study and told me to forge ahead and take the test. "If you don't take a chance, how will you find out whether you're qualified?" That taught me a new lesson, this time an American one, "sink or swim".

On one occasion I was walking on campus between classes, an ice cream cone in my hand and books under my arm, when I ran into Dr. Richard, a young professor whom I had been told had served in the China Theatre with the U.S. Air Force. "Are you settled down now?" Richard asked. "Oh, yes!" I replied. "And do you like it here?" Richard continued. "Certainly," I said. "Better than China?" he asked. That last question hurt my pride, and I answered, "Be it ever so humble, there is no place like home." Richard was so surprised and asked where I had learned that expression. Then, somewhat embarrassed, he confided, "I served in the China Theatre during the war. I am glad to see that you have adapted so well." After this exchange, Richard became one of my closest friends, teachers and confidants through the years at Penn State.

Happy Union

In 1948, just a year after I left China for the United States, I learned with much joy that Yu Yi had been granted a scholarship to Lindenwood College in St. Charles, Missouri. I was in my second year at Penn State. However, despite Yu Yi's many friends and fellow alumni in Nanking, it still took her tremendous effort to secure a passport and visa and make travel arrangements. Funding was one major problem. Finally, help came from an uncle on her mother's side living in Shanghai. Yu Yi's Uncle Jiang, a well-known Chinese physician, was kind enough to offer help with the travel costs. She booked the voyage from Shanghai to San Francisco on the General Gordon, the same ship that I had traveled on a year earlier. Uncle Jiang gave a farewell party in honor of Yu Yi. In addition, Jiang gave Yu Yi $100 in pocket money for miscellaneous expenses.

Even though Yu Yi and I were both in the U.S., we could not see each other immediately as we were both occupied with our respective heavy study schedules. Also, travel was too expensive for either of us in those days. Not until Christmas did we finally meet, in Memphis, Tennessee, where Dr. and Mrs. Rudolph Shields had settled after returning from Shandong. The Shields welcomed us with great kindness. Mrs. Shields remembered what a good friend Yu Yi's late mother had been, and both of the Shields knew Yu Yi well. Although it was the first time I met them, they welcomed me into their home with open arms as they did Yu Yi.

Yu Yi and I were ecstatic to see each other after a long year of separation, and the Shields unobtrusively allowed us private time together. We walked along the bank of the Mississippi River, admired the great water and recalled the song of "Old Man River". The Shields later moved to Virginia to be close to their children, and we continued to visit them on numerous occasions. After Dr. Shields passed away, Mrs. Shields moved to a nursing home and lived to advanced age. She was always pleased to see us when we drove to Winchester with our children to see "Grandma Shields" in later years. Another of Yu Yi's dear friends, Miss Bell, lived in Cleveland, Ohio, and worked for the city government there.

After completing her degree in social work at Lindenwood in 1949, Yu Yi was accepted in the fall to an occupational therapy program at Western Michigan College of Education in Kalamazoo, Michigan. During the school recess, she found a summer job at a hospital in Cleveland. As this was much closer to Pennsylvania, we found time to meet in Cleveland several times and finally decided to marry. When we shared our engagement with Miss Bell, the close friend in Cleveland, she offered us the use of her home for our marriage ceremony, which took place there on August 28, 1949. A Chinese minister presided over the ceremony in the presence of a few friends.

After a three-day honeymoon at Niagara Falls, New York, we had to separate again, each to our respective schools. Yu Yi went to Kalamazoo to complete her OTR (Occupational Therapist Registered), and I returned to Penn State to complete my Ph.D. It wasn't until Christmas that we were reunited as man and wife. Yu Yi took the long bus ride to University Park, Pennsylvania. To surprise me, she purposely took an early bus, which arrived on the scheduled day, but early in the morning. Upon entering the house, she raised a finger to her lips, signaling Mrs. Donelson, my landlady, to be silent, and then she tiptoed to my room. It was indeed a pleasant surprise! We later rented a house in the neighborhood just for that Christmas holiday in 1949. There we held a delayed wedding party to celebrate our marriage with our friends at Penn State. My friends and Prof. Jensen's family were enchanted with Yu Yi.

We endured our separation for another year. By early 1950, I had completed my Ph.D. work at Penn State and moved to Lancaster, Pennsylvania, to work with Dr. Walter Frankenburg. Meanwhile, Yu Yi had completed her OTR and found a position at a hospital in a small town about an hour's bus ride from Lancaster. We could not yet afford a car. Yu Yi spent her weekdays at the hospital, and traveled to Lancaster by bus so we could enjoy our weekends together. It was a lonely route and we worried about safety and bad weather since she had to wait outside along a rural road for the bus.

Chapter 6

Learning, Working Hard, and Recognition in the Academic Fields

Learning the Basics of Research

As I completed my final oral examination, my advisor and the other committee members congratulated me, addressing me as "doctor" for the very first time. I was in seventh heaven.

I had to decide whether to return to a new China or do post-doctorate training. I thought I knew all there was to know about tobacco and was ready to fly home. However, a little knowledge is a dangerous thing, my advisor Jensen counseled me. He suggested that I needed more training and recommended that I work under Dr. Walter Frankenburg at the General Cigar Research Laboratory. I took his advice with some doubt, though it turned out to be the best education I would ever receive in my entire professional career. Frankenburg was well known in the field of enzyme chemistry, particularly catalytic chemistry. The two years I worked under his guidance familiarized me with disciplined German-style laboratory procedures. After several weeks, I found out the hard way how little I knew about tobacco, even within my thesis area. In 1950 and 1951, I learned not only how to be a scientist, but also how to be an honest man with vision. Certainly, I was fortunate to have the guidance of two such giants in tobacco research, first Dr. Jensen and then Dr. Frankenburg.

Frankenburg gave me a small independent project under his close supervision. Frankenburg required every new scientist in his laboratory to start from the beginning. At first, I was assigned to learn the research basics by working with technicians, all young girls, who were directly out of high school. I was not too happy about the assignment but I agreed to share the same bench with them. There was no room for error in analyzing a small sample, beginning with fractionation, followed by identification. Most samples were from newly purchased fresh cigar filler leaves or different stages of leaf fermentation.

I was assigned to work on alkaloids, including nicotine and its relatives, of which little was known in published documents. Frankenburg insisted on one hundred percent return of the original material we started, from fresh to fermented products. He asked each of us to keep two recording books, one for ourselves and the other for him. He took his book home every night for review, examination, or as basis for next day's discussions. I experienced trouble in getting 100 percent return because during fermentation, dry matter is lost. One day at lunch, I mentioned the problem to him. Actually, he was expecting this question from me. So, he asked me, why not try using something that does not lose weight? He then told me to use calcium instead of dry matter as a base. The problem occurred often in tobacco research, publications, or presentations, but few people cared to look for the answer. If I had not worked on the bench with those technicians, I might still be in the dark.

History, Frankenburg taught us, has recorded many "discoveries" stemming from error. Frankenburg tolerated no errors in his laboratory. Nonetheless, a study occasionally went astray. There was such an error during the development of an innovative product called "homogenized leaf tobacco". A young technician failed to complete her assigned test before leaving for a date. She put her test material in the refrigerator, intending to finish the test the next morning. When Frankenburg arrived the next day, he was upset to learn that the young women had failed to complete her assignment on schedule. When he asked to see the material, the frightened young woman showed him the overnight settled mass; he realized that they had stumbled on a way to make tobacco paper from tobacco waste material. There it was, the discovery that he had been waiting for was in hand!

The early 1950s was the dawn of academic tobacco research. Frankenburg's Lancaster Laboratory, Jensen's Penn State Laboratory, and the U.S. Department of Agriculture's Philadelphia laboratories were among the foremost tobacco chemistry research centers. Prof. Dawson at Columbia was also known for his research on the tobacco plant. Other industrial laboratories were at the early stages of development and other universities were mainly conducting tobacco breeding or agronomic studies. It was through the joint efforts of these research leaders that joint tobacco research seminars began to be held in Philadelphia and then at Penn State. Those open exchanges later became formalized as the Tobacco Chemists Research Conference (TCRC), currently changed to Tobacco Science Research Conference (TSRC). I had the honor and opportunity to organize and chair several of those meetings in later years. In fact, I initiated the much-cited reference series, Recent Advances in Tobacco Science, in 1976 when a trade journal refused to print the symposium papers in full.

Research at USDA Beginning with a Fellowship from the State Department

I worked in Lancaster under Dr. Frankenburg for two years, 1950 and 1951. In late 1951, I received a letter from the U.S. Department of State. Dr. Fisher at the Chinese Scholars Placement Office was inquiring whether I was interested in working on tobacco for a year at the Beltsville Agricultural Research Center of the U.S. Department of Agriculture with a State Department grant. I was surprised and elated because Beltsville, Maryland, is known as a leading research center, and also because only U.S. citizens can work in that government facility. Neither Frankenburg nor I knew how the offer had materialized. He was preparing me for other tobacco-related projects. Yu Yi and I decided to take the opportunity and move to the new location in Maryland. She would continue her studies and I would begin my professional research career.

Again, it was by Greyhound bus that we happily arrived in the Beltsville-College Park area. It was a few days before Christmas of 1951. I reported for duty at Beltsville after the New Year 1952, and remained there for more than 50 years. Being a scientist has enabled me to earn a living doing what I enjoy most and made me be appreciated and known for what I have accomplished.

Beltsville is home to many pioneering scientists and laboratories. Dr. W.W. Garner, the "father of tobacco science", had founded the Tobacco Laboratory. He had retired two years before my arrival. The laboratory had authorities in genetics, breeding, physiology and chemistry. Only ten of the lab's thirty professional scientists were stationed at Beltsville. Others worked at various state universities and experiment stations. I began as the smallest fish in a big ocean and had to work extremely hard. I was keenly aware that I would be judged for what I could contribute and how I conducted myself in this "holy temple" of tobacco.

When I reported to Beltsville for duty, Dr. J. E. McMurtrey was in charge of tobacco research after the retirement of Garner. McMurtrey was a second generation Irish immigrant. He asked me to continue my work on chemistry with Jeffrey, a plant chemist. Little did I know how lucky I was, Jeffrey asked me to work on tobacco alkaloids, the exact area I did under Frankenburg.

So in January 1952, we moved into a semi-detached apartment connecting to the big main house of university professor Dr. and Mrs. Cory, in College Park. The house was on Dartmouth Avenue, only one block from the streetcar line. I could easily ride to work at Beltsville, and Yu Yi could walk to the campus to be a graduate student at the University of Maryland's Department of Human Development. We learned later that Dr. Cory's family had some Chinese blood generations ago, and both of them were most kind to us. It was during that period that Yu Yi began to use her American name Margaret, which was of course much easier for school and for our friends to use.

I took the streetcar every day to the nearest stop and then walked two miles to work at what was then-called the Beltsville Plant Industry Station. I did this six or seven days a week and I worked at least ten hours each day. I had to prove my ability as a researcher within the one-year the State Department fellowship allocated to me.

I was assigned to work on tobacco alkaloids, the main one being nicotine, to discover nicotine's family members and relatives, both in the plant in the field as well as in the cured leaf. It was a challenge I gladly accepted. I would need at least two years to find a lead, yet I had to prove myself within only a single year! I worked long days and through weekends. I often had two or three tests going at one time without any assistance. Frankenburg joked that the U.S. Department of Agriculture (USDA) hired me to steal his secret technology and for cheap labor!

I had my first breakthrough in only nine months, thanks partly to luck and partly to hard work and the cooperation of many fellow alkaloid scientists. I developed a new way to extract, separate and identify tobacco alkaloids. I found 23 relatives of nicotine, with a third of those being identifiable by an easy process. This finding proved crucial in the tobacco science community, and geneticists, breeders, physiologists and the industry would pick it up. By the end of October, I had a major manuscript prepared for publication.

Frankenburg and his whole laboratory staff came to Beltsville to visit and congratulate me for this accomplishment, which was a great honor and deeply impressed McMurtrey, Jeffrey, and the whole Beltsville campus. Soon after, industry and academic scientists came to visit Beltsville tobacco research. Some offered to become research fellows at Beltsville and work with me even before the end of my one-year fellowship. It was another lucky break, and this time I knew it.

By the end of 1952, I had completed my one-year term at Beltsville. Many academic institutions showed interest in my services. I considered continuing my work at Beltsville. However, without U.S. citizenship I could not hold a permanent government position. The head of tobacco research, Dr. McMurtrey, asked me to remain at Beltsville, saying that Beltsville would find some creative legal way to allow it. The way he eventually found was to ask the University of Maryland to hire me as an associate professor and then assign me to Beltsville for cooperative research. Beltsville would then provide funding to the university agronomy department. And so it was arranged. As I enjoyed the people and my research at Beltsville had gained momentum, I was happy to stay. My obligation was to be on Maryland campus once in a while, join the weekly seminar, and present the subject of my research to students when needed. Further, Margaret could complete her graduate study in University of Maryland. What other lucky breaks can one hope for? Those opportunities made me work harder.

After 1952, many of my other key findings followed, mostly in cooperation with other subject authorities on the research campus. Industrial and academic researchers from the U.S. and abroad came to work in my laboratory for short or long periods. Well-known scholars approached me for cooperative or joint research, and my Beltsville laboratory expanded with more assistantships and funding. Through the years, my research papers continued to be eagerly sought after by scientific journals.

When our life began to settle, after hope and prayer, we dared to plan a family. When Margaret was carrying Betty, we were in a tight budget status and had to prepare baby's essential needs in a thrifty way. We went to shop whenever and wherever there was a sale, as long as the shop was close to the streetcar line. Once we went to Washington D.C.'s Hecht Company to buy a baby crib, it was in the early morning and we were at the front of a big waiting crowd. However, when the store doors began to open, every one tried to get into the store ahead of others to find a better bargain. We were so scared that the pressure might hurt our baby, but we were already in the midst of a mass, there was no other way out. We stayed together to offer some protection to each other as much as we could. I do still not remember how we two got the baby crib and even a punch bowl and safely returned home by streetcar.

Our first Child, our daughter Elizabeth (Betty), is a gift from haven. She was born on May 4, 1953. She immediately became the center of our life. Betty was a very beautiful and bright child. She was so active that once

104

she rolled out of her scale which was about four feet above the floor. Fortunately she was not hurt. That event scared Margaret and me, thus we decided no more weighting. Margaret stopped schooling to devote full time to her, especially the task of night care. I could only help after work. We enjoyed pushing the baby carriage along streets whenever possible. All the neighbors got to know us and loved us, including some campus students. At Betty's one-year birthday, we held a big celebration dinner party sharing our joy and thanks at the main hall of a near-by church. Many Chinese friends helped us, preparing various Chinese dishes to entertain almost one hundred guests. It was a great party in the eyes of all. In fact, Margaret and I always liked to entertain friends, co-workers at our small apartment for dinner. We ignored the American custom of formality or decoration for the event; we wanted only a practical, good meal. We usually cooked many favorite dishes for our guests. If our card table was too small to hold the food we prepared, we simply put dishes on the floor or even on stairway steps for guests to serve themselves. Gradually our friends got used to us and appreciated our informality, and invited us to their homes for wonderful meals. Our only requirement was that we took Betty with us, no baby sitters.

Because of our old Chinese family tradition and especially our own experiences at war and in many narrow escapes, we were used to facing troubled waters and tolerating hard conditions. Margaret and I always keep the principle of "being small rather than big, being low rather than high, being poor rather than rich, and being humble rather than proud." Margaret and I both were hard working, and provided ourselves with simple but comfortable living, while treating our friends and neighbors with helping hands and love. It was then, and it is now.

Betty was indeed a blessing to us and she was a happy and bright child. She gave us all the joy and love. At that particular period of time, there were many Chinese scholars living in the College Park and Washington, D.C. area, mostly scientists of modest means with temporary visa status in the States. We communicated with each other, helped each other as a big family. Betty was the only Chinese child among the small Chinese circle, and always the center of attention and love.

To meet the need for essential transportation as our family grew, we had to buy our first used car, an old Buick. Margaret received her Master's Degree in Human Development, from the University of Maryland with honor, and returned to work again when Betty started schooling. In 1955 we moved to a small home in Berwyn Heights, which is on Blackfoot Road, and is closer to the USDA Beltsville Center than College Park. As Margaret was a devout Christian since her China days, we attended church regularly, and decided to join the Berwyn Baptist Church at its old location and enjoy the brotherly love. The church held its Sunday Bible study in its basement, with three or four different classes separated by movable curtains and we could always hear the group next to us if the teacher happened to speak loudly. Children's classes were held either in nearby private residences or a public hall. At Christmas time, neighboring members from the Berwyn Baptist Church visited our new house to play Santa to Betty. At that period the church members began planning to build the current new structure, first the fellowship and worship hall, and later the Church Chapel in two stages with donations, bonds, and loans, It took about 5 years to complete. It is our other family ever since.

Continued Struggle and Taste of Success

Learning is a lifelong continuous process. It is my belief that we should not let our formal education interrupt our lifelong learning, and we should not stop in the middle of our lifelong quest for knowledge. A student who has the illusion that he or she has reached the pinnacle of learning will soon be left behind.

Life is a continuous struggle. I was fortunate to have learnt from and worked with many excellent scholars in the best environments. They helped to show me ways to pursue my dreams in the wide-open field of tobacco research. I was not a top student in my undergraduate years. Constant worry about the war, my need for financial support and my missing family were only parts of the reason. In hindsight, I see a main factor limiting my success at that time because my approach was to take just one step at a time. I had no higher goal in mind as to where I wanted to go and what to do.

The education system in China encouraged students to just count their credits rather than aiming for higher objectives. Actually, because the University of Nanking was a U.S.-sponsored missionary school, in this respect it was much better than other public schools in China. Most universities served students a fixed curriculum for each class year and did not give students freedom of course selection. Some Chinese universities still use this fixed curriculum system. Teachers often refer to this system as "tube feeding". Another advantage of studying at a missionary school was that we used English textbooks and some teachers lectured in English. My exposure to Western literature, in addition to classical Chinese writings, kindled in me a fondness of reading, especially of contemporary Western authors. When I was under pressure or feeling low, I would usually read such literature for comfort and relaxation. For example, I admired Sir Winston Churchill for his writings more than for his wartime achievement. He used a few simple words to express deep emotions.

In the mid 1950's, because of the need for modern technology using isotopes in plant research, I asked Beltsville to send me to the Oak Ridge Nuclear Research Center to master the use of isotopes in plant study. That training gave me additional wings to fly into a space almost unlimited. After Oak Ridge, with a new tool in hand, my research on alkaloids became easier. I made rapid progress in studies on biosynthesis, biogenesis, loci of formation, transformation and organic metabolism in tobacco. I realized during this productive research period that isotope technology could be applied to great benefit for a large number of crops.

My research using triple-labeled isotopes examining the organic metabolism of plant compounds became a milestone in the plant science community. The research was reported by the National Geographic Magazine in 1958. It received broad attention. Under that limelight and although I enjoyed the fame, I never relaxed or thought that I had achieved success.

There were too many giants ahead of me! The period between1952 and 1960 was certainly my most creative and happy time as a basic research scientist.

Publications were then, as they are now, the lifeblood of a scientific career. It was during this time that I found I had made the transition from the "first stage" in my publication life, to the second and even the third stage. Stage one is that of young scientists, new in a field, and eager to have their name in print. To get published, such newcomers try to associate their research with established scholars. For example, new scientists invite an experienced scientist to co-author a research paper, even if the experienced scientist had nothing to do with the research project. The second stage is reached when a scientist and collaborators work together with mutual respect to obtain and document solid scientific results they find worthy for publication. The third stage is the reverse of the first. That is, when an experienced scientist receives an invitation from a newcomer, even if the experienced scientist had nothing to do with the study at hand.

In 1960, the U.S. Congress, responding to a request from the tobacco industry, asked the USDA Beltsville laboratory to start research on a new material to control the growth of "suckers" in tobacco plants. Suckers are auxiliary buds that emerge after the tobacco flower has been removed. Usually of little value, suckers draw precious nutrient from plants. This research project was rather different from my previous work in that it was applied research. At first, my immediate supervisor led the study. However, when he passed away suddenly, Beltsville asked me to take over the project. Some 3,000 compounds available at Beltsville had to be screened in cooperation with the many field stations of USDA's Agricultural Research Service (ARS) and scientists of tobacco producing states. Finding the growth regulator would be a real boon to tobacco farmers. It would greatly reduce their labor since it would eliminate the need to remove the suckers from the plants by hand. Moreover, sucker-free plants would generate more profit and produce better leaf usability for the industry as a whole. However, the problem turned out to be a rather difficult one. None of our compounds at Beltsville proved effective. Inspired by a story I had read on the use of lard and oil, I proposed screening fatty compounds in different chemical forms.

Here my experience at the Frankenburg Laboratory proved a great benefit. I had retained the habit of keeping two full sets of record books for my primary concepts and my daily progress in the laboratory. On behalf of the USDA/ARS, I requested a particular group of chemicals for testing from an industrial supplier. One of the chemicals in that group proved effective in regulating sucker growth! But when the results become known, the supplier of the chemical informed the USDA/ARS that it would apply for patent protection to market the compound worldwide. In a hot debate that followed in the ARS Administrator's office, the company representative in my presence remarked, "Government scientists write their dreams only in their record books. Then they shelve them to collect dust." That particular compound, he said, had been tested at the company's initiative and therefore the company should have the patent rights. I was insulted by such a statement, and boldly suggested to the administrators that ARS should fight to keep the patent rights. As I saw it, our reputation and honor were at stake. Also, an USDA/ARS-held patent would benefit tobacco farmers and the tobacco industry, because the chemical company would otherwise monopolize the supply. Two years of court battles ensued, regrettably taking me away from my research much of the time. Finally, however, we at USDA/ARS won the suit and the patent right.

In 1964, while I was eager to return to basic research, the U.S. Surgeon General's Office had released a tobacco and health report linking tobacco smoking to certain diseases of smokers. Suddenly the future was in doubt for the whole tobacco research community, and especially for us at the Beltsville laboratory. Some scientists requested transfer to other crops. My view was that tobacco research would intensify to solve the problem on scientific grounds, and this situation was not a crisis but an opportunity. Too many questions were as yet unanswered, but I was convinced that solutions could be found. My prediction was that tobacco research funding would increase instead of decrease; and cooperation between government agencies and the tobacco industry would be strengthened.

During that period, I conducted research on mycotoxins from tobacco mold, on radioactive elements from chemical fertilizer, on soil and air, and other related studies. One of these studies aimed to establish a theoretical model for a safer tobacco. I analyzed the association and transgression of more than 500 variables in tobacco leaf and smoke. This was only a tip of the iceberg for there were some known 4,500 compounds at that time. These studies attracted the attention of scientists of the then U.S. Department of Health, Education and Welfare (HEW) and also from tobacco industry leaders.

In 1967, the U.S. government finally took action on health-related tobacco research. That year President Johnson requested in his health message that a task force on lung cancer be set up. However, because this task force and its subgroups were only concerned with research on various aspects of lung cancer, the Surgeon General established a separate group on smoking and health. This latter group concerned itself with education and motivational studies. Among the working groups under this task force was one to investigate the possibilities for less hazardous cigarettes and to review plans and develop further strategies and activities to reduce the health risks of smoking.

No funds were appropriated for fiscal year 1968 to the group for less hazardous cigarettes, and only $1.4 million was allocated for 1969. Members of the group were selected primarily for their scientific expertise rather than organizational representation. The director of the National Cancer Institute invited me, on behalf of the HEW, to participate in the group's first meeting set for March 11, 1968. Following that meeting, which was attended by ten members, the subgroup decided to name itself the Tobacco Working Group (TWG) so that it could include the tobacco industry. Industry had the most information and manufacturing technology for product development. I was asked to serve as the only plant scientist in this group. The USDA approved and authorized my participation as its chief representative, working with various government agencies, industry and academic institutes related to the tobacco and health project.

This 1968 major turn of events shifted my research direction and changed my professional life from then on. By then, many administrative leaders and senior scientists from several agencies of U.S. Department of Health, Education and Welfare (HEW) had visited Beltsville. They learned about our research achievements and current activities, and discussed our national production research on tobacco and health. As an expert on phytochemistry and production research, I firmly believed that a less hazardous cigarette was achievable; in other words, I believed that though absolute safety might not be achieved, the risk factors could certainly be reduced. This conviction reflected my appreciation that, in our world, nothing is risk free, including the food we eat each day.

In our first joint session with the National Cancer Institute (NCI) leaders at Beltsville, I reported that in the agricultural area we were investigating sources of alpha particles, mycotoxins, and common pest control and suckering agents. All those who attended the briefing session felt that critical risk factors could be easily identified and removed. I was asked to draft a total plan, from the plant science side, on our approaches to solving this problem. Knowing little about the complexity among leaf, smoker, and environment, plus politics, I was innocent enough in preparing a master plan in achieving this huge task. Based on my above belief (in our world, nothing is risk free), I proposed to the group an outline for manipulation of leaf tobacco at the stage of plant production.

In this proposal I listed four key approaches. First, identify the undesirable or potentially risky factors, using chemical and biological tests. Second, carry out positive genetic changes. Third, perform changes during the growth stage, including modifications of production inputs, shifts in the dynamic balance of chemical components, and regulation of biosynthesis and biogenesis. Fourth, induce and control senescence and curing metabolism in a more favorable direction.

The eleven active years, 1968-78, in the TWG, and the five additional years to 1982 that I spent leading USDA/ARS cooperative research were the most challenging and busiest of my professional career. Tobacco health related studies greatly broadened my vision and arena of research field. Which leaf components might affect health in smokers? How to remove them from the plant without changing the usability requirements? What are combustion products of leaf tobacco? What are the effects of soil, the chemicals including fertilizer applied to the field, the water, and the air? What are the biological effects to smokers of any material generated from combustion, singly and collectively? USDA was responsible for answering most of those questions in coordination with other federal and state agencies, and academic institutions around the world during the active ten year period of TWG. Soon I learned hard facts: To meet the smokers' need, complete combustion is not an alternative.

Much of our research attracted broad cooperation. I visited national and international institutes, and discussed projects. In the process, I befriended many bench scientists and their research leaders. We examined the radioactive elements in fertilizer and soil, every input material used in production, every tobacco plant type, every species, even leaf positions. We studied chemical changes in genetic plant tumors from inter-species hybridization, removal of risk components by altering curing methods and reconstitution. We studied how to identify toxic risk substances such as aflotoxin A and B, and we ran many other projects.

Preparing leaf samples for study was a relatively easy part of the whole evaluation process. Starting from learning the genetic background, leaf materials had to be analyzed at each stage of growth and post-harvest handling and processing. We followed that by cigarettes tests including, mechanical smoking, analysis, and bioassay. We used many study methods—from the most simple, such as cell mutation, to the most complex and difficult, such as animal inhalation. Animal tests are expensive, and long-term, and expert interpretation of bioassay data often disagrees. Also, animals are wise enough not to inhale. They hold the smoke in their mouths and "exhale" later. Using negative pressure to force an animal to "smoke" is totally different from inhaling voluntarily, as humans do. The search for fair and accurate scientific conclusions on which to base opinions and decisions for our next steps thus proved frustrating.

Our research on plants was no easier than animal testing. To evaluate a single targeted compound, we had to ensure that a tobacco leaf had grown in an isolated, absolutely uncontaminated environment. For this special project, we enlisted the cooperation of the government of Canada, which allowed us to grow tobacco on virgin land on Prince Edward Island. We found a special location where no crops had ever grown. This, we expected, would ensure a tobacco leaf free of any possible contamination. However, after harvest, our samples leaf analysis showed a small level of DDT! The chemical had been prohibited in Canada for over two decades, and DDT had never been applied near Prince Edward Island. It was sobering to realize that air or other means had likely carried the pesticide to every corner of our earth.

Among many findings, we isolated fraction-1-protein (F1P) from leaf tobacco and therefore reduced a major precursor of certain harmful products, plus the fact that F1P is of high value for nutrition and also for medical use.

That TWG period was a wonderful experience for me from the mid-1960s to late 1970s. Although I did propose a theoretical model for a "safer" tobacco, later we realized that it is not achievable. As a scientist, I have to conclude that there were no risk-free smoking products. However, this does not mean that we should stop all research on tobacco, or using tobacco as a research tool in biological science.

In addition to our intramural projects, USDA/ARS had many cooperative projects with scientists in tobacco producing states. Some projects were for purely academic needs, and others were politically oriented as a way to channel funding to a specific region. We made the best use of the available research funds, building an excellent cooperative program and recruiting many brilliant scholars. We also collaborated with HEW on many projects. Those activities provided opportunities for me to visit health-related research institutes and industrial research centers across the globe.

It was at this time that my friends began to tease me that my initials, which had become my name, T.C., actually stood for "Tobacco Chief".

During my professional career, my name appeared on more than two hundred scientific publications, and fifty-two U.S. and foreign patents. I received awards and honors from academic societies, industry and government. Two U.S. Presidents, one Democrat, one Republican, recognized my achievements. Those were the years that tobacco research was still politically correct. The political winds began to shift from 1978 onward. Congress gradually discontinued funding for tobacco research, and in some cases made scapegoats of renowned research scientists. The wisdom to distinguish academic research from politics seemed rare indeed.

Looking back at my publications in those years, some were certainly "breakthroughs" in terms of the science we applied. On others, my name should probably not have been included, or perhaps some publications should have never been published. The same is true of many of the honors I received. At the USDA, I advanced to the meritorious rank of U.S. senior executive service, which meant that agencies other than the USDA could request my services. I took early retirement in 1983, and soon the Tobacco Research Laboratory was abolished. However, the USDA/ARS continued to keep me in service as an honorary advisor, or "collaborator", to its National Program Staff.

I must add that those years were the most joyful and challenging times of my life. I received almost all the honors and recognition a research scientist could receive. I had the privilege of being appointed a charter member of the Senior Executive Service (SES) by President Carter in 1979. In 1983 President Reagan awarded me the rank of Meritorious Member of Senior Executive Servia.

On Glass Ceiling and Discrimination

A question frequently asked of me by friends and strangers, scientists and non-scientists alike, is do foreign-born nationals face a glass ceiling in the United States? And if so, how did I break through it? To be honest, I was too busy during my professional life to observe any barriers. Or perhaps my sailing was too smooth for me to feel the waves. Yes, I observed racial discrimination as soon as I arrived in San Francisco, especially when I saw the signs "Colored" and "White". My first confusion was a practical one, "which was I?" In fact, I usually took the nearest door, or the one that first caught my eye, white or colored. Many people laughed at me for that.

To me, discrimination seems mostly to originate from, and be conducted by, people of lesser education or of lower social status. I never sensed discrimination in the classroom, at the university, in the research laboratory, or in my professional activities. Once a senior scientist at Beltsville noted to me that our tobacco laboratory was a collection of talents from around the world: Irish, Jewish, Chinese and American. In fact, I found many advantages to not being a native-born American. I simply told myself that I had to work harder to achieve more. This drive helped me to earn respect and recognition in my scientific community and from my organization. In my case, standing tall, or short, had nothing to do with my origin. At the international conferences in which I frequently participated, I felt that somehow my oriental origin enabled me to gain even higher respect and more friendship among international audiences. Perhaps this, in fact, can be interpreted as another kind of "discrimination".

Yes, there is always discrimination. Discrimination against a sex, a race, a religion, a type of conduct, or certain manners will always exist. But as a scientist, I followed the mantra "prove yourself first". Don't worry about a glass ceiling. Aim at the stars.

National and International Activities of Interest

I devoted 42 years to tobacco research from my undergraduate days up to 1983 when I retired from my position as Chief of the Tobacco Laboratory at the Beltsville Agricultural Research Center. It was indeed a rewarding career, which I would not have been able to achieve had I remained in China. Various groups representing widely divergent interests sought after my expertise and leadership. I organized and chaired symposia and conferences of national and global scope. I was a member of the Tobacco Working Group, a member of the President's Lung Cancer Task Force, a member of the Smoking and Health Review Board of the National Cancer Institute, and a member of the Technical Advisory Group for many U.S. states. I also served as an advisor to public and private industry, domestic and abroad. Over the years, I received honors and awards of the highest level. I felt the warm esteem of my colleagues in phytochemistry and within national and international professional societies.

My scientific stature brought opportunities to travel. My travels and the exchanges and discussions they brought were rewarding, as they led to new ideas and cooperative efforts. During the most active stage of my research career, I was involved in projects with collaborators in England, Germany, France, Japan, Canada, Philippines, Taiwan, and many others. During the 1980s, the scope of my activities extended to mainland China, South America and Africa.

My association with Japan in tobacco research could be traced to an occasion in 1951 when Dr. Onishi visited Frankenburg's laboratory in Lancaster, Pennsylvania. Dr. Onishi showed us a "volatile oil" flavor fraction, which he had isolated from tobacco. Onishi unscrewed a tiny tube that then emitted a very strong odor in the room that remained for days. Later, Dr. Onishi, Dr. Tamaki (Wada) and many others from Japan not only became my respected professional associates, but also good family friends. These and many other Japanese colleagues visited the U.S. often and they invited me to Japan many times.

Once when I was Dr. Onishi's guest in Japan, after a full day of professional exchange with Japanese associates, we went to Atomi for one night of relaxation and rest in the warm springs. The resort house was maintained by the Japan Tobacco Monopoly and frequented by the Japanese royal family. As Dr. Onishi and I arrived a polite young lady attendant who spoke only Japanese received us. Apparently she was waiting for us. She showed us the beautiful rooms, served drinks and withdrew. Dr. Onishi told me to prepare for some relaxation before dinner and he also disappeared. Soon the lady reappeared, bringing a kimono. She laid the kimono on the bed and gestured to me with a charming smile. After I waited another few minutes, Onishi still had not shown up, and I noticed that the entire house was very quiet. Then I found the lady was standing at the door looking at me mysteriously puzzled and gesturing, but she spoke only Japanese. I could not decipher it. Suddenly the lady approached in a rush and before I realized what was happening, she had removed my tie and was busy trying to unbutton my shirt. This happened so fast I cried out for Onishi's help. Soon Onishi was located—wet and in his hastily donned kimono. He laughed until tears came out when the embarrassed young lady tried to explain what had happened. It seemed that Onishi went ahead alone to the warm spring bath and had already immersed himself. When he realized that I had not followed, he asked the attendant to hurry me into my kimono and bring me to join him. It was close to dinnertime before I enjoyed a bath in the warm spring.

On a separate occasion, my whole family was invited to Japan for a tour and a two-week scientific seminar and discussions. My friends and hosts were considerate and had formulated a detailed plan for our stay. They had arranged a few days of sightseeing for the family before the seminar and professional meetings began, in addition to a three-day "break" between the professional sessions. It was understood that, during the scientific discussions, I would be fully preoccupied in business. A retired Japanese friend was invited along to look after my family so that I could concentrate on my work. Knowing this, I had my materials well prepared for the two-week exchange. I put all essential materials on slides, including chemical formulas, data, laboratory schemes and field pictures, and was looking forward to a rewarding and enjoyable working vacation. A family vacation was long overdue.

I had sent the slides and other lecture materials by U.S. government diplomatic pouch to the American Embassy in Tokyo two weeks ahead of our travel began. Everything was on schedule, like clockwork. The day before the science session, to my surprise and shock, a messenger came from the American Embassy and informed me that my materials and slides had not arrived. My Embassy friend, Agricultural Officer Davis assured me that the package definitely was not lost, but might be wrongly routed. Davis suggested that I go ahead with my lecture and that he personally would track the materials until they were found. There was little choice for me but to proceed. The first day started with some pressure but generally went smoothly. I was nervous that evening in preparing the next day's materials. Without slides I had no data, no chemical structures, no guidelines; common subjects suddenly became complicated.

On the third day, I felt my fingers were less sensitive, my train of thought became slow, and my speech frequently became incoherent. My host, realizing this difficult situation, asked me if I wished to put off my talk for a few days and wait for the slides. I also received a routine physical checkup from a physician. To my amazement, my blood cholesterol level was at an unusually high level of 410 mg/dL. It had been 180 at my physical check up before the trip. I assumed it was an error and chose not to be concerned. Fortunately the slides reached my hands that very afternoon, three days late. The presentations went smoothly from then on. At the next stop of our trip in Taipei, JCRR physicians checked my cholesterol level and indeed it was 410. This incident taught me two lessons -- first, always carry lecture slides myself, and second, stress could raise my cholesterol level drastically.

In 1976, Japan hosted the CORESTA (Cooperation Centre for Scientific Research Relative to Tobacco) Congress. The excellence of the organization and the arrangements it made for the meeting impressed all in attendance. They even had professionals at hand to redesign visuals for speakers who did not have good quality slides for their presentations. It was on this occasion that I delivered my well-publicized report on the use of tobacco for food as well as for "safer" smoking material. Two years later in 1978 in Sophia, Bulgaria, CORESTA awarded me the first International Tobacco Science Prize. Yu Yi was with me on that occasion. Before our trip, The Chinese Ambassador Han Xu in Washington, DC, had been kind enough to notify the Chinese ambassador in Sophia about our planned trip and asked the embassy there to help us in case of need. During our stay in Bulgaria, Hungarian Goulash was the main dish at dinner, day after day. All other Hungarian meat and most vegetables, including tobacco leaves, were shipped to the then-USSR. From time to time, Yu Yi and I escaped to the Chinese Embassy in Sophia to enjoy a good Chinese meal. There was not a large Chinese population in Sophia. The embassy had only four employees other than the ambassador and his wife, and there were only two Chinese businessmen in Sophia at that time.

The following year, 1979, I was invited to tour the Philippines and lecture on tobacco for one week. Col. Tabije, Director General of the Philippine Tobacco Administration (PTA), served as my host. They put on such a red-carpet welcome for me that I was overwhelmed. Fifty or more tobacco scientists and students with banners and cheers met me in the middle of the airfield when the door of the plane opened. This reception made me forget to go through the official immigration process, which almost prevented me from leaving the island. On my tour of Luzon Island, I rode with the colonel and his wife in a long limousine. At a brief stop on the road I noticed two armed jeeps were traveling with one in front, one behind us. Both were poised ready to fire machine guns if needed. That evening after one of the many welcoming parties and lectures was over, I could not help thinking, "What on earth am I doing here!" In 1980 the CORESTA Congress was held in Manila with Col. Tabije, President of PTA, serving as chairperson. Before President Marcos of the Philippines delivered a speech welcoming the CORESTA Congress to Manila, every attendant, including all CORESTA members, was required to pass through a metal detector before entering the meeting hall.

It was in the 1980 Manila meeting, through my efforts, that Chinese tobacco scientists from both sides of the Taiwan Strait had their first direct contacts. My encouragement for China to promote international activities and cooperation resulted in the next CORESTA congress meeting in Guangzhou, China. It was the first international meeting China ever hosted. From then on, I made frequent trips to China on tobacco and agriculture projects, sometimes making 6 trips a year for various missions. I had made a total of 116 round trips between the U.S. and China up to 2005.

Special Benefits and Obligations at Beltsville

Being in Beltsville has many advantages. USDA's Beltsville research area is world recognized for its pioneering research leadership and significant achievements. There are 400 or so active research scientists in various research laboratories, some are world renowned, and I can communicate with them all the time. Especially in the early period, several Pioneering Research Laboratories were located at Beltsville. World authorities of academic field were just in the next building, and one could conduct discussions or seek their wisdom. Beltsville was considered a "holy" place in agricultural research. Foreign and domestic visiting scholars or scientists on sabbaticals or fellowships were always there, working on joint projects.

In addition, foreign political leaders who had an interest in agriculture frequently visited Beltsville. Nikita Khrushchev, Party General Secretary of the former Soviet Union, emperors and heads of state from several African countries, presidents, ambassadors, etc. visited Beltsville. They usually took general tours, but frequently asked to visit specific areas. For example, several of my old friends in agriculture visited two laboratories in one day, and continued visiting for one whole week. We had to serve as local hosts. Several ambassadors from China, or their science specialists, dropped by our laboratories to learn new areas of activities.

Beltsville also had its obligations from being close to the Capital. There were frequent inquiries from congressional members as a focal point in agricultural research. Through those years, by request or invitation, I had to attend many international meetings and conducted special projects in an advisory capacity in and out of the tobacco area. Occasionally, I was asked to serve on the board of international agricultural centers, such as the Asia Vegetable Research and Development Center (AVRDC). In addition, I had to respond to special requests from foreign countries.

I am not a politically oriented person. However, by living close to the Capital, one cannot escape the opportunity to witness some historical moments. We moved to Beltsville in 1952, and frequently visited Washington either sightseeing with visitors, or visiting museums. It so happened that one time, I received a commercial "invitation" with two tickets for the Inauguration of President Eisenhower. With another scientist of Chinese origin from Beltsville, Paul Cheo, I went downtown for this event. When policemen asked if we have tickets, we honestly said yes, and showed our tickets to them. When we two walked to the corner of Pennsylvania Avenue and 16th street, people were already four layers deep. My friend is taller than I, and he could see from the ground but I could not. I helped myself by climbing onto a tree branch by the sidewalk and had a perfect view watching the presidential car. In fact, I could have easily touched the heads of either president with another branch. At that very moment, I suddenly realized that I was in America, and I was witnessing democracy in full swing. On the way back from Washington to Beltsville with my friend, we knew that we had learned a lesson of democracy.

My memory also took me back to 1929 when I was a sixth grader in Wuchang, China. It happened one day that the main street near my school was full of armed soldiers with guns ready to fire. They lined up on both sides of the street facing the people on the curb. They stopped all usual street activities, even walking was forbidden. It continued for 30 minutes and then a chain of big, black limousines passed by at high speed. It was Generalissimo Chiang himself.

Policy Sensitivity and Tobacco Research

Tobacco has been a controversial crop since it was introduced to the civilized world more than five hundred years ago. Moreover, tobacco has been a valuable plant science research tool for almost one hundred years. I happened to be involved in research using tobacco most of the past sixty years. Many countries depend on tobacco for a major source of their national revenue though they may have differing policies regarding control of tobacco usage.

According to German Chancellor Otto von Bismarck, politics is not an exact science. To me, science is an accumulation and summarization of common sense into a simplified but beautiful language. Being a scientist who used tobacco as a research tool throughout my professional career, I experienced the policy ups and downs of tobacco research as a part of plant science. Having contributed to the supporting research findings, I am fully aware that tobacco smoking is a health hazard. However, I cannot agree with those experts in the science community who discourage or avoid using tobacco as a research tool.

It is unfortunate that a recent major agricultural journal which printed hunger signs of six crops on its cover, did not include--or even mention--tobacco. It is indeed regrettable that today's concern for political correctness could blind the scientists-or even worse that the writer did not know about those milestone studies. Furthermore, I know many established tobacco research scientists who branches of the U.S. government treated as though they had committed high crimes. On another instance, the integrity of wording in a respected scientific publication was questioned during litigation. If the science community and certain branches of government allow such unhealthy mistakes to continue, the future development of science in any country will suffer a tragic loss. It is with this deep feeling that I, a plant physiologist and phytochemist, wish to make a clear statement: the potential benefits to be realized from using tobacco as a research tool are only at their beginning; and tobacco research must receive due respect. Research institutes and funding institutions must learn to separate politics from academic research.

With this purpose in mind, I wrote a monograph entitled "Policy Sensitivity and Tobacco Research". Attached to this Memoir as Appendix A, the monograph is not a technical publication in the classic sense, but it does report past tobacco research contributions that paved the very foundation at

122

the dawn of plant science research. Tobacco has great future potential for food, medicine, and continued development of the biological sciences. Yes, we need to; we must treat tobacco research with respect.

The Three Wise Men in My Life

During my life I never thought that I am successful, or a person of fame, although many of my friends believe so. One way that I am at peace with myself is that I always try my best on any project or mission assigned to me; and anything that I can do today is not delayed till tomorrow. I always hand in my meeting notes and expense reports while my memory is fresh at the completion of a mission whether flight or train or hotel. Therefore, I feel free in spirit and ready for the next challenge.

I have contacted literarily thousands of people, and befriended them in the world academic community as well as in China. Many of them inspired me and helped to make who I am today. A grain of sand or a drop of water is of no significance; but accumulations of thousands and millions of grains and drops result in the land and the sea. I cannot honestly identify who provided the most teaching and inspiration to me. If I name one, certainly I will miss many, many others. Here, I wish to mention one name in each of the three areas representing science, service, and character, because those areas are the basis on which a person is valued today. I have stood on their shoulders to reach where I am today.

Dr. Walter G. Frankenburg

In the area of science, I wish to mention Dr. Walter G. Frankenburg. He escaped to the U.S. from Germany in the earlier Hitler days, and he used his expert talent in catalyst chemistry to direct tobacco research as Director of the General Cigar Research Laboratory. Within the first ten years in his new field, Frankenburg established himself as the authority of tobacco chemistry. Several of his early papers are considered classic documents that all tobacco scientists must read, even today. Upon completion of my Ph.D. at Pennsylvania State University in early 1950s, my advisor, Professor C.O. Jensen, recommend that I continue my learning as post-doc at the Frankenburg laboratory. It is of interest that Jensen and Frankenburg held different academic theories on tobacco fermentation. Frankenburg accepted me to work with him on a salary of $10 per week. Those two years, 1950 and 1951, were the most important and challenging period of my training as a tobacco scientist.

In that period, Frankenburg conducted research on alkaloids, fermentation, and tobacco reconstitution. In alkaloids, he knew there were many relatives of nicotine yet to be separated and identified. My interest in alkaloids sprang from him. Frankenburg considered fermentation to be a mainly chemical process, and used copper as a catalyst to promote the process. He considered that fermentation involved two major processes. The primary one is chemical or catalytic process and the secondary one is the biological process. Now we know that both are major factors. On leaf reconstitution, Frankenburg initiated the technology to make better cigar fillers from ground tobacco leaves, residues, and other binding materials to form homogenized leaf tobacco (HTL). In all three areas, he was in the forefront, and he opened many doors for younger researchers.

In addition to Dr. Frankenburg's broad academic knowledge, I benefited by his scientific ways of approach in conducting research. One example is his insistence on obtaining 100 percent return on all and every fraction of the organic material from the very beginning. In other words, to search and understand the fate of each fraction, the dynamic changes during fermentation, especially under the condition of dry weight loss. He made it easier for us to reach the 100 percent return by using calcium as the base for calculation. Another example was that Frankenburg requested that every scientist keep two complete sets of laboratory notebooks, recording in detail every step of the research, or experiences. Those approaches helped me greatly in my professional career.

Frankenburg and his laboratory were among the most well known tobacco research institutes, and they attracted world attention. Famous university professors, internationally known tobacco authorities and scientists came to Lancaster, Pennsylvania, to visit the rather small laboratory, and of course to talk with him. Accordingly, I had the opportunity to meet many nationally and internationally recognized tobacco scientists who were doing related research.

Frankenburg had extreme curiosity in any new knowledge of tobacco, his mind moved fast and he was impatient with most of us. Whenever there was a seminar or a conference on tobacco, he was always there. He sat in a front seat, and asked the first question before a speaker had finished the last sentence. Because of his stature, many speakers were awed in his presence and became nervous in deliberation. He did not realize this problem until several of us called it to his attention. (Some twenty years later, people told me I had the same habit. But I learned to control myself and discuss questions with the speaker out of the conference room.)

Frankenburg distinguished himself not only as a great scientist, but also in kindness and consideration as a human being. Margaret and I were frequent guests in his home with his family. He showed us the furniture they brought from Germany, his study, and of course his ever present big steak for dinner. They took their beef rare, while Margaret and I could not eat meat with blood. Still, we had to finish what was on our plate. Years later, when Frankenburg visited us at Beltsville, I told him that story. He said they might have been so occupied in enjoying their own steak that they overlooked our lack of appetite.

In 1951, when I received a note saying that my father was in jail in China and asking me to pay U.S. dollars for his daily needs and possible release, I was very troubled. The demand was so great and impossible to meet for a post-doc with $10 per week in salary. When Frankenburg learned this, his immediate suggestion was to ignore that request. He told me: "I learned from my own experience with Hitler, the more you pay, the longer your father will be in jail". Still, he understood my concern that if anything happened to my father because of my part, I would regret it all my life. Without my knowledge, he told his secretary that I could receive some advanced salary; also he arranged to borrow from others to partially meet the demand. True as he said, the second demand came soon after they received the first payment. This time it was for my father's daily food payment in jail. Now Frankenburg put his feet down; he told everyone in the institute not to help Dr. Tso to keep his father in jail. He said that he had been foolish at the first time by allowing me to send the money. At that moment, I borrowed from many friends in the States to send to China. Later, some unidentified source in Hong Kong informed me that my father had died on a labor farm.

Dr. Norman E. Borlaug

The one who inspired me on service is Dr. Norman E. Borlaug. I know and am friends with many Nobel Laureates, but the one who impressed me most is Borlaug. He is proud but humble; he speaks with authority but listens to others with an open mind. He received the Nobel Peace Prize in 1970 because of his contribution in agriculture and is well known over the world as the "Father of Green Revolution". But he considers that his mission is just at the beginning.

Borlaug visited China often, the first time in 1974 in the midst of the Culture Revolution. When he first heard the word "hybrid-rice", the other members of his delegation said the interpreter made a mistake, as it is not possible to hybridize rice. Borlaug whispered: "I believe China has had a breakthrough in rice breeding".

We shared our interest on China, on Chinese agriculture, and the important role China could play on the world stage of agriculture. I cannot recall where and when we first met, but I am sure it was in a conference where Borlaug was the keynote speaker, and where I made a presentation on certain area of Chinese agriculture.

Borlaug has a vision of a world "free from hunger", and is devoting his total effort toward that goal. Four years ago, when I mentioned to him my concept to compose a book on the vision of Chinese agriculture in 2050, he looked at me in a somewhat surprise manner and replied, "I have had that in my thought for at least 20 years, but have had no time to do it. If you could take the lead, I will support you". It was the very beginning of the book-"Dare to Dream: Vision of 2050 Agriculture in China".

We traveled together in China many times, mostly to the poor southwest and far west, in addition to meetings in Beijing. Each time he insists on visiting fields to see crop production firsthand, to visit with local scientists, to share his experience, and to talk with farmers.

In Beijing, Borlaug frequently made recommendations to the very top on important policy issues, on urgent needs, and on international cooperation. On subjects such as wheat rust, airborne diseases involving various crops, on nutrition in food and in feed, on supporting less-developed countries from China, on national coordination and international cooperation, he made repeated suggestions to Chinese leaders in writing or face-to-face discussion.

Once we were in Guizhou to see the growth and use of QPM (quality protein maize), Borlaug was moved to see farmers eating and feeding animals with QPM, and he told them that they would use less feed and get better growth. He frequently reminds me that Chinese scientists must use the original QPM to develop local varieties to control diseases in different areas.

He is concerned with the lack of coordination among scientists and provinces in China. Once he spoke strongly that disease spores do not know the borderlines among countries and provinces, they are carried by airflow all over the world. How can one area isolate itself from others?

Borlaug is always in demand for lectures, meetings, keynote speaker at important international gatherings, and to serve as an honorary member of board, etc. His schedule usually is full one year ahead. However, his top priority is "freedom from hunger", especially for Africa. He is a teacher, a researcher, a promoter, and some would even say an "activist". To him, a hunger-free world is a mission, a crusade, and an achievable target.

Everywhere he goes there are always people wanting to see him, to talk with him, and to discuss some projects with him. Local hosts usually keep his room number, even hotel name secret in order to conserve his energy. In public occasions, I generally stay away from him when there is a crowd.

Once in Texas, Borlaug and I had something important to discuss, we had to drive far away to a local small restaurant for breakfast at 6 o'clock in the early morning. While in China, however it is somewhat different. We generally traveled together, stayed in the same hotel, and had private meals together. What inspires me the most is his total dedication to his dream of a world free from hunger, and his total effort to work toward it. Never in any occasion, public or private, did he mention that he has done enough, satisfied with his achievements, or use his age as an excuse.

People who have heard of or met Borlaug greatly respect and admire him. On several occasions, I knew the host was taking advantage of his fame and worked him too hard. If I happen to know the host, I'd suggest reducing the load in order to give him some rest. If I did not know the host, I indicated to Borlaug that he had worked overtime. He just cannot say "no" to any one.

How many people know that Borlaug pays a heavy price for his mission? Officially, he shares his time between CIMMYT (International Maize and Wheat Improvement Center) and Texas A & M University each year, but actually he is on the road most of the time. Even his secretary often cannot tell for sure where he is at a specific time or location. On his 90th birthday day celebration at the State Department in 2004, he had to leave for Africa that evening. Once when he was invited to China, he had to make a stop in Japan. He is at home only between Christmas and New Years, and he has to schedule his medical care around that time.

Mr. Fu Anming

On the character area, I was most inspired by Mr. Fu Anming, a Chinese scholar. We came from the same university, the University of Nanking, but

128

did not really know each other or our families well until we met again in Washington in the early 1950s. Anming served with distinction for many years as the Secretary to the late Ambassador Hu Shih of the Republic of China (ROC), a world-renowned Chinese scholar. Later on, he served in the U.S. Navy Map department and became a map specialist. Anming directed the total survey of Taiwan mapping, which is one of the keys for "Taiwan experience" in agricultural and economic growth, and in security.

Anming inspired me by his broad knowledge; his achievements in literature and history; his in-depth analysis of any event past or present; his view of how to treat one's self correctly; his "forget one's self" philosophy; and his devotion to his faith. All the above are easy to preach, but rather hard to practice. Anming practiced those principles all the time. Anming was always smiling, humble and never lost his temper on any condition. On one hand, he taught people how to treat themselves right, and on the other hand, how to be unselfish. Anming was a philosopher, a scholar, and a gentleman in every sense of the word.

Years ago, one of his sons, his daughter and her husband and Anming's two young granddaughters returned home to Washington for Christmas from Cornell University. During their late evening return to Cornell, their car crossed the centerline and crashed head-on with an on-coming car. All occupants of both cars were killed instantly, with the exception of the two granddaughters, who were sleeping in the rear of their parent's car. When the police called to report this accident, Mrs. Fu had fainted. Anming told himself that he must keep calm at this tragic moment, taking down the location and time. He asked the police about the condition of people in the other car. He told me later that he was sadder for the others because they were the innocent party.

When I visited Taiwan, Anming and his wife were gracious hosts. While in Washington, they were brother and sister to Margaret and me. When Anming was around, it felt like bathing in the spring breeze, always fresh and relaxing. He always saw many other ways when we had a difficult question. If I did something wrong, he only suggested gently that I may wish to consider alternatives. He never ceased to praise someone who contributed to the benefit of the society, to scientific achievement, or to statesmanship.

Anming was an authority on recent history of China, especially since the Opium War in 1840. He could analyze any event that happened to or in China and provide good explanations. He spent years writing "The Recent History of China", but we could only read the first volume at his death. It was indeed a great loss to all.

In the early stage of the opening of China, Anming asked me to visit his two sisters in Nanking to see what they needed and how he could help. Although sometimes they took advantage of him, he only felt bad for me, he understood that we are in much better condition than his sisters. A few years later, they finally reunited in China.

When Anming and his wife returned to Washington from Taiwan, we had more time to visit with each other. Mrs. Fu gradually lost her memory and her sense of direction. On one occasion, she left the apartment and wandered in the streets. When Anming found that she was missing, he ran to the streets where they usually took walks. Fortunately, he found her and she was safe. In his last few years, Anming told us of his two prayers. One was that his wife dies before him, so he could take care of her till her death. Another prayer was that before her death, she would announce her faith so that they would be together again after death. Both prayers were answered to his satisfaction.

I was in China when Margaret called me and said "Anming is gone". It was so sudden that I asked "to where"? Anming died while delivering a speech to a big crowd. The title of his talk was "How to treat yourself rightly".

Yes, Anming treated himself rightly, treated his friends rightly, and indeed treated society rightly.

Anming was always very considerate, thinking about other friends who I wished to see. For example, he always arranged time for me to meet old friends when I visited Taiwan. Several times I stayed at Anming's residence as his houseguest. He asked Y.S. Tsiang to bring Chinese traditional hot "take out" and join us at an early breakfast to enjoy a private moment.

Sometimes we went to the opera together, and sometimes we visited the rare "cultural" sites, such as the old residence painting room of the late most-famous master of Chinese painting, Chang Da-Chuan. These are indeed fond memories, but these men passed away years ago.

This Memoir is not intended to record the details of all my activities, my friends, to glorify myself, or to make excuses for uncompleted missions. Through those years of innocence, struggle, sorrow, laughter, success and defeat, I have tolerated and accepted blame and experienced the need to beg for support. I was and still am much blessed with many friends who guarded me, helped me and guided me to fly high or low with my own wings.

Of many friends who helped me and supported me on many projects, the readers may note I mostly mentioned a few who have either passed away, or are no longer active. This is by intention, not an oversight, because of the fact that I do not wish those friends to appear in this writing since this book might be considered too sensitive to some.

However, outside of the professional area, I want to mention a special warm friendship and concern for Dr. Chia Liangyi, who always took care of my health, especially in China. In June 1985, I had done most of the organizing work for an international symposium on agriculture to be held in Beijing. Sponsored by the SSTC (State Science & Technology Commission), the symposium had invited several world-renowned scientists. Though I had undergone sextuplet bypass heart surgery barely three months before the symposium date, I felt obligated to be there, and Margaret decided to travel with me. Dr. Chia at first suggested that I stay at home. After I decided to travel, he flew in from Hong Kong to care for me right from my arrival at the Beijing airport. He watched me at the international symposium while I presided over the opening session and delivered my address, and accompanied me on all official functions all the while carrying emergency equipment. In addition, Dr. Chia arranged special hotel visitations with two well-known Chinese medical authorities, President Wu of the Union hospital, and Dr. Fan, who was known in China as the "palace" medical doctor. All of them are my friends. Dr. Chia, his wife Dr. Zhou, and their family treated us like family members. They looked after me all the time not only in health matters, but also in many other activities, sharing their family care and love.

In the agricultural area, I have noted many friends who shared their wisdom and cared for me at various occasions. In the tobacco area, many past and current friends always took care of me. This began with STMA (State Tobacco Monopoly Administration) leaders Li Yisan, Ni Yijin, Jin Maoxian, Zhu Z.Q., and continued to the current leadership. In particular, Ms. Mao Baohong and Ms. Li Ying's whole family always have been very kind to me over the many years I traveled to China. It is their constant care and concern that made my contribution possible.

I must express my thanks to hundreds of other scholars and friends who cared for me in every way, whether in China, the U.S. or elsewhere. I am indeed fortunate to be in the receiving end. In IDEALS and in the UCCA operation, people supported these international projects without pay; they earned my great respect.

Chapter 7

China—Split by the Taiwan Straits

Closed Doors and Dark Ages in the Mainland

On January 31, 1949, the Communist army marched into Peking and the People's Republic of China was established on October 1, 1949. The Nationalist government retreated to Taiwan, reestablishing the base of the Republic of China.

A few Chinese friends returned from the U.S. in early 1950 for the sake of caring for their parents. One case was Dr. and Mrs. Chang, Professors of Geography and Sociology respectively. They went to Henan University with their two U.S. born sons, and a third expected child. Once they were out of the U.S., no further information was available about them, and no one expected to hear from them. During this period, due to both internal political and external hostile forces, the so-called "bamboo curtain" was gradually drawn closed to insulate China from the outside world. The U.S. government applied economic sanctions, and imposed embargo and military containment policies toward China. The U.S. 7th Fleet patroled the Taiwan Straight, and the Taiwan Straight would separate PRC and ROC for years to come. The U.S. began to restrict Chinese scientists with advanced training from returning to China. Meanwhile, the Chinese government began to restrict its citizens from traveling abroad and to limit free exchanges. International personal communication was restricted and began to cease. Any correspondence flowing in or out of China was under the guidance and surveillance of the communist authority. As time went by, eventually, China was effectively

133

isolated from the rest of the world.

The establishment of the People's Republic of China in 1949 generated hope for all Chinese that they would have time for needed peace and rest, to reconstruct their houses, to educate their young, and most of all to make a living again. However, more suffering was still waiting ahead of the Chinese people. Land reform was completed in 1952, and, as a result, each poor tenant peasant got a small piece of land taken from landlords. Later these small pieces of land were coalesced to form "co-ops", a concept taken from the "collective farms" of the USSR. At this time, the peasants still had property rights to the land they had recently received. But in 1958, the government merged all co-op lands into the "People's Commune" system, and all farmland then became "public" property owned by the state, as was land throughout China. By this time, no private land property existed in China. All Chinese land had been "nationalized".

In 1950-53, during the Korean War, China paid a heavy price in human lives and national economic strength to protect North Korea against the U.S. The Soviet Union, meanwhile, stood by without active participation while collecting every penny from China for "contributions" or arms sales.

In the meantime, the Nationalist Taiwan enjoyed the three-year breathing time to regroup, to rebuild, and to make changes of major policies for social and economic stability. Coincidentally, the Nationalists having learned from their loss of the mainland began their land reform in Taiwan, thus establishing a solid foundation for Taiwan's agricultural and economic growth. Those changes were the beginning of the so-called Taiwan experience.

In the mainland after the Korean War, China had to squeeze every penny and resource to satisfy the demands of its "old big brother", the Soviet Union, who had sat on its hands while the bloody conflicts were going on.

Amid all those happenings, Mao Zedong began a series of political purges in the name of proletariat revolution, through the 100 Flower Blossom movement in 1956, the Anti-Rightists campaign in 1957, and the Great Leap Forward movement in 1958. All those purges were actually small wars against whoever might not be 100 percent obedient and have surrendered to Mao, the absolute highest ruler. No scholars and intellects, educated people, landlords, merchants, friends or foes could escape his demand for total authority. Many people were liquidated during these purges.

After the death of Stalin in 1953, Mao began to covet the ideological supreme leadership of all communists of the world, a status Lenin and Stalin enjoyed. Nikita Khrushchev, the Russian Communist Party boss, of course did not like the idea. Conflicts between the big-old-brother Soviet Union and China broke open in 1958, and finally resulted in total split in 1959. The Soviet Union expected China to become its colony and to obey its orders and commands, to satisfy every demand from the Soviet Union. Like all other Communist countries, China was to contribute all its products and resources to the Soviet Union. This was a condition even Mao could not tolerate. Along with the termination of "brotherly" cooperation, the Soviet Union withdrew all its technical personnel, equipment and even blueprints for any on-going projects. As I can see it today, the Soviet Union did China a big favor by freeing the country from permanent dependency on the Soviet Union. Meanwhile, however, the Chinese people had to struggle even harder, suffer even more, and clinch belts even tighter to pay for what the SovietUnion said that China "owed" to her.

Under these conditions, the best or the worst character of the Chinese people became evident; the nature of being tolerant, accepting whatever happens as "fate". The "three natural disaster years" between 1959-1961 were a total economic failure, whereas crisis and famine resulted from the reckless Great Leap Forward, with which Mao impatiently tried to accelerate industrialization and agricultural productivity "twenty years in a day". Households had to turn in everything containing metal, such as useful tools and cooking wares. Collected items moved on to crude, peasant-built, street "foundries" for conversion to useless, porous "steel ingot". There were no tools left for farmers to plow the fields, no doors or windows in the houses, no cooking wares to cook. On top of all this, the climate was unfavorable for agricultural production during those three years. Further, old-big-brother's hands were all over China to collect the debt from the Korean War. The fact that the Chinese population tolerated this total thoughtless madness, and that most of the population managed to survive is nothing short of a miracle.

However, Mao's political movement and liquidation processes kept going on one after another despite all those happenings. In 1966, the "Cultural Revolution" began. Mao exhorted his "Red Guards" (naive youth) to attack his political enemies within the communist establishment using a campaign against old ideology, old culture, old customs and old habits (the "Four Olds"). The Red Guard purge shut down most of the education system, especially higher education. Everyone had to "self-criticize" openly to announce errors or crimes he or she had committed against communist ideology, the Party, or against Mao. This political turmoil set family against family, husband against wife or vise versa, children against parents, students against teachers, creating total madness and chaos. Red Guards searched people's homes and confiscated family valuables and books in the name of purifying society and strengthening communist ideology. Many Red Guards led their Red Guard group to their own homes and forced their parents to admit their guilts, etc. Many known scholars could not tolerate this and committed suicide. One suicide was a friend who could not tolerate his daughter's behavior to him, her lovely father.

Some families bonded together for safe passage through this period. One old friend of mine was a famous professor. He had returned from the U.S. after 1949 to help re-build his country. His elder son, with the prior understanding of his parents, one day led his Red Guards group came to his parent's house. He openly criticized his parents, broke one valuable "old" vase, and gave them a lecture. Those actions protected his parents from further sufferings, and kept many of his father's valuable books from being burnt. In the midst of this movement, the Red Guards gradually became reckless and too out of control even for the Communist Party, and they began to create headaches for Mao. To restore some kind of order, Mao called for the urban youth to go to the countryside, "to learn from the peasants".

No one escaped this historical turmoil, not even the president of China,

Liu Shiaoqi, who was appointed as the heir to Mao in 1959. Liu was purged and denounced as a capitalist roader, counter-revolutionary and traitor, and died in prison.

First Contacts With My Family

By late 1950, after a long period of silence and no news whatsoever from China, I suddenly received an urgent letter from a cousin in Shanghai pleading for help in saving the life of my father, Yafu. The letter said that the communist authorities had put Yafu in prison because of his past "irregular" financial activities involving the former 197th Division. The Division Commander, Ting, had died and the Division was liquidated by "friendly" forces before the Japanese surrender. Now, the only surviving person involved with the 197th was Yafu. Not only had the communist authorities asked for cash payment for the "irregularities", but they also asserted that those who were held in prison needed money to provide for their daily food. My cousin suggested that a payment of at least of $2,000 U.S. was badly needed. At the same time, word came from Hong Kong that my Uncle Yaoshu was under house arrest and was awaiting trial for his alleged "anti-revolutionary" activities. The sky was falling on my whole family and me!

Because I was new on the job, and thus had no savings reserve, I was lost as how to handle these matters. My first thought was to go immediately back to China, but I knew in my heart that that would be no solution at all. First and foremost, the authorities wanted money that I did not have. Knowing all this, Dr. Frankenburg had a frank discussion with me. "I know how you feel", he told me, "If you do not send money to rescue your father, you will regret it the rest of your life should anything happen to him. However, as an experienced person and having escaped from totalitarianism, I can assure you that the more money you send to China, the longer your father will be in jail." He continued, "Your sending money would not help in his release. However, if you insist on doing so to ease your conscience, we can advance you $2,000. I would personally consider it a foolish waste, if you choose to send the money", he concluded.

Even under those conditions, there was no reasoning with the practical. It was a matter of the heart. I decided to borrow the $2,000 and forward it by the fastest method to China. At the same time, I wrote to people in China I hardly knew, begging them to provide daily food to Yafu, no matter the cost. Three long difficult months passed. Another letter came from my cousin in Shanghai. Dr. Frankenburg was right--the authorities were demanding more money even before the "trial". And, on top of everything, Yafu was sick in prison and I was asked to pay for medical and prescription bills.

This time Dr. Frankenburg put his foot down; he gave me a stern lecture, which went like this: "You are an intelligent person. The first time I helped you, I knew it was to ease your conscience, but I realize now that I am responsible for making you act like a fool in paying ransom to these people. I cannot allow it anymore; otherwise, we will all be fools. Neither one of us should help the totalitarian, not knowingly anyway. Do not send any more money; it might actually be the only way to keep your father alive." If indeed my father was truly sick and possibly even hungry every day, how could I not comply with the demand for money, even if I honestly knew Dr. Frankenburg was right? Somehow, I borrowed another $500 and sent it off. Dr. Frankenburg learned about it later, but he only cautioned all my co-workers, "Do not help T.C. to keep his father in jail."

Three months passed, and there was no news. By then, communication between the U.S. and China had been shut down completely. One more month passed, and it turned into the year of 1951. Word came from Hong Kong that my father had died of "malaria" in jail six months before. The Shanghai cousin had been forced to keep silent and continue to request more money even when he knew Yafu had died. Messages by word-of-mouth were passed through Hong Kong to me to ignore further requests.

More sad news followed the tragic death of my father Yafu—Uncle Yaoshu was dead at the hands of the very people who talked him into returning "to build a new China". Yaoshu had put his trust in those who never knew the meaning of the word truth. He indeed could have been a brilliant leader in building a new China, but he was never given the opportunity. I was deeply saddened for his innocent death and mourned the double tragedy.

Another story in the aftermath of the deaths of my father and my uncle Yaoshu was no better: The Communist government started another movement to eliminate the Black Five. At the top of the five black list were landlords and the anti-revolutionary. Once blacklisted in such a way and being classified as "enemies of the people", Yafu's and Yaoshu's families became the lowliest class of the low, the untouchable, according to communist society ranking. They were believed to be guilty when the party cadres said they were guilty for whatever charges that might be lodged against them; and the masses were required to believe they were guilty. There were no hearings, no trials and no recourse. Each member of their families had to swallow their disbelief, their pride and tears, accept the insult and shame and manage to bury their sorrow as best as they could. They were deprived of the privileges of schooling, employment and housing, and had to suffer all sorts of humiliation. This was 1951; and it was only the beginning of the "red terror".

Tightening the Ring

During China's isolation period, anyone who had contact with family members outside China, especially in the U.S., came under suspicion for being an enemy of the State. This outrageous paranoia put my family in total confinement. This was especially true during the Korean War period from 1950-53. Those who had U.S. connections whatsoever automatically drew attention as possible spies, anti-revolutionaries, puppets of imperialists, etc. All doors were closed to the outside world-except to other communist countries. My family did not dare to write to me; neither did I dare any attempt to contact them. The bamboo curtain indeed had closed in on China. Only through occasional foreign press reports would I learn fragmented news of major happenings in China.

The "Let a hundred flowers blossom" and "let a hundred schools of thought contend" movements led by Mao in 1956, enticed many intellectuals into speaking openly. Yet "openness" was used against intellectuals during the anti-rightists campaign. In Mao's words, "The snakes were tricked out of their hiding holes." Government credibility appeared to be of no significance as long as the "enemies" were crushed and Mao's political objectives were achieved.

After the Land Reform, there were frequent conflicts among various peasant factions in rural society over land use, water use, rights-of-way, project coordination, etc. In August 1958 the concept of commune living emerged. The Communist Party decided to establish People's Communes with all-around management of agriculture, forestry, animal husbandry, fishery, and side occupations in order to merge industry (workers), agriculture (peasants), commerce (tradesmen), education (students and teachers), and military (armed forces) into one. This led to total social change and rural and industrial reconstruction. The rural land property rights were aggregated to the State and became "public property".

Chapter 8

The Early Taiwan Experience

Agriculture Reconstruction Led to Industrial and Academic Growth

When the Nationalist government retreated to Taiwan in 1949, the political situation there was far from stable. Conflicts and mistrust remained between the "Taiwanese" and the "Mainlanders" Chinese. Taiwanese are Chinese people who had lived in or migrated to Taiwan before 1945. Mainlanders are Chinese people who had migrated to Taiwan after 1945 or had fled the mainland to avoid the Nationalist government or to escape the 1949 take-over by the advancing communist army.

There was even distrust among the mainlander leaders. The memory of the February 28th uprising in 1947 remained fresh in everyone's memory, particularly the native Taiwanese. Much blood had been shed and many lives lost on the island because of Chiang's effort to hold on to his military dictator power and to eliminate any potential political rivals. The difficulties in Taiwan were no better than those on the mainland.

Learning the bitter lessons from their total disastrous defeat on the mainland, the Nationalists tightened their control as soon as they arrived on the island in 1949. The armed forces retreating from the mainland to Taiwan were ordered to disarm before they were granted permission to land. A total reorganization followed. No one could enter or leave Taiwan freely. People's living was hard and the island space small. The presence of communist forces across the Taiwan Straight was a constant and serious threat. Native Taiwanese residents, newly freed from the 50-year Japanese occupation, worried now about Nationalist pressure and possible communist occupation. General poverty and poor agricultural productivity permeated the countryside. The burden of feeding huge numbers of military troops of the Nationalist government was almost too heavy for the small island to bear.

China's agriculture was characteristically traditional; it consisted of multiple cropping and labor-intensive operations usually augmented by raising small animals, mainly pigs and poultry, and other side-line businesses. Taiwan echoed this tradition. Taiwan's agricultural productivity improved little during the 50-year Japanese occupation.

In 1943, U.S. President Franklin Roosevelt initiated the "World Food and Agriculture Conference" in anticipation of food shortage in the postwar world. China participated in this initiative as one of the four world powers. The following year China proposed a joint U.S.-China agriculture cooperative program for postwar rural reconstruction in China. To start, in 1944 both sides agreed to form a joint agricultural technological cooperation team to study the situation and to formulate a concrete plan. This study took place in 1946 under the joint administration of U.S. President Harry Truman and China's President Chiang. The joint team visited various parts of China for 11 weeks and spent another 5 weeks preparing its report. This report was the basis of the March 31, 1948, U.S. legislation establishing the Sino-U.S. Joint Commission for Rural Reconstruction (JCRR). The U.S. agreed to fund 10 percent of the rehabilitation plans. As a result, the JCRR was officially established in Nanking on October 1, 1948, with five commissioners. Dr. T. H. Shen was one of the three Chinese commissioners, and Dr. Y.S. Tsiang was the Secretary General.

In 1949, when the civil war spread throughout mainland China, the JCRR moved to Taiwan in August. This move proved crucial for Taiwan and for the Nationalist government that had fled and settled there. Initially, the JCRR's objectives included improvements in production efficiency and farmers' livelihoods, reforms of land policy, expansion of water systems, provision of agricultural finance, and initiatives in other technical and production areas. Later the program was expanded to include animal husbandry, fishery, forestry, rural health, training, credit and economics, and broadened to include all segments of rural society. It was further expanded to research on new products, agricultural extension, farmers' cooperatives and mechanization. The JCRR was designed to remain flexible. The program could thus be adapted to the current state of Taiwan's agriculture, and it was indeed backed up by provision of new technologies and new aid legislations in the U.S.

The JCRR's most important achievement was the implementation of the land reform in Taiwan. This land reform was entirely different from that on the mainland. Taiwan's land reform was implemented in three stages: farm rent reduction, sale of public lands, then land-to-the-tiller programs. It began in 1949. Reduction of farm rents, limiting rents to 37.5 percent of the value of the annual yield, greatly benefited tenant families. In 1951, public lands were sold to incumbent cultivators on an installment payment plan over a ten-year period. In 1953, the government executed a program of compulsory purchase from private landowners of their excess tenant lands for resale to the incumbent tillers, also based on a ten-year period to complete the payment. Through this, rural livelihoods were greatly improved. Farm youths attended school for the first time, and social and economic activities were greatly invigorated. At the same time, former landowners used their influx of cash to invest in industry. Industrial development brought further improvements in agriculture, which ultimately spurred overall economic growth and social stability.

In the 1950s, Taiwan had an agricultural economy. By the 1960s, industrial development had progressed so fast as to make the island a mixed industrial-agricultural economy. By the 1970s, industries began to dominate. The key to the JCRR's success in promoting both agricultural and industrial growth was the stabilization of agricultural prices by increasing production, improving agricultural exports and increasing raw materials to fulfill industrial needs.

The return of Taiwan to China after its 50-year Japanese occupation was a monumental historical change for the Chinese people. Besides the fleeing Nationalists and their army, and refugees who preferred not to remain under a communist government, many companies and higher education institutes also evacuated to Taiwan. This migration of masses of people to Taiwan from mainland China brought capital, financial, intellectual and technical talents, and a strong determination to succeed. All of these factors greatly improved the island's social, cultural and economic development. In addition to strengthening Taiwan's higher education institutions, many public and private organizations sent students, scientists and technicians for advanced training abroad. Most Taiwanese graduate students training abroad studied in the U.S. Many became brilliant scientists, managers and administrators. Some took up leadership positions in the U.S., while others returned to become leaders of their chosen fields in Taiwan.

JCRR leaders were proactive in cultivating Taiwan's future leadership. For example, Dr. Y.S. Tsiang searched through the names of Taiwanese agricultural scientists and names of Taiwanese university graduates and located where they were working and how well they were performing. He even interviewed them in person whenever the opportunity arose. In so doing, he identified many potential talents of Taiwanese origin for promotion and training. One Dr. Tsiang's protege, an agricultural school graduate, found to be teaching English in a rural school was sent abroad for graduate study. Another with a masters degree was sent for Ph.D. training. Years later, both became top leaders in Taiwan.

Outside Taiwan, the political and economic setting favored Taiwan's development and growth. The U.S. was at that time involved in conflicts in Korea and later in Vietnam. Taiwan's leadership was wise enough to grasp the opportunity to pave the way and build a foundation for future growth. Most people to this day view Taiwan's economic growth as nothing short of a miracle. They speak with pride of the "Taiwan Experience". There is no doubt that it was indeed a tremendous achievement.

First Visit to Taiwan

In 1958, Taiwan's economic base was still very weak, including its rice production. Government relied on taxes from tobacco and wine as major financial revenue resources, and put them under the control of the Taiwan Tobacco and Wine Monopoly Bureau (TTWMB). Sugar export also contributed some income, which was used for purchasing food and feed grains. However, locally grown tobacco was of poor quality and yields were low. Thus, most tobacco leaf or cigarettes were imported, draining scarce hard currency from the country.

By 1958, I had been gone from China for 11 years, and had established myself as a well-known tobacco scientist in chemistry and physiology. The September 1958 issue of National Geographic Magazine reported on my work in an article titled "You and Your Obedient Atom". My picture ran, and the accompanying article reported that I had used triple-labeled isotopes to study organic metabolism in tobacco. The same year, I was elected to serve as the President of the Phytochemical Society of North America (PSNA). The news traveled. Dr. T.H. Shen from JCRR and the Agriculture College of Taiwan University, of which Dean Paul Ma was also an old friend, issued a joint invitation on behalf of the TTWMB for my family and me to visit Taiwan for three months. All of them anticipated great recommendations from me though most of my professional work had been limited to laboratory benches, greenhouses and growth chambers.

Our daughter Betty was only six years old, and we were expecting our second child Paul in early 1959. Margaret and I decided to accept this invitation. We took Betty with us, but had to return to the U.S. before the end of November of 1958. Indeed, this three-month stay was very productive for all of our family. Margaret took the opportunity to learn Chinese watercolor painting and had her first solo exhibition in Taiwan with great success. Betty learned to speak Chinese fluently with the help of a young girl who kept her company all the time. I traveled around the island to see, examine and discuss tobacco field production and began to understand the agricultural problems and opportunities in Taiwan.

In my final report to the Advisory Council of TTWMB, which involved almost all the known agriculture scientists and authorities in Taiwan, I made

145

detailed evaluation on existing problems and drastic approaches needed to improve tobacco and food grains, both in location and in seasonal cultivation. For example, I suggested moving tobacco from the north to the south part of the island, from heavy soil to sandy loam, from winter to spring, etc. Implementing this measure, I said, would relieve the pressure of food shortage by freeing up land in the north for grain production year around. Those recommendations were well accepted in their entirety, and indeed solved several problems.

During this trip, in addition to my agriculture work, we made many good and valuable friends. Among those friends, I wish to mention Margaret's teacher, Cao Weizuo, a well respected scholar, artist, and educator, Wu D.K., Director of TTWMB, an economic expert and industrial leader who later led wine grape production to increase farmers' income, and many tobacco and agricultural experts, including Wan H and his wife.

We also had the opportunity to renew our friendship with many scholars whom we knew before we came to the States, including many from the University of Nanking, such as Y.S. Tsiang, Y.G. Jin, H.T. Chang, and many others.

The 1958 trip to Taiwan led to many, almost annual, follow-up trips. Because of my relationship with Taiwan, I was later asked to serve as a member of the Board of Trustees, representing The U.S. to the Asia Vegetable Research and Development Center (AVRDC). I served two consecutive terms, giving me opportunities to visit both sides of the Taiwan Strait, the mainland and Taiwan, several times a year. Occasionally I served as an unofficial bridge among old friends and relatives who were separated on opposite sides of the Taiwan Strait. In addition, I used my AVRDC position to initiate agriculture exchanges between mainland China and Taiwan. I used my tobacco position to encourage other scientific exchanges, and I encouraged both sides to participate in international conferences to the extent that the political climate permitted.

The Three Dreams

On a memorable occasion in 1958, I had been invited to address the annual convention of the China Agriculture Society in Taiwan. President Jin Yang-kao, an old friend and Nanking alumnus, informed me that Professor Hu Shih, a renowned Chinese scholar, who had recently returned to Taiwan, would share the stage with me. Hu was known to every Chinese and also was the President of Academia Sinica. I begged off, although it was a distinct honor. I reasoned with Jin that such arrangement would definitely not work well. If Jin placed Hu's lecture ahead of mine, people who came to hear Hu would walk out after Hu's speech, and I would be left there alone. If Jin placed my talk ahead of Hu's, people would come early merely to hold their seats and pay no attention to what I had to say. Either way it would be embarrassing for me. Jin agreed with my assessment. He put Hu's lecture in the morning session and my report in the early afternoon. At the morning session, the huge convention hall was crowded with people. Some even were standing or sitting on the floor to listen to Prof. Hu. At the afternoon session, a third of the seats were empty.

Professor Hu's speech inspired us all. As the president of the Academia Sinica, he stressed the need to strengthen academic studies. The Nationalist government was too poor to fully support the institutes of the Academy. Hu, therefore, suggested other sources of support. What he proposed would be remembered as his famous "Three Dreams" speech. His first dream was that the Taiwan Tobacco and Wine Monopoly would support the Institute of Chemistry. The second dream was for the Taiwan Sugar Corporation to support the Institute of Botany. And the third dream was for the JCRR to support the Institute of Social Sciences.

After my presentation that afternoon, Director General of the Tobacco and Wine Monopoly D.K. Wu joined me to make a courtesy call on the Governor of Taiwan, Governor Chou. Aside from tobacco matters, the governor inquired about Hu's speech. I took the opportunity to describe the three dreams that Hu had talked about and sought his active support of them.

The JCRR support could certainly be arranged if the Taiwan Provincial government would agree to allow the Chemistry and Botany Institutes to be supported, respectively, by the Monopoly and the Sugar Corporation, as those two organizations were under the governor's authority. I laid out my case to the Governor, "It would be a welcomed gift to Professor Hu, as this is his first speech and his first open request since his return to Taiwan. Hu's giant stature would promote the academy's image nationally and internationally." The Governor turned to Wu and asked, "How much would it cost, do you know?" "I don't think it would be too much of a burden for the Monopoly," Wu answered, "Furthermore, the Chemistry Institute can help us in conducting many research projects, particularly in the fermentation area for wine research." I then added, "The same is true for the Taiwan Sugar Corporation--a small investment in the Botany Institute could produce great returns." The governor nodded with a smile, "We don't have to be concerned with JCRR. I am sure it can support the other institute."

It happened at 5 o'clock in the evening at the governor's mansion. I was scheduled to join Professor Hu for dinner that evening at a private party hosted by Professor Chao. Eager to pass on the good news to Hu I asked, "Governor, do I have your permission to inform Professor Hu this evening that his 'dreams' will soon be realized? It would be great news for him." Governor Chou, looking at Wu, exclaimed, "So soon?" To which Wu replied, "We can do it, if you agree." I was extremely happy and excited to relay the good news to Professor Hu that evening. Obviously, he was pleased with this quick, positive response. There were toasts around the table in celebration of the swift realization of Hu's dreams.

That evening, Prof. Hu happily autographed a title and his name on one of Margaret's Chinese brush paintings. It was my wife's first painting exhibition.

Chapter 9
Raising of Bamboo Curtain

Crack of the Door

In early 1971, I experienced some mysterious events that have not been clarified even today. At first, the U.S. Department of Agriculture told me that the U.S. Information Agency would like to interview my family and me and to take some pictures for professional use. That period was a very active stage of my professional career, so I naturally thought the photos and interviews were just routine publicity. Later, a team of interviewers, photographers, and others repeatedly appeared at my office and laboratory, and later at my home. They asked questions about my family and me and about relatives in China. They took pictures of the whole family, including the children and their pets. I wondered and worried about the purpose of all of this. The interviewers told me that a U.S.-related agent would release the materials to mainland China. I wondered if they were talking double talk. The exact intention was never revealed to me. Rumors had it that the U.S. government was considering a mission to China and, since agriculture is not politically sensitive, I was being considered to participate. However, no such mission ever came about. A fraction of material from those interviews was published in Hong Kong, for whatever purpose, in 1971. President Nixon's historic visit opening the doors of China took place in February 1972.

First Exchanges in 1974 Between U.S. and China

The first official science delegation from the U.S. to China took place in 1974, in the midst of the Cultureal Revolution. Dr. Norman Borlaug was the only agriculture scientist among the U.S. delegates. Borlaug received his Nobel Peace prize in 1970, and is well known as the Father of Green Revolution. Since his vision is a world free of hunger, he was especially interested in the agriculture situation in China.

At the University of Minnesota, where Borlaug did graduate study and received his Ph.D., one of his best friends was Lu Chen Hou, a brilliant Chinese scholar and Ph.D. in plant physiology. Lu had returned to China during the war against Japan, and Borlaug was hoping that they might have an opportunity to meet and catch up the past years. However, the delegation's "security" was so tight and the "fear of personal foreign contact" was so great in China that Borlaug dared not even mention Lu's name. It was taboo for Borlaug to admit knowing of Lu's whereabouts or whether Lu was dead or alive for fear of bringing Lu unnecessary harm. It came as total surprise to Borlaug when he noticed Lu Chen Hou among the Chinese scientists receiving the U.S. delegation. At that emotional moment, Borlaug and Lu knew to control themselves, both aware of the danger of even a simple conversation. An occasional eye contact between them was all they could do.

I heard this story frequently from Borlaug and from Lu. Almost 25 years later, while I was in Beijing, the China Agricultural University held a banquet for Prof. Lu's 90th birthday, and I was invited to attend. I informed Borlaug about this. He faxed me a letter of congratulation and asked me to read it aloud at the banquet. This was a very touching moment for all attendees.

Also in 1974, as an exchange, an official Chinese agricultural delegation visited the U.S. This was the first group of high-ranking government officials and senior scientists from Communist China to visit the U.S. in 26 years. Both governments were careful not to allow anything to spoil the visit. In particular, the U.S. government was unsure of how its citizens would react to the Chinese communists. The State Department went to great lengths to ensure the visit's success, including providing security guards to tour with the group. The National Academy of Science, which served as the host for the guests, sent its chief China experts to accompany the tour. The USDA asked me to accompany the delegates on their three-week visit. There were 16 delegates in the group. Among them, I knew the chief delegate, who was a professor and cotton specialist, and several senior scientists. Some were old friends and even former classmates.

U.S. officials took precautions at every step. For air transportation, the delegates sat in an arranged isolated section of the aircraft. They boarded the plane only after the other passengers had been seated and the plane was ready to take off. They deplaned after others had departed, and were immediately whisked aboard a chartered bus. At hotels, they occupied a separate section and used a special dining room. They marched in and out of the dining room as a group. Even the seating was assigned. Throughout the first week, I found that there was no small talk; we had no personal conversations or contact, except to convey that most of the guests were unhappy with American meals and longed for Chinese food. Seated in an assigned seat next to the chief delegate, I offered to help change the restaurants menus whenever possible. I also provided some canned Chinese delicacies for the group. This helped somewhat to break the ice, but I was far from winning their confidence.

In the following days, I was occasionally able to inject some words, comments or suggestions during our dinner conversations when the subject turned to U.S. agriculture. Soon, the guests began to ask me direct questions, but still they did not invite me to their respective hotel rooms. One day I intentionally went to the dining room early and took a seat other than that assigned to me. The security guard from the State Department motioned for me to shift to my regular seat. I told him that I planned to move around freely to get better acquainted with the delegates. When the chief and others entered the dining room, they immediately noticed what had happened and voiced no objection at all. From that time on, I knew that I had probably broken the ice and dispelled my "enemy" status. After this, I participated in discussions more frankly and frequently, and the atmosphere became slightly more relaxed.

Professor Wang, known as the "Mr. Soybean" in China, and I had been classmates at the University of Nanking. We had a mutual friend, Dr. Shao-lin Chen, who was then residing in Milwaukee and he was eager to talk to Wang. Wang was able to get permission from the chief of the delegation for a social telephone call from my hotel room. When the time arrived, Wang, at the last minute, invited a third person, Professor Li, an authority in maize, to join him. I knew that this was his caution to alleviate any possible false accusations that might arise in the future as to what was discussed. This third person was, in other words, a witness to what would be discussed. Throughout the trip, delegates allowed only an occasional glimpse of thin emotions. Since most of them were trained in or had visited U.S. universities many years before, each one had requested to be allowed to pay a return visit to his old residence or laboratory, even though that place might well have been drastically changed or even no longer exist.

One day near the conclusion of the tour, the delegation chief invited me to join him for a "chat". When I entered his hotel room, I found that the deputy chief and Professor Wang were also present. I noticed another scientist was pacing outside the window, but the chief stopped me from inviting him into the room. We sat down at a round table, and the deputy chief carefully arranged two cups of tea on the table before me and asked politely, "Dr. Tso, do you recall these old Chinese traditions?" I was touched. I immediately stood up, thanked both the chief and the deputy chief sincerely, and expressed deep appreciation for their courtesy. An old Chinese custom was offering tea to a guest as a common courtesy, but asking for your choice of green or red tea before serving it is yet a higher form of respect. Without asking any questions, I had been served both green and red tea at the same time. That was the highest form of respect they could show. Then, and only then, did I know that I had the confidence of my Chinese colleagues! After all, we came from the same roots, shared the same tradition and culture, and were devoted to the same field of agricultural science. The ideological difference no longer posed a big gap between us!

The Awaking and Open Door

Soon after the 1974 tour other exchanges took place in earnest. The bamboo curtain was gradually raised, communications opened somewhat and many restrictions were relaxed or removed. With the opening of liaison offices between the former enemies, additional channels were made available for formal and informal exchanges in various areas of science, particularly in agriculture. As a result, I frequently received requests to promote exchange and cooperation between China and the U.S.

Beginning in 1975, each year at Thanksgiving, several agricultural specialists of Chinese origin from different parts of the U.S. gathered at our home in Beltsville, Maryland. For two or three days we would have free exchanges and discussions. We commented on and made suggestions for better Chinese agricultural reform or for improved U.S.-China agricultural cooperation. Those scholars included Hui Chiang, H.H. Cheng, S.D. Kung, George Liang, T.L. Yuan and occasionally others. Those open expressions of scientific views were passed on to Chinese counterparts each year. Recognizing the sincerity and value of these exchanges, requests came from mainland Chinese scientists, agricultural leaders, liaison officers, and later Chinese ambassadors, ministers and once even an entire Chinese delegation, to participate in such meetings. All were private guests of our family. These early gatherings sowed the seeds for IDEALS (the Institute of International Development and Education in Agriculture and Life Sciences), a nonprofit, nonpolitical service organization that many Chinese and American scholars and I jointly established and founded in 1983.

In 1977, China finally opened its door to my family and me. We received an invitation from the Chinese Academy of Agricultural and Forestry

153

Science, which later became the Chinese Academy of Agricultural Science (CAAS), to visit our motherland on a working vacation. The timing of the proposed trip was at the end of the Cultural Revolution. The Gang of Four had been recently arrested. Deng Xiaoping had resumed office. The colleges had been reopened and urban youths who had been exiled into the countryside to be "re-educated" in the Mao doctrine began to return to the cities. However, the "die-hards" were still in evidence, and the political situation as a whole was not yet stabilized. Despite all of this, with a mind of reconciliation after almost three decades of waiting and hoping, I eagerly accepted the invitation.

Margaret and I were excited at the prospect of revisiting China, but at the same time were concerned about the great unknown in front of us. The Chinese Liaison Officer at Washington was Mr. Han Xu. He later became the third Chinese Ambassador when the U.S. and China re-established diplomatic relationship in 1979. He assured us that all would be in good order for the trip.

Prior to the travel, the State Department and the USDA briefed us regarding preparing lectures for Chinese study groups, understanding China's tobacco situation and, most importantly, navigating our visits with family members. Many of our friends asked us to make contact with their family members and to take them small amounts of cash or gifts. My feelings at that time were indeed mixed. I had no idea what to expect. Would it be a fulfilling and satisfying trip or a heart-breaking experience?

Chapter 10

Mainland China Revisited After 30 Years, 1977

The Long Wait

Years of war, years of training, and years of working had passed. I had for long years experienced sorrow and pain for myself, my family and my country of birth. As time passed and my life moved on, new developments diluted the impacts of the past as circumstances changed. The Christian faith teaches, "pardon for sin and a peace that endureth." Yet it was difficult for me to reconcile what had happened so long ago in China while I had determined to achieve my inner peace in the years to come. The healing process had to be slow and long; the scars were too deep. My feelings about Japan were an example of my still ruptured emotions. The Japanese had surrendered to China and the allies in 1945, and since that time I had made many personal and professional friends who were Japanese. Some of these were dear, respected friendships which had stood the test of time. Deep in my heart, however, the question burned of my full forgiveness of Japan's treatment of China as a nation.

We could not, or even cannot, forgive Japan's crimes committed in China. Our feelings towards mainland China were different, but not necessarily easier. Both my and Margaret's families were still in China. China held our roots. It is our motherland, no matter what kind of government it had. Since Nixon's historic visit to China in 1972, there had apparently been some relaxation in the general climate. Indirectly, we sometimes learned tidbits about our family members and their whereabouts. But we could never

155

be absolutely sure of the validity of the information.

In the wake of the 1977 Cultural Revolution, 30 years after I left China for advanced study in the United States, my family and I received an invitation from the Chinese Academy of Agricultural and Forestry Science. My 1947 voyage on the "General Gordon" in 1947 took 25 days from Shanghai to San Francisco. During those 25 days, I was full of dreams, hopes, and ambition. I was so sure of myself and believed that I could conquer the world. However, my world at that time consisted mostly of China in the period after the defeat of Japan. Even now, I had not regained my inner peace about the happenings of my motherland. Thirty years later in 1977, I made the trip in 26 hours. Although I had by then established myself as a scientist of some renown and I was a man happily married with a family, I knew nothing about what China had become except for fragmented information from family, or what was left of my family in China. The broken dreams and lost hopes for China that had occupied me many years earlier mattered no more. No longer was I sure of what I could do for my motherland. The one ambition left in me was to seek out members of my original family and contribute whatever I could toward a better tomorrow for them, if indeed I was even to be allowed to fulfill this dream.

Because there were no direct flights between the U.S. and China in 1977 due to the U.S. policy of embargo and blockade, all travel had to be routed through Paris, which meant long hours of flight time. The Air France flight from Paris to Beijing was filled to capacity. Margaret and I occupied aisle and center seats. During a brief stop in Athens, a young mother with her baby boarded and seated herself two rows ahead of us. The baby was crying and the mother tried to comfort him with little success. It caused considerable disturbance for the entire trip between Athens and Karachi. Upon landing in Karachi for refueling, all passengers deplaned to stretch our legs. The weather was hot and humid and there was no air conditioning at the airport. When at long last the plane again took off, the baby started to cry once more. This continued throughout the flight and for several hours there were loud complaints.

Finally, we heard the voice of flight captain, "Ladies and gentlemen, we are now entering the air space of the People's Republic of China. Please pack your cameras as no pictures are allowed." Immediately a hush fell over the cabin. Even the baby stopped crying. People not only packed their cameras and other belongings, but everyone seemed to sit rigidly in their seats and speak in low whispers, though the plane was still hours away from Beijing. There was a new tension in the air. Apparently no one knew what to expect.

Another two or three hours passed. The voice of the captain was heard again, "We are entering the Capital Garrison Region of China. Please remain in your seats." I noticed only total silence in the cabin except for the drone of engines. The passengers seemed to freeze. I felt the plane slowing but could see nothing out of the window. It was 2:30 p.m. local time.

Another long 20 minutes passed without incident. Again, the pilot's voice came to his passengers authoritatively. "We are cleared for landing. Please remain seated. Do not leave your seat until we receive permission from local authorities." Now I was totally immersed in the tense atmosphere and a strange feeling of nostalgia. Glancing outside as the plane approached the runway, I saw small farmhouses, crops and one or two moored planes. When the plane finally came to a stop in the middle of an open field some distance from the tower. I saw many uniformed people moving about. Another five to ten minutes passed before the doors were finally opened. Several armed soldiers came aboard and proceeded to search the aisles with fierce probing eyes. Without exception, the passengers were silent, effecting a patient and obedient attitude.

Two to three minutes after the soldiers departed, the captain finally gave orders to deplane. Margaret and I gathered our carry-on luggage and gradually moved toward the door. As I breathed again the air of China, I deeply yearned to take a photograph to commemorate my return, but it was forbidden. As I took my first tentative steps in my motherland, I dared not bend low to kiss the earth as I had long dreamed of doing. Soldiers were lined up on either side forming a path and waved the passengers through. As uncompromising as they were, I suddenly bent, pretending to tie my shoe and used both palms to imprint on the runway. I had expected to shed tears, but they did not come. Something else, heavier and hard to define, took over my emotion. It was 3:30 p.m., June 15, 1977.

As we approached the terminal, a huge portrait of Chairman Mao that hung in front of the building caught everyone's eye. I saw several hands waving at me and knew my hosts were as good as their words in meeting us. The customs and immigration officers were courteous but firm. Margaret and I carried one watch more than was allowed. To clear customs, we would have to pay tax on one small item of medical equipment meant as a gift.

We were officially met by a group of four government officials. I knew one of them from the 1974 Chinese delegation to the U.S. Our hosts were reservedly polite and sincere, but appeared to be understandably distant. I hoped it would not be long before we would become friends. They offered to carry our luggage and led us through an impressive hallway with a larger-than-life statue of Mao, a white marble imposition on a bright red carpet. On the walls there were enlarged, framed writings of Mao's poems and quotations. I was impressed by the immediate surroundings and quite automatically slowed my pace. My host immediately suggested taking a picture in the splendid hall with Mao as a very dominant background. Looking ahead, I noticed another quotation of Mao, which proclaimed, "Our friends are all over the world."

Grand Tour in Six Weeks

Everything had changed in China and in the world. Everything seemed gray. People with gray faces and forced gay smiles wore unisex gray uniforms. They lived in gray houses, walked on gray streets, and everyone seemed to be in a gray, gray mood. There were no streetlights, even in Shanghai. Only a few automobiles were available for special occasions. Drivers used lights only for a split second when they sensed something ahead. Margaret and I had a strong sense of being watched all the time. We too began to feel gray, even in our hotel room! Prior to the trip, I had been warned of these things--that hotel rooms may be bugged and personal documents may be searched. I made up my mind to keep my integrity intact despite the uneasy feeling. After all, I had nothing to hide. Wouldn't you be scared? Wouldn't you be concerned? Wouldn't you be willing to offer some help to improve the situation? I recall wishing that we were at the seashore, picking up colorful seashells.

This trip, I delivered talks on five subjects on tobacco, some repeated at different locations. And I gave two lectures on general agriculture. The hosts copied all of the slides and papers that I brought with me. On tobacco, I reported on: (a.) state of the art, including major trends between 1965 and 1975, the period of the Cultural Revolution; (b.) smoking and health research and the development of a less hazardous cigarette; (c.) production research involving para-sexual hybridization and leaf usability; (d.) advances in manufacturing technology. Lastly, I discussed (e.) my vision for the tobacco industry towards the year 2000.

In the area of general agriculture, the Chinese Academy of Agriculture and Forestry (later re-named the Chinese Academy of Agricultural Sciences Science) sponsored both of my talks, which were delivered at the Beijing Hotel. Forty to fifty scientists attended. I had to begin on subjects related to tobacco, but did mention some major agricultural breakthroughs in the outside world, such as DNA research, the Green Revolution and other areas of pioneering research and developments around the globe. I could sense that my audiences were feeling lost after 30 years of isolation, although no active discussion was possible or allowed following my reports.

As an agricultural scientist, I naturally had a particular interest in tobacco plant physiology. My wife, Margaret, was interested in health care. Our tour included Beijing, Shandong, Shanghai, Hangzhou in Zhejiang Province, Wuhan in Hubei Province, Zhengzhou in Henan Province, and the famous Dachai in Shanxi Province. Shanghai and Wuhan were targeted for visiting our relatives. The remaining locations, with the exception of Dachai, which was a trip born out of curiosity, were visited for professional interests.

Most of our travels within China were by train, with some by air. Our first flight in China between Beijing and Jinan in Shandong Province was quite an experience for us. We flew in a small propeller plane made in the former Soviet Union. The plane's cooling system either did not exist or did not function. Shortly after take off, moisture condensed in the cold air to form a dense fog inside the cabin. That some passengers were alarmed would be an understatement. The young stewardess valiantly tried to allay fears by announcing, "Don't worry, this is only condensation; we fly very low, don't worry."

I was to learn that the standard formula for professional visits such as mine began with a formal briefing by the host. The briefing, typically including statistics, history, achievements and future plans, with emphasis on how poorly every facet of life was conducted before the People's Republic of China was established in 1949; how much the country had since achieved under the "Party" guidance and how many breakthroughs had been made possible based on Mao's ideological teachings. A guided tour was usually followed by a reception. I soon became aware that the reception gave the visitor an opportunity to express any thoughts, views or "critique". Prior to this trip, I was told that technical people in China, after 30 years of isolation, were eager to learn from and communicate with outsiders. So, at the first welcoming banquet in Beijing, when I was told to be prepared to "empty my professional pocket"to my Chinese peers, I was ready and willing to do so. I was also encouraged by the eagerness and hunger I sensed for knowledge among colleagues I had met during the tour. But at the same time, I was aware of their seeming fear of overstepping the party line by showing any inferiority or "loss of face".

The Beijing central government had assigned two guides to accompany our tour, one professional guide and one security guard. They stayed where we stayed, traveled where we traveled, and when I toured at the provincial level, I was provided with two provincial guides in addition to the ones already in tow. And, it got worse! There were prefectural level guides, district level guides, commune level guides, brigade level guides, and production unit level guides. Thus, when I was visiting a tobacco field of a certain production unit, which meant that I was touring at the seventh level, an entourage of 14 official guides might well escort me. This, of course, was in addition to various and sundry managerial, technical and support personnel. This could, on any given day, amount to ten or more vehicles crammed with the necessary accompaniment of guides and hosts. It was easy for me to lose count of who was who, except for those who had been with me from the very beginning. At the close of a tour day, the guides banded together and reviewed the day's events in preparation for their evaluation report on me as their foreign visitor or guest. This report was duly transmitted to their respective supervisors and superiors. The evaluation was usually sent onward to the next location as well and sometimes embellished with remarks and comments by that location, too.

Thankfully, before long my professionalism, ethic and sincerity won respect and true friendship among my hosts. They communicated more freely, and occasionally a guide even begged off some routine function. As it was 1977, the Cultural Revolution was barely over, and most people were still nervous and fearful, and paranoia was everywhere. Most authorities were still under the purview of the party secretary of the organization.

The guides had been instructed from the highest level to protect the visitors' health. They were admonished to ensure that nothing undesirable happened to any of us. One day in Shandong, I felt some stomach discomfort due to a heavy intake of banquet food the previous night and requested that the afternoon's discussions be postponed to the following day. Immediately, two medical doctors from a provincial hospital were called in to care for me. An EKG was moved into my hotel room and tests performed on the spot. Then the doctors took a detailed health history from my wife and me, followed by medication and close monitoring overnight. Wiser from this lesson, I proceeded to quietly tolerate any minor inconveniences, and participated in each and every appointment scheduled from then on.

These visits continued in a routine fashion until we reached the Hsu-chang Station in Henan Province. There Margaret caught a light cold and was resting in the guest room. Blocks of ice were swiftly moved into the room in addition to floor fans. A woman was sent in to attend her and prescribe medication. I noticed that it was the same woman who had recently joined our tour group. Curious, I questioned her about her ability as a plant scientist to administer in a nursing capacity to my wife. The woman smiled and gently replied, "I am a heart specialist and was sent to accompany your tour from the time of your sickness in Shandong. I am glad that you are doing fine."

The efficiency of politically-oriented communication in China amazed me. During our visit to an old cigarette factory in Wuhan, an elderly gentleman who was a top party official and his young assistant conducted the briefing. It became all too apparent after just a few minutes that the old party secretary knew little about the factory or the technology concerned. After a short walk through the building, the group returned to the briefing room. I knew it was now my turn to comment. I had not been at all impressed with what I had seen and observed, and I remarked, frankly, that I felt that there should be no smoking permitted inside the manufacturing area. I commented that discarded cigarettes had been scattered on the floors and cigarette paper and shredded tobacco covered much of the floor area. I further indicated that the workers should avoid any waste of raw materials, and take precautions not to let paper and tobacco fall to the floor and accumulate there. They should also be more circumspect in their use of time, by cutting down on chatting during working hours and especially between shift changes. These suggestions were gracefully and politely accepted. I returned to my lodgings at a hotel across the Yangtze River in Hankou, and mostly forgot my remarks at the factory.

After dinner, Margaret and I went for a walk along the riverbank, about two blocks from our hotel. As we left through the hotel door several young students playing Chinese chess stopped to watch our progress. One young girl called, "Are you the expert from America?" I acknowledged that I probably was. She continued, "Did you make three points of criticism at the factory today?" She then told me how they were planning to address the problems. I was amazed and wondered out loud how she had learned of the encounter as it had taken place less than three hours before. She replied, "It was announced on the factory speaker system and my elder sister works there."

In China at that time political "discussion", "learning" and "study" sessions took place on a continuous basis among workers and party leaders, in schools, factories, farm units and government offices. I had noticed at a "learning session" I had visited that about half of the participants were dozing off and the other half were reading newspapers and other materials. I hoped that the one in the cigarette factory had been a serious discussion of my comments rather than window dressing.

Our visit to Dachia in Shi'anxi Province was another experience that I would never forget. The agriculture "model" came from one of the poorest areas of China, and suddenly became a showcase for visiting heads of states, scholars and students. The stories they told at briefings were amazingly convincing. Actually, it was a phony show, because the government subsidized all of the "achievements" just to show the greatness of Mao's leadership and the success of Communism. Who would have ever discovered the truth about Dachia if the Cultural Revolution were still going on?

Family and Friends

News of our return visit spread fast and furiously. It coincided with China's long-awaited change of course: the end of isolationism and the cautious beginnings of the "open door" policy. However, the aftershocks of the Cultural Revolution and the great earthquake that struck the city of Tangshan in Northern China in July 1976 were still casting long shadows over the population.

I was not alone in my puzzlement and curiosity. People on both sides were straining to see through the small crack in the door ajar. Those from the outside wanted to know what was really happening in China, and those in China were equally eager to find out what was happening in the outside world. There was a great need for communications between the two sides of the "bamboo curtain". However, it was risky for Chinese citizens to associate with a "foreigner" simply because no one knew which way the wind would blow in the future. Having outside connections or having foreign friends could perhaps trigger some criminal charges against a Chinese citizen. This could begin with as little as an expressed wish to meet a relative or a desire to have a small gathering of friends and acquaintances.

To meet friends or family members, prior approval was needed from the cadre in charge of the residential area, the lane, the street or the party leader at work. Party members had to be told of the purpose, results and benefits expected of any meeting or visit. Before granting such permission, they might question in detail how you came to know the visitor and the circumstances surrounding and the nature of your relationship, your visitor's political ideologies, and finally, your friend or associate's potential to become "an enemy of the state".

I bore witness to party leaders' penchant for questioning about correspondence with almost anyone. How frequent was the communication with this person? Every 10, 20 or 30 years? By what means? Through whom? Etcetera, etcetera? After this long inquiry, comrades would discuss the pros and cons of a request and then make a final decision. Only if the decision were favorable would the request be forwarded to the host organization, through every step of the organizational hierarchy and the security apparatus. In my cases, final arrangements on where, when and how the meeting would be conducted were decided by the local host together with the two top Beijing guides.

A visiting guest could request to meet with relatives or friends, but, as I found out, a lot of lead-time was needed. The handling of a guest's request is slightly speedier, but frequently the response was simply, "John Doe is not available"; "He is traveling"; or perhaps, "Your health is the most important thing, so we suggest you try to see him the next time you are here." Even when all of the clearance conditions were met, there were last-minute "interviews" before a Chinese was told he or she was going to meet a foreign guest. Most likely a guide who would keep track of the time would accompany my meeting with a visitor. Upon the conclusion of a meeting, it is likely that my visitor was debriefed, to examine what had been said, what gifts had been exchanged, and a multitude of other meeting details. Despite all these handicaps and risks, however, requests to see and talk with me were numerous from one stop to the next. This made the guides tense and uneasy at first. Control and screening were tight. Gradually, after coming to grips with the situation and getting to know me better, guides relaxed restrictions.

Professor Ding taught genetics in Shandong University for many years. He was trained at Cornell University and was a serious scholar who longed for new knowledge after many years of isolation. His initial request to meet me, his college classmate, was denied. I had brought him a new U.S. textbook on genetics, and had requested a visit to Ding in Beijing. After my patient prodding, permission was finally granted for a five-minute meeting in the Beijing Hotel in the company of another host member. Both Ding and I were moved at that brief reunion, but could not say what we yearned to say. We each said to the other "Take care of yourself" while shaking hands. It was not until our later meetings that I learned that the gift textbook had been searched and examined thoroughly before Ding was allowed to accept what became a treasured possession and, furthermore, he immediately used it as "new" knowledge to rewrite his lecture notes.

It was an open secret that most if not all of the hotel rooms for visiting foreigners might be bugged. No doubt, some may even have had hidden cameras. One evening in Beijing a high-ranking government officer, Mr. Tong, and his wife came to visit me. We had known each other from our university days in the U.S. and came together as old friends. While inquiring of each other about friends in common in the States and speaking about nothing that could have been construed as sensitive in nature, Mrs. Tong turned the radio loud and suggested that we should move out to the balcony to get some "fresh air".

This trip in 1977 was somewhat pioneering and adventurous for me, and though official invitations had the blessings of the liaison offices of both sides, I knew that I must watch my step at all times. I had put in long hours before departure attending U.S. briefings on what I must and must not do when visiting China. I had taken instructions from the Chinese liaison offices in Washington, D.C., concerning the protocol of touring China. Many friends from the States had asked Margaret and me to find out about parents, relatives and friends in China. Many Chinese Americans were anxious and looking for information on lost sons and daughters in China. Some had asked that I be the bearer of cash and small gifts to loved ones there. Under these circumstances it was indeed an emotionally exhausting time for Margaret and me.

While in Hangzhou in Zhejiang Province, I requested a visit with the father of a friend. This gentleman was over 80 and resided in a place at a good distance from where we were lodging. After several long discussions and negotiations, the local host finally agreed to allow us to meet him for five minutes, but then asked the elderly man to come to my hotel. I was genuinely appalled. It was far too long a journey for a person of that advanced age. The host guide insisted and promised that he would provide the transportation and make all arrangements for the gentleman's comfort. When the appointed hour arrived, there was no sign of the visitor. I was told that the elderly gentleman was on his way. Actually he was being interviewed by the guides, which went on for 30 minutes. When finally, my friend's father appeared, a guide advised me that, because of the late hour, our visit should not be more than 15 minutes. After that brief visit, the guide insisted that I remain in my hotel room while he saw the older man home. I later learned that the elderly visitor was debriefed before being allowed to go home and then required to make his way back to his village alone.

Mr. Neeley, the Agricultural Officer of the U.S. Liaison Office, left word at his Beijing office that he would meet me enroute to Jinan, in Shandong Province. When I arrived at my hotel in Jinan a young Chinese gentleman was waiting for me. Mr. Chang was the son of a friend. The elder Chang was trying to help his son get into the U.S. The young man had graduated from college in 1968 and was working in a remote area of Shandong. He had permission but seemed to have little patience with all the red tape involved in meeting with me in Jinan. He had traveled for two days by train and bus

166

and was finally at his wit's end. He was complaining loudly in the guest room. Although I hinted to him that the rooms may be bugged and that authorities might likely be listening to every word we said, the young man seemed oblivious to my hint. I then suggested we walk in a garden adjoining the hotel. That was when I realized there was someone else present. A Western gentleman cast concerned eyes toward us, obviously understanding our conversation in Chinese. From my attire, the man would certainly know that I was a foreign visitor. The gentleman approached my young visitor and me and introduced himself as Mr. Neeley. He was the first of many U.S. Agricultural Officers that I would meet in China. To return to young Mr. Chang, he and his family, his sister, and her family are now all citizens of the U.S., established in their professions.

Both Margaret's and my families were contacted well in advance of the meetings to take place in Shanghai or Wuhan by arrangement of our local hosts. My family, sisters, brothers, cousins and more, were widely spread throughout China, from Fujin to Shanghai, Wuhan and Xinjiang. Margaret's family was located in Sichuan and Shanghai. In Shanghai we hosted two different dinner gatherings each for about 20 people. Our hosts also arranged for my elder sister to get much needed medical care in Shanghai. Visitors were allowed to enter our hotel compound only when accompanied by a hotel guest. One evening Margaret's brother and sister were blocked from entering until I arrived to meet them. It was a sad episode in an otherwise happy time for the reunions with our respective families.

In Wuhan, I told my guides that I would like to visit one of my sisters at her living quarters, which were located in a dormitory of the hospital where she worked. Several days elapsed, before I was granted the permission. We set aside an entire day for the much-anticipated reunion and the accompanying sumptuous dinner. Hospital co-workers, neighbors and friends all contributed time and effort to help fete the Western visitors. It was about this time that I realized I had created a small crisis. The government and hospital party bosses requested my sister to have her living quarters cleaned and painted, including the furniture therein! But it was too late to halt events. I invited the guides and some local officials to join us for the reunion dinner. They politely declined.

When the day arrived, Margaret and I found ourselves at a banquet in the official style. The table was set up, using connecting boards, to three feet in width and extended at least 15 feet in length. The makeshift table was then laden with every sort of foodstuff--a very expensive undertaking--with 25 to 30 people sitting around it. But, unfortunately, we had little time to visit nor did we have much appetite. At the end of about two hours, I felt even worse because I realized they had no refrigeration for all the leftover food in the hot weather. But at least all these good people who had contributed this rather lavish banquet divided and bundled up the food among them and returned home with it. Margaret and I could only hope that they and their families enjoyed the rich and rarely prepared food that had been presented for the visitors that day. I inquired of my sister how she had managed this party, and she gave credit to friends, neighbors and local officials for the honor bestowed on her brother and my wife.

I saw no bedroom or bed in my sister's living quarters and assumed they had been removed to make space for the dining table. Some years later I learned that this very dinner was "suggested" by the party boss and the director of the hospital (who may even have made it mandatory) and that the expenses were deducted from each host's salary for several years to meet the costs of the party.

After long isolation and numerous "movements" and purges, little trust was left among the Chinese people. There were no real "heart-to-heart" exchanges, even among family members. My family claimed they had good jobs, sufficient salaries and maintained a decent living. "The Party takes good care of us," they said. When Margaret and I took them out to a "friendship" store (stores established solely for foreigners and which accepted only foreign exchange certificates), their attitude changed somewhat. Clothing fabrics were at the top of their shopping list. In addition, each family desired and needed a sewing machine, which was identified as a "Honey-Bee" brand name in Shanghai. These machines unfortunately were not available in the stock. Through much effort, my host located two of the sought-after brands. The particular sewing machines were much more expensive than their counterparts in the U.S., but the American-made machines were inadequate for the local sewing needs.

Upon our return to Beijing and only one day before our flight to France, Margaret and I, along with our original guide and the security officer, were traveling by car from the train station to the Beijing Hotel. Margaret, feeling relaxed at long last, remarked, "Now we have only 'the gang of four' left." The guide, Mr. Zhou, who had become a friend after six weeks of touring together, was shocked. His face turned pale and he said, "No, no, we are four friends! Never say gang of four." A lighthearted joke had almost turned into a serious incident for Margaret and me. Unfortunately, both Mr. Zhou and his wife died of cancer in later years. At the conclusion of the six-week tour, I was confused and exhausted. The ever-present Mao statue, Mao writings, "party guidelines" and absolute party control were at the top of my mind. The poor living conditions, inadequate transportation, low education standards and many other aspects of the situation in China appalled and disgusted me.

On one hand, we had witnessed with our own eyes open-cranial surgery performed with only acupuncture applied as anesthesia. We had seen a "production unit" of commune farmers using anther culture for plant improvement. We met with "barefoot" doctors and saw healthy, happy children in nursery schools. On the other hand, however, we had seen the poor livelihoods, low-housing standard, inadequate facilities, deficient and dysfunctional management and dull working spirit in the factories and on farms. Which was the true picture?

Because the door to China was only slightly ajar, the answers to the questions racing through my mind would have to wait years for solutions and understanding.

When I returned to the U.S., I felt as if I had just toured a strange "foreign" land, although it was actually my motherland, where my roots were. People had been friendly but cool, polite but distant. Even family members, apparently happy with their lot, were reserved, probably because no one knew what their reunion would bring to them tomorrow, for better or worse.

Professionally, I had met with tobacco production and research teams and a few technical persons. In addition to the Dachai Brigade, which was upheld as the "model of agriculture" during that political period, I heard many fairy tales from agricultural "experts". The Dachai story was reiterated so frequently all over China, no one dreamed of questioning its reliability and authenticity. Was there any likelihood of progress in the near future? Apparently, the answer was yes, since the great majority of the population had looked healthy in the rural areas. Would there be progress in agricultural science and technology in China? To this, I had no answer, as I had not been allowed personal contact with agricultural researchers at the bench level. Nor did my few-minutes visit with two old friends in the agricultural science and education community provide a definitive answer. The day before my return to the U.S., our Beijing political guide asked me whether we had more "wishes". When I said that I had hoped to meet with higher agricultural officers or research administrators to learn about agricultural policy and strategy, the guide was apparently shocked. Losing his usual polite demeanor, he walked out of the room responding coolly, "You are fortunate this time; do not overdo it." He then closed the door behind him.

Tears and Laughter

On following trips to China, many events were bitter or sweet, sad or funny, though they were deadly serious at the moment.

The I-Dou Tobacco Research Center was located near Jinan of Shandong Province. The main hall was covered with a huge painting of Mao, with a cigarette between his fingers. He was visiting a tobacco field in Henan, which Mao called the "Capital of the Tobacco Kingdom". All members at the center had high expectation of my visit, and treated us royally. Even the guest suite we occupied was reconstructed with modern facilities, including new shower and toilet system. All of us involved in this project, the host, staff member, research scientist and ourselves were somewhat nervous, because we knew not what to expect at such a new situation. The very next morning, Director Sun opened the program with a welcome address and a briefing of the Center's activities. Mr. Sun spoke with heavy local accent and my Chinese hearing was rather rusty, which made it rather difficult to catch Sun's presentation word-by-word. Sun kept using the word "Huang-Gou" which confused me. After a few moments, I could not help interrupting him, asking: "What has 'yellow dog' (huang-go) to do with tobacco?" At first, Sun was stunned, but immediately he caught my question. What he had said was "Huan-Gou", which means "deserted furrow", not dog. The entire audience burst into wild laughter, and soon the atmosphere was relaxed for all. Sun was reporting on their efforts to utilize wasted land for tobacco production. From then the fence between us disappeared, and we even became good friends and I cited this story in many occasions.

After I-Dou, we began to move to the South. Our first stop was Xiao Shijiazhaung, to see field production and we would stay overnight at the commune's Guest House. When we arrived at the tobacco field, I suddenly saw a familiar face; it was Mr. Dong, a tobacco specialist who worked with me in 1944 when I was in the university and later in 1947 in the Tobacco Bureau. We knew better than to meet as old friends, but met with our eyes. In the tobacco field, I did find an opportunity to exchange greetings with him. I saw they were growing a type of multiple-leaf tobacco, which may produce double or triple leaves, but is of very low quality and usability. I purposely asked why that type of tobacco was used, because I knew Dong was against that type in the past. As a senior tobacco scientist, Dong stepped forward and said, "It is the government policy to produce the highest yield as possible." Later on at the commune banquet, Dong joined this official function for welcoming us. Both Margaret and I did not have much appetite at this feast, but consumed much peanuts and millet, which we had missed for years.

After dinner, we were guests of honor at the showing of a movie, a CPC classic story repeated thousands of times. After the show, we returned

171

to our room for rest. Soon we heard a sound of knocking at the door. As I opened the door, I saw a black shadow running away from me, and there were two small bags left at the door. One contained peanuts, the other millet. We knew and appreciated this demonstration of friendship at the cost of considerable risk. We immediately understood that it must be Dong but said nothing about it. Not until 10 years later, did Dong acknowledge his kind and brave action.

At the time, there was an "eight words agricultural constitution" dictated by Mao. They were: water, fertilizer, soil, seed, closeness, responsibility, labor, and management. In order of importance, the ten crops include grains, cotton, oil crops, flax, silk, tea, sugar, vegetable, tobacco, and fruits. Tobacco was ranked ninth of the ten; high-yield varieties, planted close together were required. Speaking of tea, we visited the "best" tea-producing unit, called "Meijiawu," in Hangzhou of Zhejiang Province. It happened to be a raining day. The head of the Commune insisted on a demonstration to show us how the green tea is baked. It is the common knowledge that tea leaves should not be harvested during rain, because tea could not be 'baked' with water on its surface, especially green tea. However, the lady in charge said, in the Chinese Commune, we treat heavy rain as light rain, and light rain like shining days. So, they used some cloth towels to 'dry' the surface water on the leaves, and immediately put the leaves in a huge pan for the quick baking process. We did not know how those tea leaves turned out, but did receive two cans of the famous "dragon-well" green tea as gift.

The Mao 8-word constitution and the order of 10 priority crops were obeyed absolutely. They were recited repeatedly at any occasions. All farmers and scientists were asked to follow those teachings, and learn from others. When I visited the Dachai Commune, the very model of Chinese agriculture at Mao's time, I was told an old story. Once Madame Mao, one of the Gang of Four, visited the cornfield in Dachai. She asked the farmers to learn from the practice on tobacco production in order to gain yield and quality. She was in Henan and observed that the farmers practiced "topping" of tobacco in the field, or removing the tobacco flowers for higher yield and quality.

She told the farmers to do the same for corn. Fortunately, Dachai leaders did not follow her advice; otherwise, there would be no corn to harvest. There were similar cases in China around 1977; only some of them were made known to me, a foreign visitor.

Looking back to the years prior to the trip, and years after that trip, many deadly serious but comedic events happened. Some I experienced first hand and some I heard from people involved. We may share the tears and laughter today, but they were life and death when they happened. Here I wish to mention only stories in which the players have either already passed away, or are totally inactive.

At the final years of Mao's life, he had a team of famous and well-known "palace" medical doctors serving him. Among them, one (here I give his name as Ping) may have been too much of a scholar to enjoy the favor of Madam Mao, Jiang Qin. Jiang had a very hysterical and volatile personality, either love or hate, either live or death. For some unknown reasons, she wanted to get rid of Ping. Ping, however, was totally unaware of the danger he was in. The late Premier Zhou En-Lai, Ping and two other doctors attended an important meeting called by Jiang on Mao's health. Jiang intended to take action against Ping at that moment, but another matter drew her attention away and she had to step out of the room for a few minutes. Zhou took that break and ordered Ping to get out immediately for a narrow escape. Soon after that, Mao and Zhou both had passed away, and the Gang of Four, which included Jiang, was arrested. Ping had many other narrow escapes; he survived a plane crash, losing everything except his life. In later years, Ping continued to serve as a palace doctor. During a public review of the armed forces in an annual national holiday parade, Ping was asked to dress in army uniform and was seated by the very side of the leaders.

In my 1980 trip to China, I visited my hometown Wuhan, the capitol of Hubei Province. It was immediately following my meeting in Beijing with the Vice Premier Wan Li on agricultural issues, which had been widely reported by the media. The late Ambassador Han Xu was also present. Wan, during our important agriculture discussions, jokingly asked me if it was time for him to smoke again, and I answered that he had to wait. Several days later, I received royal treatment from local leaders in Wuhan. The First Secretary and Governor Chen Pi Xian asked me in advance two things. What would I like to have of my native dishes, which I missed, and which particular friend I wished to invite to join the official welcome banquet? I mentioned 2 or 3 dishes that I usually enjoyed from the street stands, and I named one special professor, Dr. Chang, with whom I worked on tobacco. To my surprise, most of the banquet dishes were most expensive, likely flown in from outside, and my requested "specialties" were presented as small side dishes.

Dr. Chang was present and seated next to me. Chang had totally changed to a different person. In the early 1940s when he returned to China from Minnesota, he was a handsome, brilliant, ambitious scholar with a new Ph.D. Now I saw next to me a thin, physically weak person without that old confidence or charm, although I still occasionally caught his bright eyes. Chang was a professor at the Wuhan University together with his wife who was the head of the English Department. Chang asked permission from the Governor to invite me to be his family guest the next evening in a private dinner. Governor Chen kindly promised that I could go; he also ordered the restaurant to prepare all banquet dishes to take to Chang's residence the next evening. Chang and I insisted that we only wished to have time together to catch up the old times. We would have only a very simple meal. Upon my arrival to Chang's university dormitory, I met his lovely family but found a big table ready for another banquet. It was not from the Governor, but the Party Secretary of the University. In courtesy, the University Secretary came to join us at the end that evening. That event, I believe, was the first time a U.S. visitor was allowed to a private residence of a Chinese professor. However, two years later, Chang was still not invited to participate in our open exchanges on education reform.

Through the years, I experienced great trust and friendship from ambassadors and mission members at the Chinese Embassy in Washington. Here I wish to recall some happenings from the earlier two ambassadors, who I call friends. The very first Ambassador, Chai Zemin, had the

174

background of armed services. He was frank, honest and straightforward. He mentioned that once he was out of food and water for three days. And when he finally found dry bread and water later in a village, he ate and drank without thinking. As a result, the dry bread expanded in his stomach, causing him to suffer many days after. Chai put agriculture as one of his important missions, and he visited Beltsville and me often. He usually stayed for a whole day, visiting various laboratories followed by questioning.

Chai had a strong, heavily built body. Once he put his hands at the newly developed instrument measuring meat fats to see how much fat he had. He could not tolerate the "rare" steak at official functions, so he made frequent requests to our home for well-baked hams. Also, he asked us to prepare bushels of blue crabs that he would enjoy with his associates. Each time they insisted on bringing their own ginger and vinegar of Chinese origin. Chai's native town was Shi'anxi, which is famous of its special "knife-cut-noodles". The dough, when ready, was placed on top of the cook's head, or on his arm. It then was cut with sharp knife at high speed, allowing the noodles to fall directly into boiling water. Chai hired an expert chef from Shi'anxi at the Embassy for special treatment of the Washington society. That chef arrived in Washington in the later part of Chai's term of mission. Chai was so much in demand for farewell parties that he could not find an opening in his schedule for us to experience the special treat at the Chinese Embassy. A few days before his return to Beijing, Chai and several of us were sharing a ride after a formal party. We joked that the Ambassador did not keep his word in inviting us to that special treat of knife-cutting noodles. He immediately ordered the driver to go to Embassy for us to enjoy a night treat. However, that chef did not expect such a sudden order, and was not in the kitchen. The substitute chef, being not an expert and in a hurry, did not do a good job. Chai then promised me that any time I visit Beijing; he will take me to the famous Jin Yang Restaurant to make it up.

Chai always kept his promises, and frequently invited himself to join our other functions in Beijing. When I returned to Beijing the first time after Tiananmen Square, Chai visited me at my hotel. He was surprised at the extremely strong reaction from the outside toward the Chinese Government's action, and that several of his old friends had protested at the door of the Chinese Embassy the morning of June 4, 1989. Obviously, many people in Beijing did not know the details of what happened, and they miscalculated the effects of that tragedy on the Chinese image.

Ambassador Han Xu came from a diplomat background. Han and his wife, Ge, are dear friends to us. Han was not only brilliant, but also very considerate, attending every detail with great vision and judgment. In things big or small, he always cared for the team he worked with. Han was the Chinese Ambassador when the Tiananmen Square tragedy happened. I can only image his deep feelings when he saw with his own eyes that many old and trusted friends came to the door of the Embassy to protest. Beijing did not inform all foreign missions of its policy, if any, at that critical moment in time. Han had to request that all mission members be calm, waiting for guidance from Beijing. He had nothing to base his views on except the news from People's Daily. Most unfortunate, it was the last year of his U.S. mission. The number of attendees at his official farewell party in the Chinese Embassy was much less than expected. Later, on a separate occasion, eight of us, Han's close friends in the academic area invited the Ambassador and his wife to a private dinner as a personal farewell. It was a hard time.

On one occasion in Beijing, then-Minister of Agriculture He Kang and I were invited for luncheon by Han at the International Club. Since the three of us knew each other well, He and I decided to arrive early for more time to chat. It was not a formal occasion but we knew for sure that Han would be waiting for us. To our surprise, Han was not in the dinning room. We knew he must be there somewhere at the Club. Soon, Han showed up, apologized for his absence upon our arrival, because he had been visiting the kitchen staff, offering his thanks. That International Club is under the Ministry of Foreign Affairs, one of the thousands under its supervision. Ambassador Han died before his time from a disease resulting from one of his many friendly missions to underdeveloped countries. We all miss him.

TC at Nanking, 1947

Margaret at Nanking, 1947

TC and Margaret's civil
wedding at Bell's house in
Cleveland, Ohio, 1949

177

TC as post-doc at Dr.
Frankenburg's Lab,1951
(Frankenburg at back center,
TC at his left)

TC at Beltsville USDA
Reseach Center, 1956

Margaret's first painting exhibition
in Taiwan, Mr. D.K.Wu, TC and
Betty at right, 1958

TC receiving USDA Superior Service Award, with Secretary Freeman, 1968

TC received the First CORESTA Prize, 1975

TC receiving the USDA Distinguished Service award from Secretary Bergland, 1977

179

Reunion with teachers and friends at Dr. T.H. Shen's house, Taipei, floor in front of Dr. Shen, Shen extended his hands on TC's shoulder), 1978

President Jimmy Carter conferred TC as charter member of the US Senior Executive Service, 1979

Partial Family reunion at Hankow, Hubei, Chnia, 1980

Walking with PRC
Premier Wan Li
(Betty and Margaret
behind TC), 1980

Official photo
with Wan Li (R2
Betty, R4
Margaret), 1980

Minister of
Agriculture He
Kang visited TC's
home in Beltsville,
MD, USA, 1981

Official photo with Premier Wan Li at the opening of Chinese Agricultural Education forum (front row L4 Margaret, Wan Li, TC, 2nd row R2 Paul), 1982

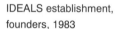

IDEALS establishment, founders, 1983

TC spoke at his USDA retirement banquet, 1983

Dr. Y. S. Tsiang and Anming Fu
in Taipei, Taiwan. 1984

Drs. Chia Liang Yi and
Zhou Zhong Fan with TC &
Margaret, 1984

The President of the United States of America
has conferred on

TIEN C. TSO

the rank of Meritorious Executive
in the Senior Executive Service
for sustained superior accomplishment in
management of programs
of the United States Government
and for noteworthy achievement of
quality and efficiency in the public service.

1983

Ronald Reagan

President Reagan awarded
TC Meritorious Executive
in the U.S. Senior Executive
Service, 1984

China National
Tobacco Corp.
invited TC as Sr.
Advisor. (CNTC
President Li & TC),
1985

TC receiving CNTC
International S & T
contribution award,
1992

TC receiving the first
International Science and
Technology Contribution
Award from State Science and
Technology Commission, PRC
with Ambassador Han Xu (left)
and Minister He Kang (Right),
1993

TC and Margaret attending the
International Fertilizer
Conference banquet, 1994

TC with Dr.
Norman Borlaug,
1994

Tianjin government invited TC as
Agriculture Advisor, with Mayor Sun
Hailing, 1995

TC meeting with PRC
President Jiang Zemin, 1995

Betty's appointment as
director of ER at University of
Maryland, 1999

Elizabeth Tso, M.D., has been named clinical director for Adult Emergency Services. Tso oversees a team
of attending emergency physicians, resident house staff
physicians and support staff. The adult emergency
department treats 38,000 patients each year, 7,500 of
whom are admitted to inpatient services.
    Tso is heading a joint Medical System-University
Physicians task force to improve the registration and discharge processes for emergency services.
    Tso succeeds Wade Gaasch, M.D., who has taken
on an expanded role related to corporate EMS initiatives. In addition to his clinical duties, Gaasch is medical
director for Maryland ExpressCare and the Baltimore
City EMS/911 system.

Whole family toured
Tibet, Betty, TC,
Margaret & Paul, 1999

186

TC with CNTC Vice
President Jin and Dr. Zhu,
1999

Charting the water
resources of China, TC,
Borlaug & von der Osten,
2000

TC meeting with
People's Congress
President Li Peng,
2000

TC revisiting Shanghai Park Hotel
with Betty (where TC stayed in 1947
before the trip to USA), 2000

Meeting with CNTC
Leaders 2000

Bridging Taiwan and
mainland tobacco scientists
in Taiwan, 2000

Meeting with CNTC
leaders, Ni, Zhu, TC
and Jiang (left to right)
2001

Meeting with Premier
Wen Jiabao, 2001

Visiting Jilin soybean
research station with S.
D. Kung, 2001

189

Paul, an organ transplant surgeon at Emory University since 1999

TC and Paul at Paul's wedding, 2001

Paul and Denise's wedding, 2001

TC and two sisters at
Fujian China, 2005

Paul, Denise, Andrew
& Emily, 2005

Family reunion
(TC, Margaret,
Denise, Andrew,
Paul, Emily &
Betty), 2005

TC receiving Life Time Achievement Award from Dr. Bush at Tobacco Science Research Conference, 2005

TC inducted to ARS/USDA Hall of Fame, 2005

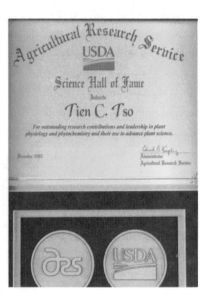

TC negotiating with water on a floating bamboo raft in Fujian, 2005

The Third Thirty Years
1978-2006

..staff as privilege of old age:
at seventy, privileged to carry a cane in the capital;
at eighty, privileged to carry a cane at the royal court.
-according to the Book of Orders, a Chinese Classic-

at ninety, do what your heart desires, there is no limit in the book.
-according to TC, this is just for fun in this quotation-

Chapter 11

Moving Toward Modernization

In the years following Nixon's 1972 first visitation to China, the political climate thawed between China and the outside world, and the spirit of reconciliation between mainland and overseas Chinese also improved. An official Chinese party celebrated the 1979 normalization of diplomatic relations between the U.S. and China at the Mayflower Hotel in Washington. This was a remarkable event attended by hundreds of "who's who" in political, social and academic circles. It marked the beginning of a new era. It was also in 1979 that I was invited to visit China again, this time at the joint invitation of the Chinese Ministry of Agriculture and the Chinese Society of Agriculture.

Though it was merely two years after my first return to my motherland, the difference in reception was enormous. This time, I was sought out to attend many discussions on agriculture with the country's highest-ranking officials and academics, including members of the State Council, ministers, presidents and provincial governors. I presented speeches and informal talks, and even openly reported on the Taiwan situation, which had been an extremely sensitive topic two years earlier. In fact, upon learning that I would travel on to Taiwan after Beijing, many old acquaintances sent regards to their long-forgotten friends there. After 1979, a stream of government officials, agricultural scientists and leaders, provincial governors, party cadres, research scientists and educators from China began to visit the U.S. with regularity, enjoying an open society. As agriculture was a key to China's modernization, Chinese visitors to the U.S. invariably chose to tour our USDA

Beltsville Agricultural Research Center in Maryland. Since Beltsville was my place of employment and also my place of residence, the USDA or the Chinese Embassy often asked me to participate in briefings for visitors and to accompany them in their further travels in the States. As a result of this, I became well known in China, not only for my tobacco science profession, but also for agriculture in general.

In these years, I lobbied tirelessly for agricultural improvement in China, for exchanges of mutual benefit between the U.S. and China and for bridge-building across the Pacific as well as the Taiwan Strait. I traveled between the U.S. and China three to four times a year, sometimes even six times. I served in various capacities on various occasions in these travels, and I met government leaders on many of these trips. Some of those leaders won my respect, despite our differing personal views.

The 1982 Agricultural Education Forum

An event happened in 1982. Deputy Minister of the Chinese Ministry of Agriculture Mr. He Kang made a great effort to organize a U.S.-China Bilateral Conference on Chinese Agricultural Education within China. I was invited to lead a team of nine Chinese agricultural scientists from the U.S. to meet jointly with Chinese counterparts. Most were university presidents, deans and senior professors. The U.S. team included H.H. Cheng, Hui Chiang, S.D. Kung, George Liang, Tony Huang, Bill Tai, Steve Yen, T.L. Yuan, and me. Our task was to examine and evaluate the Chinese current agricultural education system, the curriculum, facilities, teaching materials, selection and training of students, college structure, extension and research. We were then to submit constructive recommendations for improvements. It was a very important assignment and the group took it seriously. Vice Premier Wan Li received our group and declared strongly that he would put our recommendations into practice.

The total tour and conference took five weeks, including visits to several "key" agricultural colleges, which later became agricultural universities. We wrote and submitted detailed recommendations. Unfortunately, we later learned that the bureaucracy in China had prevented some university presidents from receiving final copies of the report, though they had participated in the conference.

The four "key" locations where our delegation visited were the Beijing Agricultural College in Beijing, the Central Agricultural College in Wuhan in Hubei Province, the Nanjing Agricultural College in Nanjing in Jiangsu Province, and the Zhejiang Agricultural College in Hangzhou in Zhejiang Province. At each location, we had old friends who looked forward to our visit and our report on what was going on outside of China. The discussions, however, were only attended by a few selected people who had no "political risk" to China, even though it was five years after the Cultural Revolution.

One sad story I must mention here. After we had completed the mission in Wuhan, our host chose to take us by a ship to our next stop, in Nanjing. Several of our group stood with me at the ship railing watching workmen untying ropes and removing the gangplank to the shore. Suddenly we saw an old man, carrying a small bag on his back and waving with both hands, race toward the ship. We realized with surprise and sadness that the man was Dr. C.C. Chang, who earned his Ph.D. in Agronomy from the University of Minnesota and was teaching in Wuhan. As I mentioned earlier, he had been my guest at Governor Chen's banquet in 1980. He was not allowed to participate in our three-day discussion, also our host kept him in the dark of our travel schedule. He learned at the last moment of our departure. Chang was my former supervisor in the Tobacco Improvement Bureau in Nanking, a bright scientist, educator, administrator, and dear friend to me. He carried a bag of fruit, without any means of transportation, and had walked and run a long way to say goodbye to us. At that emotional moment, many delegates who knew his name and his scholarship could not hold back tears while watching this unfold. We asked the ship to delay removing the gangplank, so we could welcome him aboard and hold his hands tightly while we said goodbye. I repeatedly assured him that we would see each other again, and I asked him to take good care of himself. This incident also reinforced to us the lesson that China had a long way to achieve its goal for modern education.

It was also in 1982 that the Chinese Academy of Agricultural Sciences (CAAS) presented me with its prestigious Honorary Research Fellow award in recognition of my contributions and persistent efforts for the country's agriculture. This marked the first time in CAAS history that the award was presented to a foreign scientist.

Our team worked day and night, even while our ship was sailing between locations. This fact I believed greatly impressed those high-ranking Chinese officials who were assigned to travel with us. We read and discussed the materials provided to us, including textbooks, class requirements for students, reading assignment, field experiments, etc. We interviewed current students and recent graduates working in the near rural area. We held three separate group sessions, discussing various key issues relating to agricultural education. As a result, we completed three reports: one from the Chinese team, a second from the U.S. team, and a third from the joint team reflecting recommendations for needs, priorities, and the realities of what can and should be done immediately. Our emphasis was to provide more basic science training, and to give students more time to think, to reason, to practice, and to form visions of their own.

We strongly recommended changing the prevailing current agriculture college system, which was copied from the Soviet Union. We recommended placing agriculture as a part of comprehensive university education. Unfortunately, in most cases, China only changed the name of agricultural colleges to agricultural universities and departments to colleges. Zhejiang Province, one of China's most economically and culturally developed provinces, was one known exception. Zhejiang at first upgraded its agricultural college to Zhejiang Agricultural University, and later enfolded it into the greater, comprehensive Zhejiang University.

The 1985 Science and Technology Policy Reform

In the fall of 1985, I was in Taiwan attending the board meeting of AVRDC, and Margaret was with me. In the middle of night, a call from the U.S. woke us. The caller informed me that there was going to be an important Science & Technology (S&T) meeting in Beijing organized by then-Chairman Song Jian of the State Science & Technology Commission. I was urgently requested to attend because I was the only agriculturalist available.

This was the most important policy reform event of 1985. Prof. Song Jian, newly appointed Chairman of the State Science & Technology Commission (SSTC), led the meeting. The CPC had drafted a report for reforming S&T policy before the meeting, but had not yet publicly announced the report. It was a historical break from tradition to put an S&T policy review to open discussion with overseas Chinese scholars before releasing the findings. That delegation of scholars was selected from different academic areas and I was the one in agriculture. The head of our delegation was Prof. Yang Zhen Ning, a Nobel laureate in physics.

Two items are always in my memory. One is the opening speech by Song: "This is the first time our national policy has ever been put into public discussion before its official release. If it is successful, we shall all be benefited; if it fails, I will be the second Tan Chi Tong in Chinese history". Song was referring to the scholar and martyr who was beheaded due to his suggestions for political reform at the twilight of the Qing Dynasty. All members in that meeting were deeply touched by his courage, wisdom and vision, and thus our own responsibility.

Another item I recall relative to agriculture. The draft policy suggested that research and development be self-supporting and be financed by end users. I voiced my objection that agriculture should be excluded from that item because farmers are too poor to purchase new seeds. Breeding a new crop variety takes eight-to-ten years. I was happy that my opinion was adapted after some discussion. In 2005, while the world scientific community admires the rapid progress of China's agriculture and the rapid advancement of China's science and technology, we need to give credit to the wisdom and courage of Song Jian 20 years ago. Yes, it has been a long road for us, but an even longer road lies ahead of us!

Intensive Training and Exchanges

In the very early 1980s, China's basic economic, scientific and technological foundations in all fronts were very weak. Even though some leaders decided to make drastic reforms, there were no talents or facilities, nor economic strength. For example, after the 1982 education meeting, or the 1985 S&T meeting, China needed trained experts, funding, and specific plans for local, regional and national development.

Here we must acknowledge the essential roles in agricultural development that World Bank, the NGOs, several foundations and world scholars played in providing the essential needs to make progress possible. The World Bank, in two major projects of $100 million dollars each, was the key for China's agricultural education development. Those loans targeted training, refreshing the agricultural leaders and professional scholars, and purchasing of modern equipment for teaching and research. The loans also targeted modern field production principles, concepts and practices. They also emphasized environmental protection. In addition, there were many other loans for local or regional development that the World Bank considered important. China executed World Bank-sponsored programs effectively. I later learned from the World Bank that China was the most efficient and successful of recipient countries in using the loans for identified purposes.

A big country, to make the projects a success China needed strong and wise leadership to address its huge agricultural program with such a large amount of money, and in such a limited period of time. Agriculture Minister He Kang was equal to the challenge. A visionary, He Kang brilliantly set visions and priorities, identified needs, designed the overall plan for negotiating with international organizations, and sought advice from international experts. Lastly, He Kang successfully administrated the execution of the plans and ensured the success of the total mission. He Kang's wisdom and contribution was well recognized by world scholars and the academic community, and he received honorary degrees and the Laureate of the World Food Prize. His effort for agricultural improvement and rural modernization was not limited by the period of his term as the Minister in the Ministry of Agriculture. He continuously devoted himself to rural and township enterprise development, and served as a promoter for international cooperation between China and the world.

I was privileged to participate in World Bank projects at the negotiating, planning and administrating stages. As an expert, on field trips I participated in evaluating and reviewing project progress, discussions with leaders, and making recommendations for decision makers in both the World Bank and the Chinese government.

In order to devote myself totally to Chinese agricultural improvement and promoting international cooperation, I took early "retirement" from my USDA professional position and to set a new mechanism of operation. With many scholars, we organized a non-profit, non-political, independent institution we named the Institute of International Development and Education in Agriculture and Life Sciences, or IDEALS. IDEALS was founded at the end of 1983, and officially became functional in 1984 with full support from Chinese government leaders, world NGOs, and scholars and educators from both countries. However, when the full support from the top ranks of government trickled down to low-level cadres, the actual operatives, support largely evaporated. Even with the remaining meager support, IDEALS contributed significantly to refresher training for Chinese scientists, exchange and communication channels, developing remote western regions such as Tibet and Xinjiang, and connecting scientists across the Taiwan Strait. These are some examples of IDEALS's efforts. All IDEALS leaders served without pay and with total devotion.

In 1997, I retired from active duty in IDEALS. Its future development and activities are limited only by the need to seek additional funding and to devote total effort to leadership. There is still urgent need in China to reach out to the world community, and for the expression of different voices on important national policy matters.

I helped establish two consortia, one organized by American universities, and the other organized by Chinese universities, with common interests in cooperation and exchange in agriculture. Both sides were highly supportive. The Chinese consortium was established in 1996 with the participation of seven universities, and the American side in the following year, named UCCA, or University Consortium on Chinese Agriculture, with the participation of more than ten universities. However, after the first few years, each side had its own priorities and moved very slowly toward a common consortium. The need for joint action of common interest involving major agricultural issues for both sides is still there.

Impressions of Leaders I Met

In most of my China trips, there were important projects of national interest related to agricultural science, education, policy and rural or regional development. Except the 1977 first visit, in the wake of the Cultural Revolution, in all following trips my host would arrange some special meetings with the local authorities or central government leaders, depending on the nature of the trip. I was honored to have opportunities to visit Head of the State Council members including the Premier, the Chairman of the People's Congress, Ministers, and Governors as the mission needed. It is not my purpose here to name who's who or drop names, but only to reflect my impressions of some leaders who enjoyed my high respect. Also, I mention only those I met privately or personally in real exchanges. I do not include group courtesy sessions or general meetings.

Most of those private sessions were in the Zi Guang Ge of the Zhong Nan Hai, or the State Guest House. The public sessions were in the Great Hall of the People. Those visits served several main purposes as far as I was concerned. First, I could learn firsthand directly from national authorities and express my views, which might differ from the current policy. Meetings provided me some opportunities to point out alternatives. Second, I could speak to real situations and real needs from what I observed and learned firsthand in rural and urban society. In doing so, I could express myself directly to the very top without hesitation. Third, I could report any new development from the outside world for their reference, which generally resulted in several follow-up international conferences to be held in China. Fourth, high-level visits were always reported widely by the news media, and thus indirectly helped me in promoting my mission in lower level visits, such as regional or even rural areas.

It is not my intention, nor am I qualified in attempting, to judge leaders who I was honored to meet. On one occasion or the other, I had the opportunity to meet almost all the top leaders, either in private or in group sessions. Somehow, I feel obligated to express my high respect and appreciation to those I admire greatly and sincerely. In agriculture, several top leaders impressed me with their vision, broad knowledge and up-to-date understanding of the key issues, and their sincere willingness to listen to and lead in-depth discussions, pros and cons, and even involve current policy. Chairman Wan Li, Premier Wen Jia Bao, and Minister He Kang had my admiration. With them I could feel frankness, honesty, and friendship, and discuss any subject without reservation. I have to acknowledge that some points I raised were not necessarily new to them. I could freely channel to them the thoughts of many Chinese scholars on politically sensitive subjects.

For example, as early as 20 years ago I raised the question of eliminating all taxes and "local contributions" from farmers. I even suggested increasing taxes on tobacco to replace the potential loses from eliminating agriculture taxes. I stated the urgent need to solve land and water resources problems, and I disagreed with the then-current plan to transfer water from south to north, because that would not resolve underlying problems. Instead, I strongly supported using water from the western four rivers, especially the YLZB River, for the water needs in the north and northeast of China. In land policy,

I raised the issue of tillers owning their land so they could preserve its long-term productivity. Also, tillers need secure ownership without having to worry about sudden land conscription by the local government. The land ownership policy, as I suggested, is in contrast with the current Chinese constitution.

In science and technology development including agricultural and the biological sciences, I have great respect for President Song Jian, who not only had great vision, but also actively promoted that vision. Song impressed me with his wisdom not only of engineering, but also of agriculture and international situations. We could exchange views with trust; he usually told me what could be done, what could be contemplated, and what was impossible.

I cannot recall how many such special meetings were held in my honor by national and local authorities. Almost every time, in moments I had a feel for and could distinguish the sincerity or phoniness of the host. Some had a firm handshake and made direct eye contact. Others had a touch of soft fingertips and avoided eye contact. Some were very well informed and knowledgeable on the subject matter, while others simply did not know the basics. In such meetings, I immediately knew whether it was worth my time to say anything of significance.

Here I like to mention another type of high-ranking leader on agriculture in Beijing a few years back. A World Bank leader and I visited him to discuss agriculture development. This host did not know how much of its Gross Domestic Product (GDP) China invested in agricultural development. He also was unaware of several key issues. My World Bank friend was so surprised that after the meeting he asked me how did this person get into such high position. On another occasion, this same leader was supposed to address an important international meeting on China-West at a banquet that included over 100 foreign scholars. He stayed in his room, visited an exhibition, locked all the elevators waiting for him, and finally showed up an hour late! Cases like this one certainly did not provide a good impression to foreign delegates. One of the delegates, a keynote speaker, even decided to leave the "international" meeting early the next morning!

The message I hope to convey is mostly to my young friends who in the not-too-distant future will become middle-level or top-level leaders. Please be sincere, be honest, ask yourself what you do not know, and do not show off what little you know. Most important, remember you are representing the government, the country and the people.

Chapter 12
What Price in the Name of Stability?
So Soft is the Water

Chapter 12

What Price in the Name of Stability? So Soft is the Water

What Price in the Name of Stability

There is an old saying in China, "People are like waters, they can carry a boat, or sink a boat."

Once the door opened to frequent exchanges, some scholars observed with great satisfaction and hope, yet others were concerned that the communist system might not allow reforms to go far. Nevertheless, the general belief was that reform had reached the point of no return. In early 1989, the smell of spring and the feel of hope spread all over China. People were happy. Any slight doubt that Communist leaders would turn their backs to the people was dispelled. Reform had moved too far. It was too late to turn back, even if they wanted to. "China will proudly stand up in the world again!" was the belief among the populace. The whole developing world looked to China as an example of progress toward modernization. Underneath, however, the Chinese people knew little of the power struggle going on among the leadership, nor indeed did they know the struggle had not ended. One wonders whether any power under the communist system could endure the test of time.

As the door to the world remained open and its general economic situation improved, the student-led cry for faster reform grew louder. The imminent storm became palpable upon the initiation of the campaign against "spiritual pollution" in 1983. Frequent student demonstrations commenced in 1986 and intensified with the onset of the campaign against "bourgeois liberalization" in 1987. Hu Yaobang"s death in 1989 at last triggered the event known as "Tiananmen Square Massacre".

Just before events leading up "Tiananmen Square" unfolded, President Wan of the Chinese People's Congress, an old friend of U.S. President George Bush, was leading a Chinese delegation on an official visit to the U.S. President Wan's personal physician, Dr. Chia, arrived ahead of time and was staying at our home for a few days. Chia, watching the news of Tiananmen Square on our television, for the first time learned a great deal about what was going on. He could not have learned or heard the actual facts while in Beijing. Chia was certain that the demonstrations would end peacefully, and assured us that no violence could take place in Beijing. The government would not turn its back on its people and return to the dark ages. At a reception at the Chinese Embassy honoring President Wan, I chatted and joked about our "aging" with Wan regarding which of us is older. We had met on several previous occasions and enjoyed each other's company. Wan again repeated that the Chinese government would not use force on its own children--its very hope of tomorrow.

During the following two days, Wan was scheduled to accept honorary doctorate degrees at two universities. He was also scheduled to play tennis with President Bush. Though things seemed fairly normal, friends suggested to Wan that since events were so tense in Tiananmen Square--hunger strikes resulting in some deaths--that it might not be a good idea for him to play tennis with Bush the next day. There was concern that a light-hearted tennis match would send a wrong message to the world about the seriousness of Tiananmen Square. Wan agreed to consider the advice. As fate would have it, that very evening Wan and his delegation were called to return to China immediately. All itineraries were canceled. When the delegation's early departure was confirmed, I knew something dire might happen soon, but I never dreamed it would be as brutal as the forthcoming events eventually turned out to be. Later, I heard that Wan's plane was ordered to land in

Chapter 12
What Price in the Name of Stability?
So Soft is the Water

Shanghai instead of Beijing, and Wan was immediately taken into "medical care" for the ensuing days because he was considered one of the "softies" who were sympathetic to the students.

When news of the unconscionable Tiananmen Square massacre broke, my family and I cried when we saw on TV what was happening. I was shocked, and felt that all of our efforts were wasted, our hopes dashed. What kind of leadership was this? What kind of country was this? June 4, 1989, fell on a Sunday in Washington. My family and I decided not to attend our regular church service. Instead, we joined the mass protest demonstration marching to the Chinese Embassy. When we arrived at the embassy's front gate, the door was closed. Hundreds of demonstrators were there already. Evidently, some of the embassy officials felt the same way as the crowd. The embassy staff had always enjoyed good relationships with the Chinese community. A few representatives of the demonstrators entered the embassy to present a formal text protesting events in Beijing and to ask the ambassador to forward it immediately to Beijing. It was a demand to stop the killings, to release all students and demonstration leaders from prison and to punish those responsible for the massacre.

All of us of with Chinese roots were understandably low-spirited, ashamed and despondent about what had occurred. These events were turning China's history backward hundreds of years. In the following days and weeks, I searched for the true meaning of this tragedy, but failed to find any justification. Was the blood of the students shed in vain? I did not believe so.

Winston Churchill said in the House of Commons on August 20, 1940, "Never in the field of human conflict was so much owed by so many to so few." The Chinese people certainly owed much to the students. It is also said in the Bible, Leviticus 17:11, "it is the blood that maketh an atonement for the soul." I have tried to express my feelings in the following poem.

Searching for a Nation's Soul

There was a breath of spring.
There was a stir of hope.
There was youth and fire.
There was the dream, but no fear.
Suddenly, there was emptiness-nothing more.
There was only the search for a Nation's soul!

There was a cry for freedom.
There was a chant for democracy.
There was a song of inspiration.
There was yearning, but no fear.
Suddenly, there was emptiness-nothing more.
There was only the search for a Nation's soul!

There was darkness.
There was alarm shouts and screams.
There was blood.
There was silence, death, but no fear.
Suddenly, there was emptiness-nothing more.
There was only the search for a Nation's soul!

There will be a new spring.
There will be new songs of freedom.
There will be new roads to travel.
There will be new promises to redeem.
Come! Ye Nation's soul, tears and blood may be shed but march on.
For tomorrow, tomorrow my soul, There will be new dreams to fulfill!

Chapter 12
What Price in the Name of Stability?
So Soft is the Water

Observations from Beijing and Beyond

It was late September 1989 before I again visited Beijing. I had canceled two previously scheduled trips in June and July to avoid seeing Tiananmen Square again. The September meeting was a U.S. Department of Agriculture technical mission and could not be delayed. It might be a test of water in the political sense.

James Lilly was still the U.S. Ambassador in Beijing. Lilly and I had known each other since his earlier mission days in Taipei. In September 1989, three months after Tiananmen Square, Beijing's diplomatic relations with the rest of the world had fallen to an all-time low. Condemnation came from every corner of the world. Tourism was nonexistent. The American Embassy in Beijing informed me that our delegation was the highest-ranking mission U.S. to visit China since Tiananmen Square.

I told an old friend, Ms. Lou, who worked in the Embassy, that she had appeared frequently on U.S. television distributing papers warning American citizens to quickly leave China immediately after the massacre. Her superior officer, overhearing our conversation, told me that it had been a difficult and dangerous assignment for her, but that she had handled it with courage and had done an excellent job. When I congratulated her, Lou held my hands with tears and said, "T.C., you did not see the ugliest and cruelest parts through television coverage." Later, I heard about the tank soldiers who fired wildly into the diplomatic compounds. Bullet scars and recovered spent shells provided unmistakable proof.

Within the Chinese government, the usual buoyant mood had vanished. In our meetings, key officials, even old friends, maintained solemn appearances as if at a funeral. Most tried to avoid the whole subject of Tiananmen Square. Some were noticeably depressed, while others tried hard to defend the government's action. Later I learned that even some young government employees had participated in the pro-democracy demonstrations. Their superiors did not punish these employees, except for lectures after the massacre had taken place. Most governmental functions had been affected at the peak of the crisis. Communications and transportation were blocked; buses and bicycles could hardly get through. Even inside offices the minds and hearts of most government employees were hardly on the jobs. These people longed for reform, but they had no idea what kind of reform they wanted. It is easy to defend the words "freedom" and "democracy", but it is extremely difficult to practice them without the benefit of education and experience in actual freedom and democracy.

I visited our old friend Dr. Chia in Beijing. It was he who was staying in our home just prior to President Wan's official Washington arrival and only days before the massacre. Officially he was accompanying President Wan, but he, like Wan, rushed back prematurely to China. He confirmed the account that Wan, instead of returning directly to Beijing, had checked into a Shanghai hospital when his special jet made its first stop. The reason Chia gave was that Wan needed a physical check up. This, of course, cleared Wan of any suspicion of his having any role in the Tiananmen Square horror. Chia, however, hastened to say that the situation in Beijing was not as bad as the foreign media had presented it. His hospital friends informed him that there were very few wounded or dead. Evidently, China's public servants and the nation's media were tightly controlling all communication, and most of what had happened was as yet unknown to the Chinese general public.

Chia was not alone in his lack of knowledge of the facts. One high-ranking officer in Hainan, 1,000 miles south of Beijing, said the whole "Tiananmen event" was an "Arabian Nights" story manufactured by the foreign press--it could not happen and indeed did not happen. With utmost conviction, he said that I, an old friend, should know that nothing like Tiananmen could ever take place, and that I and billions of others were being "hoodwinked". Another old friend, and former ambassador, confided to me at my hotel that they had been hearing that most U.S. people were very pro-student and anti-Chinese government. He named several mutual acquaintances, but did not include me among those who had protested at the Chinese Embassy. I remarked, "Mr. Ambassador, why are you being so polite today? You have purposely omitted my name from the protesting group." In

Chapter 12
What Price in the Name of Stability?
So Soft is the Water

reply, the ambassador asked, "Were you there? But, why?" I then asked in return, "Why not?" We continued our discussions for several minutes as the ambassador attempted to justify the government's position. I protested, "No matter what the students did, there was no justification for the government using tanks and machine guns on its own children." Two months later, being a gentleman and responsible for semi-official public relations for China, in an attempt to ease the tense atmosphere between the U.S. and China after the massacre, the former ambassador invited many noted U.S. scholars to visit Beijing.

He met with little success, however, and finally realized just how deep a wound the massacre had caused. There were many other witnesses to the tragedy at Tiananmen Square. On June 3, Miss Wang, a young government employee, while walking on a side street near Tiananmen, found trucks and wooden barricades blocking the square. She saw armed soldiers emerging from subway stations and pushing onlookers to go home. One young foreigner refused to leave, and he was consequently knocked to the ground. Wang moved to assist the foreigner by speaking English, and she too was ordered to leave and was pushed out of the way.

An American journalist and author happened to be in Beijing at the time. He had just completed a trip retracing the route of the "Long March" in preparation for writing a book marking the 50th anniversary of the famous 25,000-mile long march. He was staying on the seventh floor of the Beijing Hotel overlooking Tiananmen Square. Many Chinese leaders knew this– since he had appointments to interview several that had participated in the Long March. As the massacre unfolded, much to his amazement, he was an eyewitness to another historical event of a completely different nature. His interviews were canceled. Back in the U.S., instead of reporting on the Long March he reported what he had seen and heard at Tiananmen.

In yet another case, an agricultural scientist from America had been invited to Beijing as a guest of the government and happened to arrive late in the evening of June 3. He wondered why no one met him at the airport, but managed to get to the usual hotel on his own. He had barely settled in his

211

room when the Tiananmen assault commenced. Knowing nothing of what was transpiring he tried to reach his CAAS host by telephone. His host finally did arrive in a government car only to tell his guest to leave the country as soon as possible. By that time, the major streets were blocked and soldiers were ordered to shoot at any moving object. Using back streets to escape, their trip to the airport required three hours longer than the normal trip. His host simply dropped him there and hurried back to town. This American agricultural scientist found himself alone in an airport overflowing with foreigners without any plan or itinerary. They were just trying to get to any point out of China at any cost. Fortunately, the American Embassy had its people at the airport, coordinating with other embassies. They chartered many flights in the effort to move people out of Beijing as quickly as possible. The scientist was lucky, securing a seat for the next day. But he was still in shock when he told me of his experience much later.

The international reaction toward the Tiananmen Square tragedy was so strong that many countries doubted that China was capable of moving forward in her quest for modernization. In the United States, within government and in general society, there were many very active discussions on what to do next. In one of the multi-society meetings in Washington, which I attended, the common understanding was that we had to keep China's door open in order to promote a democratic society, especially in the academic area. Otherwise, China would become totally isolated again.

Among the many side effects on China due to Tiananmen Square was the loss of many highly talented scholars who happened to be in the U.S. at that time. They decided to stay abroad rather than return to China. Many students were in training for essential needs in China, and many of them applied to stay in the States or other countries. The estimated number reported by news media was 30,000 of top talents.

Chapter 13
Keys Toward China's Real Stability

Quo Vadis

In 2002, I initiated a project to envision China's agriculture future toward 2050, or after fifty years. I asked several world-renowned scholars to join me. They would become members of the editorial board, help select important subjects, and invite qualified authors to address various subjects. Fifty-five scholars shared the same dream, contributing their wisdom; collectively we completed the book "Vision of 2050 Agriculture in China", which was printed in Beijing and released in July 2004. We dared to envision above the tree of tradition, and to glimpse the future of China with fresh thoughts. We all agreed that China must maintain its social and economic stability, and that only stability can sustain its economic growth.

Since China opened its doors in 1972, the country has made steady progress. Unfortunately, such unexpected tragic events as the Tiananmen square massacre, unrest in rural society and widening economic disparity between east and west dampened overall success.

As a member of the world community, China's leadership, scientists, educators, industry, trade, etc., must have active communication and cooperation with the world, and China must follow the general international rule to achieve academic, social and economic growth. China cannot afford to be isolated from the world again.

What are the essential "keys" for a country to move forward towards consistent economic growth and real stability? For all developing countries, there are hundreds of issues to be resolved while marching toward modernization. Since resources are usually limited, a country must work out priorities toward its goal.

Experts in different fields will have their own views as to which keys should have top priority. I am an agricultural scientist, and I wish to place agriculture as China's top priority. China is an agrarian country in the sense that 70 percent of its population lives in rural areas. However, agriculture is the weakest link in China's economy. Here I wish to address our joint views as expressed in the Vision book, and especially state my views on important issues.

Vision and Approaches Toward 2050

The following is a summary of views from the book "Dare to Dream: Vision of 2050 Agriculture in China", edited by T.C. Tso and He Kang, published by the China Agricultural University Press, Beijing, China, 2004.

Three major concerns face the world in the next 50 years: food, natural resources and the environment. How we resolve agriculture issues and problems will have a strong impact on resolving all of these, especially in China.

Rapid economic growth has brought immense changes in China over the past three decades. In 2002, China was second only to the United States in purchasing power parity (PPP). China will surpass the purchasing power of the United States in 2023 if both countries maintain their current growth rates. By the same token, China's per capita Gross Domestic Product (GDP) will equal that of today's Japan by 2050. China has the capacity to surpass these goals if it can address key social issues and agricultural policy, harness and direct the power of education, improve science and technology and conserve its natural resources.

Key Issues:
* The Chinese population will reach 1.6 billion by 2030; and is likely to remain at this level assuming the current one-child policy continues.

* China is losing arable land at an annual rate of approximately 2 percent. By 2050, there will be a total reduction of at least 20 percent of the current area under cultivation.
* Domestic demand for food and fiber will double in 50 years.
* Environmental deterioration and resource depletion will put pressure on agriculture.
* Using current science and technology, China can no longer increase food production at the rate achieved over the past 50 years.
* Rural-urban income disparity in China is among the largest in the world and needs to be improved.

* Those issues present a number of global concerns for 50 years from now, not only for China, but also the world.
* Water and energy demand will reach the limits of global supply.
* World arable land (11 percent of total land surface) will reach supply limits.
* Biodiversity is being rapidly depleted.
* Pollution from excess nitrogen, phosphorous and carbon dioxide will further damage the environment.

In pursuing new science and technology to end world hunger, genomic research, biotechnology, information technology and bio-nanotechnology, together with resource conservation, hold the keys.

Based on what we see, our concerns and our vision, we firmly believe that the Chinese government must take the following steps to meet the challenges of 2050 for the benefit of China and the world:

* Strengthen education and agricultural research. The funding level for agricultural education (including rural education) should be at least 3 percent of national agricultural GDP, and 3 percent of GDP should be devoted to agricultural research. This will enable China to train advanced talents, compete in global innovation, and take part on equal terms in international scientific cooperation.

* Enhance partnership and international cooperation to share in the most advanced knowledge and developments.

* While promoting biotechnology, the emphasis should also be placed on an interdisciplinary approach to problem solving, including preservation of biodiversity and systematic risk assessment to ensure bio-safety.

* Genomic research is fueling new discoveries that will feed the world and improve health and quality of life. Together with biotechnology, genomic research will help sustain economic growth and preserve natural resources. China must devote great effort to increase its capability in this area. Second best is not an option.

* Intensify research and development on information and communication technologies, so as to help farmers link more closely with consumers and researchers.

* New technology alone cannot adequately increase farm incomes. Also needed are rural education, improved agricultural and land policy, updated infrastructure and improved product management and marketing systems.

Agricultural Education, Research and Extension

Education

In 1982, Minister He Kang of the Chinese Ministry of Agriculture (MOA), asked me to organize a delegation of Chinese agricultural scholars from the U.S. to visit China. We were to hold in-depth discussions and make recommendations for Chinese agricultural education. The key points of our recommendation included providing opportunities for students to reach their full potential, to develop their full character, and to put agriculture colleges of excellence under comprehensive universities so that students may receive better fundamental training. In addition, we emphasized the need for research,

216

education and extension as a unit for agricultural development. However, to my great surprise, one of the presidents told me many years later that he never received our written reports as promised, and that agricultural colleges were changed to agricultural universities in name only. Not until the late 1990s did State Councils encourage and act to establish comprehensive universities, and place agricultural colleges under this new university system. This is the best way for students to receive sound education in basic science and also receive a much broader view of sciences in general.

Many agricultural universities have greatly improved in teaching quality, academic standing and facilities since 1982. They also have strengthened basic science training and provided some flexibility for students to change or to select academic courses. However, students generally still have limited freedom for total development, as there is little time or space to develop their talents beyond fulfilling the crowded fixed requirements.

Each time I visit China, I make my best effort to visit with students or with farmers one-on-one or in informal exchanges. The reason is very simple: students hold the future of China, and farmers hold the foundation of China's stability. In both cases, I encourage them to express themselves frankly, so that I may fully understand the facts without interference.

What could I learn from them? What could I advise them? They were so pure, so innocent that they accept what comes to them without questions. I could, at the very least, channel their thoughts, their problems and their dreams to others; also share my experience with them. (See Appendix B)

In the fall of 2004, there was a special academic lecture session by four Nobel laureates at the Great Hall of the People, and about 1,200 selected top students attended. Each speaker delivered a 50-minute talk, and allowed 10 minutes for questions and answers. To my great surprise, no one among the students raised questions at all. Two possible reasons were suggested for the students' silence: too much concern about speaking English correctly, and too much fear of asking a "wrong" question. As a result, it caused embarrassment to speakers, educators and students.

Later at the Northwestern S&T Agriculture University near Xian in

Shaanxi Province, I told the students this story. I called to their attention that each student knew more Chinese than those Laureates. You have to use English because of the fact that the speaker knows nothing about Chinese. I also assured them there are no wrong questions, only wrong answers. This story made the exchange active.

I asked students to observe the following points to be better scholars, and better men or women: (a) Be yourself and do your best; (b) Be cooperative with others, sharing your ideas and wisdom; (c) Be humble, keep in mind that others may have better judgment; and (d) Be honest and straight forward, do not be afraid to express yourselves in front of "authorities".

Several students asked me this: our university is not the best in China, and I am not a top-level student, how can I achieve a good career? It was a very good question indeed. I shared with them my thoughts: Of the ten best universities in the world, eight of them were in the United States, and two are in England. Of all the Nobel laureates, most of them are not from those ten universities. There were good students and professors in every school, and bad students and professors in every school. Good or bad is relative; it is up to each individual to make maximum use of his or her talent.

Exchanges with farmers were very different. They were always under the watchful eyes of the local cadres who led me to the farm. I doubt that I really visited a farm that showed the worst poverty. For one thing, I relied on local transportation arranged by the cadres. They also accompanied me. They had the authority to show me what they wanted me to see. Even when I made a sudden request for a short stop on the road, they always had some excuses to avoid stopping if they did not want to accommodate my request. Secondly, on some occasions I could stop anywhere at my own will, such as in a tobacco field tour. The tobacco farmers I met all had better average income than farmers growing other crops. It was not that the cadres attempted to lead me to wrong impression; it is the tradition of Chinese to show off the best to guests. In the Chinese culture, embarrassment is called "losing face", something to avoid at all costs so far as possible.

To spur innovation, China must strive to fully develop the talent of each individual, stimulate students with incentives to achieve academic excellence at college and in postgraduate studies. Students need freedom and opportunities to achieve their dreams and develop their interests. In teaching and research, universities must avoid inbreeding and encourage innovative research-oriented teaching programs. Agricultural education offers key means to link farm production plans to consumer demands, as well as to productivity and value enhancing products of academia and research.

Research, Science and Technology Development

China has devoted great effort to developing its S&T and has made remarkable progress. However, as measured by indicators such as numbers of biotechnology and chemical patents and innovation index, China still lags far behind other countries. China must intensify its S&T investment for poverty reduction and for agricultural production growth. According to a recent survey, every 10,000 Yuan ($1,250) that government invests in R&D brings seven people out of poverty. In agriculture, every Yuan invested in research yields 8.3 Yuan in increased productivity. In China, the total S&T development plan for 2006-2020 (mid long-term plan) was recently announced. There was much emphasis on pioneering and basic research. Agriculture S&T, although partly practical in nature, should also be classified as pioneering and basic research. In addition, in agricultural and biological S&T grant application and evaluation, consideration must be given to the fact that such projects take longer to complete than physical science projects. Without sufficient completion time, grants generate research results of no real significance. Peer reviews to be practical must include both Chinese and international experts. Peer reviews cannot rely solely on a few big names from inside China who may or may not be the experts in a special area.

In 2003, China's R&D intensity in agriculture was only 0.3 percent, meaning that the public investment in agriculture R&D as a percentage of the total agricultural GDP is very low. World developing countries generally have an intensity of 1 percent, and developed countries 2 percent.

China can benefit from the experiences of developed countries in restructuring its S&T. In agriculture, education, research and extension must work as one unit. In the U.S., the agriculture extension system is a means of communication between farmers and S&T supported by state university and specialists funded by federal and state government. Extension provides information on such topics as: world food demand, new technology or varieties, potential disease outbreaks and how to take preventive advance actions (perhaps based on climate and world air movement). Distance education for farmers is also an important part of the extension system because farmers need to tend their farms most of the year.

Many extension specialists are professors (within an agricultural specialty) at a state-land grant university. They circulate through production areas throughout the growing season advising farmers regarding production matters. Industry extension people often are available at the farm to advise from an industrial point of view. Post-harvest management advisors recommend the best use of produce and marketing. Simply put, the objectives of the extension system are informing, educating, coordinating, marketing and distributing.

Most Chinese farmers have no opportunity to obtain basic education, which makes it difficult for them to adopt new technology. It is the responsibility of government and universities to promote rural education in classrooms or by distance education. The Chinese government must provide 9-to-12 years of free and required education all over the country, including the rural community. This, in a way, would increase the employment opportunity and narrow the wealth disparity. In addition, the agricultural extension system should not be an administrative organ, but rather connect farmers to scientists. It is essentially a part of continuing education.

The very objectives of S&T are to improve general welfare, national and international competitiveness and academic achievement. S&T capacity is built on both basic science and new technologies. One cannot be developed at the expenses of the other. A case in point is that certain universities in

China wrongly abolished general biology courses in favor of biotechnology.

With a view toward 2050, China needs sufficient supply of food and feed; risk-free genetically modified organisms (GMOs), plant-based fuels, chemicals, medical supplies, synthetic fibers, value-added GM animals for pharmaceutical proteins, and nutriceutical products. All these could be achieved through biotechnology, including transgenic plants and animals (e.g., from C-4 to C-3 plants, fast-growing and disease-free animals), quick gene discovery, and application of DNA chips. China should use GMO with great intensity, but basic science is also essential. In addition to biotechnology, other new initiatives are also needed, such as synthetic biology, information technology, bionanotechnology, biocomplexity, and precision agriculture, all of which are currently at the frontier of science.

In China, many scientists devote efforts to increasing plant yields and stress resistance. However, lack of nationwide coordination and cooperation has resulted in duplication and low efficiency. China has newly established many pioneering laboratories for basic and applied research with world-class talents. But national priorities and strategies are still needed so as not to dilute limited human and financial resources.

The Green Revolution was achieved mainly by using improved varieties, chemical fertilizers and irrigation. Today progress must be made through other types of innovations and through improved management. For example, biotechnology, which covers plant, animal, microbial and environmental aspects, can be used to the great benefit of integrated agriculture, food and health, and thus can enhance the quality of life.

Extension

Generally speaking, agricultural extension system, as we understand the term in the West, is lacking in China. The same word "extension" in China is used for channeling governmental orders or marketing needs to the farmers, and there is little feedback. Field-level operation and practice, such as new technology introduction to farmers, and field information transfer to research and education institutes are rather limited. Field-level cadres routinely follow package guides for farmers without considering differences of local specification.

In China, the current so-called farm extension system is an arm of the government administrative unit. Mostly the extension tells (orders) farmers what to grow. Some extension specialists may arrange for fertilizer without concern for quality; or collect grain for the government. Each province or region should have its own, nationally coordinated, farm extension system that is similar to that of the U.S. land-grant educational system. Some regions, because of their huge size or widely varying different climatic zones, may need several such systems to serve the public.

In a visit of five or six years ago to a cornfield in Jilin Province, I noticed farmers were using at least twice the needed fertilizers, pesticides, etc., generating waste and pollution. It is the responsibility of scientists and extension specialists to advise against using such practices on farms.

The problems of rural society, especially for farmers, are interconnected, and one cannot solve one while ignoring the others. Those problems include education, employment, population, land policy, and income disparity. Education is a top priority among them. Since 70 percent the total Chinese population, reside in rural areas, and 50 percent are farmers, there is no doubt that farmers hold the key to future Chinese economic growth and stability.

When I was with students or with farmers, I felt comfortable, and I sensed they were comfortable with me. If there is no person willing to speak out, and there is no leader to change the status quo, what will happen tomorrow? I cannot help but keep wondering on this question.

Natural Resources Development and Management

Land and water are other factors limiting agricultural growth. Only

10.2 percent of China's land is suitable for agriculture, and 37.1 percent is suitable for animal husbandry. Erosion by wind and water is serious. Most land is neither well preserved nor well utilized, primarily because tillers do not own the land.

China's supply of underground water is limited, and surface water is ill distributed, with only 20 percent in the areas where 64 percent of arable land is located. By 2050, China's total water deficit could reach 400 billion cubic meters, and China's current supply facilities offer only slightly more than 500 billion cubic meters, which is below current demand. Government has addressed these problems by various means, but solutions have proven elusive.

China is now promoting the diversion of water from the Yangtze River to the north. The plan would not benefit agriculture, however, for the following reasons:

1. The plan is primarily for relieving pressure for drinking water for the general population and for industry.

2. There are three routes for transferring this water: east, middle, and west. Only the western route is practical as its sources are the same as I mentioned earlier--not the middle part of Yangtze River, but the upper reaches of it.

3. From a resource utilization efficiency point of view, growing rice in northern China is impractical because there are no adequate water resources. Chinese always like to boast, "China can grow rice in the northern climate more than any other country in the world". At what cost? Take wheat and rice for comparison, growing one kilogram of wheat requires 900 liters water; but rice requires 1912 liters. Why not grow more economic crops that generate more cash for farmers? Why set the upper limit of grain imports? It seems politics plays a major role over economics.

Furthermore, it is questionable how much Yangtze River water can be diverted considering that 40 percent must be retained to maintain the local ecology and 20 percent is needed for additional growth. There are various plans for solving the water problem. But most plans favor using the vast supply of waters from the west for the north and east. One plan is to divert water from the upper reaches of the Jiansha, Lancang, Nu, and the Yarlong Zangbo (YLZB) Rivers. Another is to exploit the "big U-turn" of the YLZB River in Tibet. The YLZB River has an annual runoff of 165 billion cubic meters. The "narrow neck" (Pai and Beiben) across the U-turn is only 40 kilometers long, with a drop of 2,250 meters. It carries an annual flow discharge of 1,900 cubic meters per second and has annual runoff of 60 billion cubic meters. A 16-kilometer long tunnel could be built near the neck. Connecting that tunnel with local waterways is the key for successful diversion. The natural hydropower from the drop would generate sufficient power to transfer the water north and northwest. In connection with the upper reaches of three other rivers, the total capacity would meet China needs toward 2050.

Development of China West

In the past 25 years--beginning with remarks in 1979 and followed by many later discussions-I had frequently and openly expressed my view that China West is more important than China East as far as the national stability is concerned. In 1983, the first Xinjiang Region Delegation visited the U.S. Led by First Party Secretary Wang En Mou, the delegation emphasized agriculture. I was happy to meet with them and explain major U.S. agricultural research projects, particularly at the Beltsville Research Center. Wang surprised me by asking to visit the very advanced, cutting-edge Beltsville research laboratories on molecular biology and biotechnology. The difficulty was neither his interpreter nor I knew how to translate those special technical terms into Chinese as they were very new, and I knew only the English terminologies. Fortunately, Dr. Li, then-Deputy Governor of Zhejiang Province, was a visiting scholar at Beltsville, and I asked him to interpret for the First Secretary. In later years, we frequently used this story to demonstrate the lack of scientific understanding between China and the outside world.

224

Wang and I became good friends, and have maintained a mutual respect since that visit. In 1984, Secretary Wang invited me to visit the Xinjiang Region. On that and frequent follow-up visits, I fell in love with that great region, its people, its resources, its culture, and its needs. To me, there was no doubt that Xinjiang held the key of China's future, especially for economic development and national stability. I said then, and I repeat now, Xinjiang is the California of China. (See Appendix C)

When one compares the status of Eastern and Western China today, the contrasts are obvious. In general, the East is economically developed, rich and blessed with fertile land. The West lags far behind, is poor and has infertile land. The East faces population pressure and resource scarcity. The West has plenty of space and abundant resources. People in the East enjoy high-quality education and social benefits, while those in the West do not. The East is politically stabile, while the West faces difficulties with minority populations. The disparity between the East and West is wide. Yet such disparity, if addressed correctly, may be advantageous for long-term national development.

The Chinese government has invested some U.S. $75 billion in China West development. Investment of this magnitude should have led to an increase in average per capita GDP of about 8.6 percent. However, actual personal income did not increase. In fact, the growth of western farmer income actually slowed during 1996-2000 from 9.1 to 2.1 percent. This is mainly due to the misconception that development of the West is meant to benefit the East. Thus, priority has been placed on investments in heavy industry, energy, mining, infrastructure and similar sectors, mostly with benefits to the East in mind.

The first priority for China West investment should be agriculture and education. Some 90 percent of China's 80 million poor live in China West. The average per capita income in Guizhou (West) is only eight percent that of Shanghai (East). Strategically, because of its vast area and a multitude of nationalities, China West holds the key to national stability. Logistically, because of its rich resource base, China West holds the key to sustained

225

economic growth. China's future success will depend on its identifying the needs and solving the problems of the West.

After two visits to Tibet, I strongly feel that the West needs to train local people technically. Now most technical people in the West are from elsewhere and are on home leave about 25 percent of the time. Technical training in such areas as germplasm, fertilizer, and animal husbandry has much room for improvement. The long-range goal for China West should be two-fold: (1) promote sustainable economic growth, education, science and technology, social welfare and harmony among all groups; and (2) conserve and better utilize natural resources and protect the ecosystem.

The experience of conquering the American West occurred only some 100 years ago. The success is well known to the world. While many factors contributed to this success, it was mainly due to the establishment of sound policy, development and utilization of human and natural resources and preservation of land, water and ecology. California itself is the most notable symbol of this success. The state evolved from a bare desert to become the top agricultural state in the United States over a period of only 70 years in cash receipts as well as farm income. Furthermore, agricultural research, education and extension in California are among the best in the world. (See Appendix C)

Policy, Trade, and the Agri-Food Chain

Disparity of income between rural and urban people is one of the most urgent problems that China must resolve soon. In my opinion, population, education, and land policy are three major issues. Those three are practically linked to one another. Each farmer rents only a small piece of land from the public; renters cannot mechanize, therefore they must use hand labor. Most farmers have two or three children to help farm operations, but children have no educational opportunity because farmers cannot afford to educate their children.

On a recent visit in the northwest, we stopped by at a small village, hoping to talk with a few farmers. At first, two or three senior people showed up and chatted with us while sitting on doorsteps or benches. Within minutes, more than 10 had gathered. After half-an-hour, the group grew to 20 or more. Many were active farmers, and many others were school-age children. I was so surprised to find that many families could have more than one child by paying a "head" tax, and that there was no school available or school was too expensive for the farmers. As a result, there was no way to find a better job. At the time of my visit, their "housing" was very good, far above my expectation, and those families were happy and content. I did not ask how much area the house covered in comparison with the total land available to them. As the population increases, more similar housing would be needed. At current annual rate of 2 percent arable land decrease, where would farmers find land to farm? Those farmers had no complaints, no further desires, and no messages for me to forward to the authorities. They asked only to see and to touch a U.S. one-dollar bill. Fortunately, a friend from Taiwan carried a dollar bill in his pocket to satisfy their curiously, as I did not carry any money with me. It worried me then, and worries me now. If the masses do not dream for the future, what will happen tomorrow?

There is always great concern in China about agricultural self-sufficiency. It is impossible for any country to satisfy all of its own needs. One can produce only what is most suitable under local conditions and rely on trade for exchange. In China, there are as yet options for agricultural expansion. For example, there are 8 million hectares of arable land and 47 million hectares of pastureland not yet developed in Xinjiang alone, and more in other western Chinese regions. Migration to those areas could ease population pressures in the East while increasing China's overall agriculture production. Though the world generally takes a dim view of such large-scale migration, it is needed for China to improve the quality of life in this vast rural region. Another alternative is to "rent" arable lands abroad, such as in South America, Africa and Russia for Chinese farmers to use or operate under contract to meet Chinese needs. However, a permanent solution still rests on China itself, on scientific and technological development and resource development and management.

To sustain agricultural growth, vertical integration of the food chain is required. Agricultural food sector development depends upon the efficiency, commercial orientation and responsiveness of China's transportation system and of intermediaries in the agricultural food value chain. China must address the residual problems of inefficiency and maintaining unviable state-owned industry, especially in rural areas. Policies have to shift from those that establish markets at the margin to those that improve and promote the existing market activities. China, as a member of the World Trade Organization, will have to commit itself to building economies based on transparent rules and the enforcement of property rights. Its success at establishing policies that further market development and improve market players' capacity to take advantage of opportunities will serve to promote economic growth and optimal resource allocation. This, in turn, will facilitate equitable and efficient economic modernization. Establishing an efficient factor market in rural China is the key for China to succeed as a member of the WTO.

The Chinese government has for many years understood the importance of agriculture and accorded solving agricultural problems top priority. However, despite limited success in some areas, basic problems remain. Looking toward 2050 or nearly fifty years from now, even assuming that the Chinese population remains at 1.6 billion, the demand for food, feed and fiber is projected to double. But the amount of arable land will fall by one-fifth, due to non-agricultural development and use, and restored pasture and forest. Using current science and technology, it will be impossible to raise production to continue the production increases of the past 50 years. China must act now, changing its current rural development course.

When I visit a rural area, I usually go to a farm and talk with farmers. Once I asked a group of five farmers, "I am going to see the top leader in Beijing tomorrow, what message do you want me to speak on your behalf?" They answered in unison and without hesitation, "Reduce our tax burden." Agricultural tax, for example, contributes a mere 1 percent to the national coffers, yet is a heavy burden for the country's farmers. At the rural level, there are already additional costs to be paid, for road repair, water systems and maintenance of tax collector's offices. These are beyond the control of central government. Completely exempting farmers from national tax would not be a big loss to the government, but it would lead to very big gains indeed in the goodwill of the masses laboring in the fields. The Chinese government has recently announced its intention to abolish agricultural taxes beginning in 2006, which is indeed needed. I do hope that all the many various "fees" will be abolished, too.

Land reform is another way for government to reduce the burden on farmers and raise incentives to motivate them to maximize their productivity for the long term, perhaps for generations down the road. Currently peasants have few incentives to care about long-term preservation of land fertility and productivity, and the control of soil and water erosion or the reduction of pollution. Understandably, they have other compelling worries. But the main reason for their lack of interest is that the land belongs to collectives-- the farmers themselves feel like temporary caretakers. Even though these producers operate the land under long-term contracts, if government were to grant ownership to tillers that would promote their sense of security and stewardship. Tillers must have ownership of the land.

There are frequent reports of riots, protests, or even bloody fights in the villages where farmers make a living. The government can freely take over the land from farmers for other uses without concern for the livelihood of, and the consent of the farmers. Additionally, the many diminutive and dispersed plots could be re-parceled to sizes suitable for mechanization. Finally, encouraging farmers to organize cooperatives for their own interest, encompassing all steps from production to marketing would be beneficial.

There are many other factors, too, that could raise farmers' incomes: application of modern technologies, improving the credit and marketing systems, and perhaps most importantly, reducing the farming population. Rural enterprise offers vast potential for employment. But at present, rural enterprise can seldom keep up with industrial advances and competition. If, by working with farmers' cooperatives, development organizations can improve agricultural operations, post-harvest management, processing and marketing, they will not only help generate more family-farm income, but also they will simultaneously improve employment opportunities.

Advances in science and technology are bringing the world closer together. Many of the visions presented within this volume are not limited to China; and China cannot stand alone. In this new century of biology, the life sciences are undergoing transformation toward unification, including the agricultural sciences. China has experienced three major transformations in agriculture since the Neolithic Age. Its experiences of struggle and success should be shared with others. As China advances toward the economic level of the medium-or high-income countries by 2050, it must accept its responsibility to help less-developed countries in Africa and Latin America through international cooperation or even unilateral assistance.

The above-mentioned "keys" are well recognized by the Chinese scientific community, and are related to each other. However, political considerations usually take higher priority than open, scientific discussion. Take water management and long-term benefit, for example. Was the construction of the Three Gorge Dam openly or freely debated by academic and field experts? Will the current project to divert water from south to north be openly and freely debated before being put into practice? The public has not heard from many different expert voices. Important key projects should receive the public consider of various views, not just a selected few.

Chapter 14

Counting My Blessings

Suffering and Hardship are Blessings in Disguises

Year 2005 has special meaning to me. In Chinese tradition, as in many oriental countries, the numerical number eighty-eight (88) is 'RICE'age. In Chinese writing, the strokes for "eight, ten, eight" are the same as the characters for rice. When anyone reaches rice age, it is considered as a major event. I was born in 1917; therefore, year 2005 was my rice age.

To me, working hard is not the same thing as struggle, though most people consider them the same. For the first 30 years of my life, I worked hard six or seven days a week plus overtime, because I had to establish myself. In the second 30 years, I had to work hard to prove myself. In the third 30 years, I had to work hard to enjoy myself. Now, as I have reached the fourth stage of my life, working hard to me is a habit, not a necessity, but I continue to enjoy it. During my career and life, everything seems to have come so easily and naturally. Always a "lucky break" waited ahead for me, one after another. I did not experience any real difficult struggle to reach the level that is generally considered "success". Perhaps I was at the right places at the right times. Maybe I do not know what the whole mountain looks like because I am in the mountain. A famous statesman of China once said, "Anything too usual comes from very unusual beginning; any success too easy comes from hard struggle".

As I write this chapter in 2006, I have spent 66 years in my tobacco career, 59 of them in the United States for research and project coordination related to tobacco. Many scholars in the broad scientific community considered that "T.C. had it made." Frankly, although I do understand what

231

they generally mean as a kind of respect and admiration, I do not exactly understand their point of view or basis. Were those scholars counting the various honors I received, or counting my academic achievements, or counting my attitude toward working hard and devotion, or counting that I am an American of Chinese origin? I do not mind whether it is based on one or several of those bases. If I did make it, I am very grateful. However, I think the story of struggle and success needs to be told, especially in the politically sensitive crop of tobacco.

A very dear friend of mine, who is of Chinese origin, had served as an English professor, as the head of an academic department, and later on as the dean in a world- famous university, told me this and I always remember it: "There is no Asian American, no Chinese American, no American Chinese; there is only American, there is only Chinese, or at most, there is American of Chinese origin." I was not pleased to watch a recent TV program; it aired something like the success story of Chinese Americans. Why only select "Chinese" Americans? Why not German Americans? English Americans? Of course I do understand that Chinese suffered unusually hard in the past, both in China and in America. Many people asked me, how did you break the glass ceiling? To be honest, I was too occupied with my daily work to be even aware there is a ceiling.

When I was a student in the University of Nanking, one of the higher education institutions sponsored by the U.S. Missionary Board, there were many professors from America, a few from England, and one from Germany. We were taught mostly in English, talked in English, used English textbooks. No one paid any attention to where the professors came from and we ignored their origin, we judged them only by their teaching abilities, their knowledge and their character.

The term "democracy" was very familiar to Chinese students; it represented the United States of America. In my understanding at that time, democracy gave an impression of romantic and idealistic feeling. We knew the term democracy from the dictionary, but did not understand its essence.

When I arrived in San Francisco from Shanghai, the only thing that surprised me were the signs over the water fountain, on the doors of public toilets and in front of restaurants. The signs distinguished "colored" or "white." My professors had never mentioned any of those things to me. Today, after almost 60 years, I try to ask myself: Was I blind? No! Was I sensitive? Yes! Am I intelligent? Probably. Am I wise? Certainly not. Am I blessed? Absolutely yes!

My Children

We are very much blessed in having Betty and Paul, who provided us not only joy and love, but also thanks and responsibility. Margaret did more than her share in raising them with love and education. My personal research work and responsibility in coordinating national and international projects required frequent travel in the U.S. and aboard, particularly during the height of the tobacco-health study period. Margaret, in addition to caring for the children, frequently took me to the airport. Several times she did not inform me of her own illness or even her hospitalizations during my absences. I feel quite guilty about that. After Betty and Paul reached high school, she returned to work as a registered occupational therapist (OTR) in the U.S. Soldiers' Home in Washington. Margaret was devoted to the care of her patients, and her supervisor and co-workers specially recognized her work. Margaret retired with honor, and by nomination of her peers, she was invited to serve as expert advisor at the United Nations World Health Organization (WHO).

Both Betty and Paul were good, hard working students and never gave us any trouble at home or in school. Their strong Christian faith developed from childhood. Aside from class work, both enjoyed music, taking lessens in violin and piano, which provided them with broader interest in addition to school textbooks. They were members of school chorus, orchestra and participated in summer camps and tour performances.

Speaking of their music training, here is one story I like to tell. Although we had been in the U.S. a long time, and the war between China and Japan

233

was long over, deep in our hearts we could not forgive Japan's war crimes in China. An illustration of this struggle took place in the late 1960s when both Betty and Paul were studying piano. The used baby grand piano in our home was old and out of tune. Their piano teacher advised us to purchase a new piano that would do justice to the children's talents. For more than two months our whole family searched for a suitable piano, but we could not reach a decision. We were considering purchasing a six-foot baby grand. The U.S. brand was $1,000 per foot, or $6,000, while the Japanese brand was $500 per foot, or $3,000. When we still could not decide which brand to buy, the music teacher became exasperated. She knew our dilemma, but proceeded to give my wife and me a stern lecture. "Both of you are highly educated people, but your children are in the U.S. now, and the war with Japan was 20 years ago. How can you let ill feelings affect the children?" She continued, "It's obvious that the Japanese brand is a better buy since both are of equal quality. Please use your good judgment and forget your prejudices!" Soon after, we purchased the Yamaha piano. It was the only Japanese-made merchandise that we knowingly purchased to that time.

During short school breaks, Betty and Paul worked part-time at McDonald's or delivered local papers for experience and some pocket money. Both were educated in Maryland. When Betty entered the University for the freshman year, Margaret and I thought it might be a good idea for her to live in the university dormitory. She would save on commuting time, get to know more friends and enjoy campus life. It turned out not as we expected. Betty experienced that it was almost impossible to study in her room with several occupants with different interests and activities. She had to sit in the stairway to do her studying. Soon she became very disturbed with the environment, and she moved back home and commuted to school. When Paul went to college, he also stayed at home. Both of them studied medicine at the University of Maryland in Baltimore. Betty specialized in emergency medicine, Paul in surgery.

Betty later became one of the three founders of the University of Maryland's Department of Emergency Medicine. She served as department head for a few years, and is now a teaching professor and practitioner at the University Hospital. Betty devotes much of her free time to the care of hospice patients in Baltimore.

In the mid 1980s, Paul completed his training at the University of Maryland. He interned in New Orleans as a general surgeon, and began his practice in a hospital in southern Maryland. In 1993, Paul volunteered for the International Medical Corp (IMC). Paul's three-month special mission was to save lives in Somalia, central Africa, in the midst of war and disturbance. Margaret and I respected his devotion to his profession, but worried day and night for his safety. We were not supposed to know his exact location, but occasionally the IMC liaison office informed us of his condition. Our church members and we prayed for his safe return. Not until he returned home did we find out how dangerous his assignment was. There was no electricity. Surgery was limited to daylight hours and with the absence of needed medical facilities. Each trip from his living quarters to the "operating" room required the escort of machine-gun equipped guards in the front and rear of his car and on the roads and rooftops. We were most thankful that our prayers were answered, and Paul returned safely. Later on, Paul took additional special training in organ transplant surgery at the Ohio State University. After a few tours in separate hospitals, he is now happily practicing at the Emory University Hospital in Atlanta, Georgia. Paul and his wonderful wife, Denise, share medical services, and have two beautiful children, Emily Grace and Andrew Paul.

One may wonder how both Betty and Paul are so devoted to serve and care for others. Medical apprenticeship requires a long period of training, hardship, and most of all, love. Margaret came from a medical background, I am a plant scientist. Our experiences in war, in struggle, in helping others, in faith, and in hard work may have inspired them. Nevertheless, their own determination and devotion have carried them on their journey. Very rarely does our family share a meal together without interruption for professional needs.

Whenever possible, our whole family traveled together either within the U.S. or to foreign countries for vacation or to my professional meetings. Travel is a good way to understand the world and oneself, and my children benefited by it. The children have good judgment, kind hearts, work hard, and love nature and animals. They still have family dogs, which they care for dearly.

Our family frequently visited the outer banks of North Carolina, especially the Cape Hatteras area. It is a distance of seven hours drive from Beltsville. Most times the whole family went together for a few days, and later on Paul and I visited there for Outer-Bank fishing. Fishing is also a learning process for patience and for self-reflection.

We as a family are most grateful for our blessings and continue to be of service in our own respective fields.

The Impression Associating Western Imperialism and Christian Missionaries

Before ending this Memoir, I would like to address an issue that I believe is important for the outside world to understand about China and the Chinese people. The issue is the relationship between imperialism and missionaries in the eyes of the Chinese.

Many friends have asked me: Why do the Chinese people and the Chinese Communist government oppose foreign missionaries? There are political reasons of course. But I would like to share my personal views about the historical reasons. I will start with some early Chinese experiences.

Historically, the Chinese people were not xenophobes. China was one of the strongest and richest countries in the world for many centuries, and the Chinese were full of confidence in the face of foreigners. The Chinese welcomed peoples from around the world. Indeed, the Chinese capitals of many dynasties were quite international. The Chinese learnt from the world, and the world learnt from China. Indeed, the whole world benefited from such Chinese inventions as the compass, paper technology, printing technology, and gunpowder, among many others.

Moving to more recent history of China, the past 150 years in particular have had a great impact on China and the world. During these 150 years, relationships between China and the western world were redefined several times. According to the well-known scholar Fu Anming, recent Chinese history can be roughly divided into three 50-year periods. The first period began with the Opium wars that forced China to open its doors. The next 50-year period included the Sino-Japanese war, all but making China a sub-colony of multiple world powers. The third 50-year period arrived with the establishment of the People's Republic of China under Communism.

In the first period, many foreign powers pushed opium into China for the price of precious Chinese silver. The British were the biggest pushers, in volume, of the opium trade. China's attempt to stop British opium traffic led to the 1839 Opium War. But in 1842, China lost the Opium War and conceded many privileges to foreign powers. That was the beginning of the historical gunboat diplomacy. Actually, there were two opium wars. The first one was against the British invasion, in which China lost Hong Kong in 1842. The second opium war was a joint British and French invasion. That war led to opening more trading ports and the burning of Yuanmingyuan, an extremely large complex of palaces and gardens 5 miles northwest Beijing. The invaders not only burned and destroyed the 150-year-old palaces, they also removed many of China's most treasured and rarest art collections. Even as I write, some of those stolen treasures are on exhibition in London and Paris museums.

The second 50-year period began in 1894, at the conclusion of the Sino-Japanese War. Before that war, Korea was an independent sovereign country protected by China. Japan, wanting control over Asia, saw Korea as the first step toward realizing that ambition. They saw the Chinese army and navy in Korea as obstacles to be defeated. The war began with Japan launching a surprise attack before declaring war--a tactic the Japanese used in other wars. The Japanese navy destroyed the Chinese navy and took over Korea and Taiwan as well. In 1896 and subsequent years, Russia, Germany, England, France, Portugal, and Italy all had a share of spoils and gained various privileges in different parts of China, including the establishment of special "settlement zones", or foreign concessions. China was at the brink of being carved up by western powers. America, in 1899 for its own commercial interests and as a latecomer to the party, declared an "Open Door" and "Interest Sharing" policy for China, and requested other western powers' support. This policy inadvertently saved China from being totally carved up and colonized.

By 1900, foreign interventions had provoked deep hatred throughout China, leading to the Boxer Rebellion against all foreigners. However, an alliance of eight foreign powers defeated the Chinese resistance. The eight-nation alliance then forced China to accept the right of foreign powers to station armed forces and legal authorities in their diplomatic quarters as well as their provinces. They also demanded huge reparations in silver that were many times the Chinese annual government revenue. Thus, China was under foreign control politically, militarily and economically.

Also, the Russo-Nippon War was fought on Chinese soil for control of certain military and commercial interests in the Chinese Northeastern Territory called Manchuria. In the 19th century, especially the second half, through gunboat diplomacy with the weakened Qing Dynasty, the Russian Empire gradually took control of many military and commercial interests in the Chinese Northeast. They stationed an army there, built a naval port with a Russian name "Port Arthur". They built railroads to expedite trade and exploit the resources of Manchuria. The Japanese also coveted this resource-rich territory, and challenged the Russians with a surprise attack. The Russians lost naval and land battles and the Japanese took over a large chunk of the Russian interest in that part of China. However, the Russians managed to retain many interests, including the railroads. The Chinese Northeast became a semi-colony divided by the Russians and the Japanese, Russians concentrating in the northern half, and the Japanese the southern half. After the 1917 Russian Revolution, many so-called "White Russians" migrated to Manchuria, with a large concentration in Harbin in Heilongjian Province and some to Shanghai. But soon the Soviet Russian government inherited the loot of the Russian Tsar and took over their Manchurian Railroad interests.

In 1908, America began using war repayments to establish the China Cultural & Education Foundation to introduce modern education in China and train Chinese scholars overseas.

In 1911, the Qing dynasty collapsed and the Republic of China was established. Still, imperialists did not wish to see the emergence of a modern, strong China. On September 18, 1931, Japan took control of three northeastern China provinces and began instigating numerous incidents with the intention of starting an all-out war aimed at conquering all of China. Between 1937 and 1945, wide-spread, multi-nation wars with Japan led to the Japanese unconditional surrender at the end of World War II. Unhappily, civil war in China between the Nationalists and the Communists would soon resume and then intensify in 1947.

The third period began in 1949, when the Chinese Communists defeated the Nationalist government, and the Peoples Republic of China was established. The Nationalist government moved to Taiwan and initiated the "Taiwan Experience," as it is widely known today.

I was born in 1917, shortly after the establishment of the Republic of China. When I was in 3rd and 4th grade, even the very youngest students had to join government-sponsored patriotic parades. Especially in May, almost every day, we paraded and protested in the streets. Each parade was in memory of a special and separate incident perpetrated by imperialist foreigners. We shouted slogans: "Down with Imperialism!" "Down with British Imperialism!" "Down with Japanese Imperialism! And many we lambasted many others, depending on which day what country had taken advantage of China. The general public, of course, was well informed about what happened on any special day. Young students learned in the classroom to remember what happened on each incident by the foreign "devils". As a result, almost ALL foreigners were considered enemies of China. Students were taught that "there are no good foreigners; especially there are no good English people, except dead ones." Those impressions were sealed deeply into Chinese people's memories, and could not be easily erased.

When a foreign power occupied part of a city, or part of the country, its merchants, citizens, children, schools, and its religion accompanied the occupation. In occupier eyes, Chinese were opium smoking, uneducated, corrupted second-class citizens. However, they continuously sold opium to Chinese. In a Shanghai public park, known as the "Bond", foreigners posted a sign at the entrance reading: "No dogs or Chinese allowed"!

In those years, each foreign power had its own missionaries. Churches were built in the province, in schools, and in Chinese parts of the semi-occupied cities. All missionaries lived in privileged surroundings with their own people, enjoyed their own privileged life styles, and insisted that Chinese people had to be "saved". Most missionaries were tied to their own countries, their own interests, and some behaved badly. They would issue demands to local Chinese authorities that they dare not refuse, no matter how unreasonable the demand. As one example, missionaries would demand that local government evict hundreds of residents from a large desirable property, which missionaries would then claim as church property for building churches. Such disgusting and shameful behavior and "Holier than Thou" attitudes, not to mention the hated extraterritoriality, created great resentment among the Chinese people in general, and educated Chinese people in particular. The deep feelings among Chinese toward foreigners were mistrust, and unfortunately this mistrust extended to the missionaries, who were associated with, and identified as part of the imperialism. The question for many Chinese might be framed thus: You take everything from us, you kill our people with opium, you enjoy your privileged life style on our soil, you have your religion, you exploit us and our resources, you are not one of us, how can you tell us that your God is our God who has come to save us?

During those years, some Chinese occasionally visited foreign settlements, schools or hospitals connected to churches to participate in worship services. But real believers were very few. Usually, Chinese who visited settlements were attempting to connect with foreigners for their own advantage or advancement such as a privileged life of better income, better housing, better schooling or foreign-country study.

When I was in the grade school, some Chinese believers were referred to as "living on religion", or "eating on religion". They kept a distance from common people and only a few enjoyed much respect. The tie between imperialism and missionary was too great. Even though the nature of association is changed now, it is a fact that some missionaries still cannot tolerate, or accept, the local environment and ways of living. Thus they desire and arrange for living conditions far above the local people. In so doing, they have unintentionally separated themselves from the people whose souls they came to win.

As a Christian writing this Memoir today, I can firmly say that those historical events should have taught us Christians a clear lesson, and an even a stronger message to all missionaries of all faiths all over the whole world. Missionaries should absolutely not represent any special interest, enjoy any special privilege, or carry any special standard of living different from the general public you serve if you are to earn their trust. Otherwise, you are not one of "us". If you are not one of us, how can your God be our God? Only from one mind can one faith be generated. How do you reach one mind? One has to learn from another's mind, and understand another's mind to build trust with another's mind. There is no shortcut!

One may ask: Why does Taiwan, with the same culture and people of Mainland China, have many churches, missionaries and believers? Taiwan was under Japanese rule for 50 years before the end of World War II. When the Nationalist government fled to Taiwan in 1949, many of their leaders were Christians. Those included the very top leaders, high officials and scholars trained in the western world. Subsequently, as Taiwan's economy grew, its doors were open to all faiths of missionaries. The young generation was exposed to Christian teaching early, and they were free to study abroad. Most of the young people became believers and thus sowed the seeds of even larger harvests. We know that many Mainland Chinese students in the U.S. declared themselves to be believers, and most of them are planning to return to China.

I firmly believe that free will is one of the basic human rights. Personal faith should always be respected and protected.

One Grain of Sand, One Drop of Water

One of the major reasons for writing this Memoir is for me to share my faith with others. Many friends frequently raised the question, in honesty, how could a prominent scientist believe in God? Yes, I am one of the better-known scientists, and I am a firm believer.

Each one of us was brought here for a certain purpose, big or small. I pray that I have completed the mission assigned to me. It is easy to have a good vision, but always having good judgment is next to impossible.

Most, if not all, scientists shy away from discussing their personal faith openly, as it may lead others to impressions of "bias" or misjudgment of their academic efforts. Recently an article came to my attention discussing Albert Einstein's religious views. The article did not state clearly whether it reflects Einstein's opinion, or it is the author's interpretation. It reported that there are three stages of religion development. At the first stage, worship is to relieve fear; primitive people worship objects for freedom from fear. The second stage is the use of religion to establish social order, such as in Europe a few centuries ago. The third stage is to worship the Creator. That article stated that Einstein once said that he is a most religious person, but he never belonged to any church. Einstein firmly believed that there was a Creator in the very beginning; otherwise there would be no possibility for the system as big as cosmoses, as small as humans, plants, microorganisms to be maintained in such a delicate yet total balance. Cosmoses are the universe conceived as an orderly and harmonious system, living body is the utmost master structure of complicated organs, cells, DNA, yet also orderly and harmonious. What a marvelous Creator!

In the course of human intelligence development, many philosophers and thinkers avoided discussing God, the Creator; and many scientists and scholars stayed away from discussing religion. The famous Chinese Confucius once answered a question about the meaning of "death". His answer was, "How could I talk about death when I have yet to understand life?" In Confucius's teaching, he touched every subject of the society except four areas: Violence, Catastrophe, Mystery, and God, because as Confucius said, he does not know those four areas. However, Confucius cautioned worshipers to be sincere and be respectable, "when you worship you are in the presence of God".

Many of my academic friends, including Chinese university students have said to me: "You are such a renowned scientist, how can you believe in God with good faith?" My response is very simple, "my belief is based on science and faith". For example, the Dalai Lama, the Buddhist leader, has a deep personal interest in science development and advancement, he personally sponsors an annual Science and Buddhism conference at Dharamsala, India, where he currently resides.

In similar vein, the Vatican holds meetings about xenotransplanatation and the genetic modification of animals. One catholic member remarked: "The possibility of extraterrestrial life and intelligence, and the implications of cosmology for Christian ideas about the beginning and end of time, will be upcoming challenges for science-minded theologians." Take stem-cell research as another example. One Jesuit priest with a Ph.D in molecular genetics and bioethics said: "the power of new technologies is so great that we can no longer deal with them in a vacuum". There will be no doubt that organic mixed with inorganic, one species mixed with another, everything from the molecular level on up will be fluid. Science and religion must communicate. After all, there is only one Creator. To me there is no conflict between creation and evolution; it is not an issue. Creation is to create something from nothing; evolution is to evolve something to another.

Enrico Fermi had a famous question which is yet to be answered, "Where are they?" He asked why aliens, if they exist in the galaxy have not yet visited us. Ed Teller had a different argument against tachyons; he noted that if tachyons exist, why have messages not been sent? Are we to get messages in the future? However, no one tachyon has been built on earth yet. Furthermore, we need to always consider the space and time factors. Space is big, as Douglas Adams said, "you just would not believe how vastly, hugely, mind-bogglingly big". Space is continuously expanding, is there any limit? Where does the "dark" energy come from and how? Time is even more mind-boggling; do we know what is time? What is the meaning of billions of past ages vs. one second of our current clock? Our knowledge, if it can be called knowledge, is so extremely little. In the past hundred years, science and technology advanced more than past human knowledge known in total history. Yes, we are all aware of those achievements by giants who brought us to today. In my humble estimation with good conscience, our current accumulated total human "knowledge" is no more than a grain of sand on our earth, or a drop of water in our ocean. I am not talking about the Universe, which we know not or absolutely little. I am referring to our earth only. During the last year alone, scientists found evidence of signs of water on Mars, which means possible past "life"; also they found "life" in the depth of our earth thousands of feet below the surface, as well as life in the very bottom or even below the ocean depth. "Life" even was found in the sulfuric acid. Yet, a human, as the so-called "intellectual" animal, questions the wisdom of creation?

Many people can not finish reading the Bible, because so many questions come to mind in each sentence, even each word, which prevents readers to continue with "reasoning". I must admit that I had the same experience years ago; I stopped when I read the first four words "In the beginning God". How come? How come God in the beginning? Upon hearing many times the music of the Messiah, my soul was deeply inspired by its beauty, its praise, its power, and its forgiveness! I made up my mind to withhold all questions but to read, to put faith on every word from the very beginning to the very end of the whole Bible. Under that condition, I put aside whatever little "knowledge" I have. Suddenly all my questions disappeared. The first four words "in the beginning God" shock me to no end. I feel, although I do not completely understand, the difference between knowledge and wisdom, and find faith in "Comfort Ye, My people!" One can "share" personal faith with others. No one can teach you what to believe, or how to believe except yourself, and it has to come from your own heart.

Returning to our immediate selves, why do we have to eat, to drink, to speak, to hear, to sicken, to suffer, to wage war, and to die? Why are not all the creatures created free from all those pains? On the reverse side, why were we created independently to think, to reason, to love, to enjoy, to labor, and to worship? Yet, we have to do our "work" to justify all the blessings. Even birds have to use their wings to fly, to search for food, though food is made available to them. On the other hand, would you like to be created as a puppet without any sensing, feeling, or emotion? The answer is obviously not. We need to learn, to serve, to praise, and always to be thankful for we are created as what we are.

In this Memoir, sharing my faith with you is my sincere desire. It is not possible for me to shift the burdens from your or my shoulder. Yes, there will be continuous laughter, joy, suffering, crying, and bleeding in all nations.

In Isaiah, "the nations are a drop of a bucket". By faith of the Good News "the crooked shall be made straight and the rough places plain". It leads to freedom for the captive, sight for the blind, relief for the oppressed. While calling for Comfort, it is a call for all nations, including the U.S. and China, you and me. As we worship the Creator, the Messiah with good faith, we ask where is the Kingdom of God? When? How? It is as close as in your own heart, or as far as the edge of space. The questions are: Do I deserve the blessings? Do I deserve the sufferings? Do I deserve the Kingdom of God?

It makes no difference who you are; you are one of the creatures.

Year 2005

Why do I feel it necessary to conclude my Memoir at the end of 2005? It so happens that this is my "rice" year, also a year of many monumental milestones. Margaret and I have moved to a community for senior citizens to simplify our life style. There was one addition, a grandchild, to bring our family members to a total of seven. I took my 116th trip to China since 1977, made a keynote address at the 100 year anniversary celebration of the China Agricultural University, and attended the final year of my three-year term on the Science Advisory Board of the National Institute of Biological Science (NIBS), under the Ministry of Science and Technology (MOST) and Beijing Municipal Government. In the keynote address, I asked professors to give more time for students to dream, to envision, and more space for students to fly, to explore. Also, I asked students to challenge themselves for what they believe they know, and challenge academic giants on what they believe they know. My goal for the final mission to the Advisory Board was, hopefully to establish a permanent system for science project identification and achievement evaluation, also a long-term financial obligation. In addition, I received a "Green Card" from the Tianjin Municipal Government, of which I have served as an agricultural advisor for many years. In the United States in 2005, I was honored by receiving two recognitions: one from my peers, the Tobacco Science Research Conference (TSRC) for Lifetime Achievement; and the second was induction into the Agricultural Research Service, USDA, Science Hall of Fame.

I am most grateful, considering my age, for being able to travel, to reason, and to communicate with others, especially farmers and students. I also know there is a limit for everything. My Memoir needs an end point, and I believe it is right to stop here.

However, I shall not "seal" my writing pen, not yet. After this Memoir, I shall devote myself to complete a book entitled "Political Correctness and Academic Research-Tobacco as a Case in Point", in which I will encourage biological researchers to continue using tobacco as a valuable tool. I trust that the general public is wise enough to distinguish political climate from science.

As I end this Memoir, I cannot help looking back to my almost 90 years of life. Yes, it was a long journey. I received much blessing through various stages of my life, and with much love and reward. How much did I do to deserve all this?

As a servant of faith, I always know that I have not done enough for His service in my assigned missions, although my physical body is no longer able. What happened to me only reflects a grain of sand, or a small drop of water. I cried for "Comfort Ye, My People", where the word "people" refers to not only my immediate family and friends, Chinese or American, but also to ALL the people.

The vast world is still in turmoil, the suffering wide and deep. How does one make the crooked road straight? It is not by force, nor by war, nor by labor; it can only be achieved by our faith and our own belief. People always ask where is the Kingdom, how and when will the Kingdom come? My simple belief is that the Kingdom is in your heart; it is near and it is afar, all up to you.

If we can all be kind to each other, love each other, have the great faith, and share our beliefs with others, the road will be straight ahead of us.

Self Eulogy

Lord, thank you for teaching me to fly!

From creation to creation, from darkness into light,
From atom to atom, in plant, in animal, and in your image like.
While admiring the marvelous wonder,
Lord, I fear your might!

You allow me to fly low or fly high,
You watch me while I fly off course or right,

Carrying a burden, heavy or light,
Lord, you are always by my side.

Over mountains, over valleys, and over the open seas,
You allow me to taste success and defeat.
You teach me to experience hatred and violence,
Lord, your loves never cease!

You give me wonderful families, faithful to Thee,
Guide us to righteousness; guide us to be free,
You give me two countries, both dear to my heart,
In war, in peace, they are never apart!

Count your blessings; worship your might,
Ending the journey with glorious joy,
Hearing your calling, enjoy returning fly,
O Lord, what a wonderful experience, what a marvelous sight!

Appendixes

Appendix A Policy Sensitivity and Tobacco Research

Foreword
The Dawn of Plant Sciences
1. Plants and Light
2. Nutrition and Hunger Signs
3. Genetics
4. Chemical Growth Control
5. Physiological Disorders
6. Organic Metabolism

Toward Public Health
1. Radioactive Elements
2. Mycotoxins
3. Air Pollutants

Policy Sensitivity and Academic Research
1. The Mandate on Tobacco Research
2. Tobacco Research at Land-Grant Universities and Other Institutions

The Benefits of Using Tobacco as a Research Tool
1. One of the Most Valuable Tools   .
2. Most Abundant Scientific Information

Beyond the Frontiers of Science
1. Tool of Pioneering Science
2. Food
3. Medicine

Afterword: Treat Tobacco with Respect
Sources of references

Foreword

As a plant physiologist and phytochemist, I used tobacco as a research tool for almost 60 years. I witnessed the dawn of the field of plant science based on the findings from tobacco research. I also participated or led many major research projects of high scientific value on plant nutrition, organic metabolism, and growth regulators using tobacco during the early development of the sciences of plant physiology and biochemistry. With tobacco as a model plant, USDA scientists also advanced virology, and they found several groups of compounds effective in biological control.

In 1965, soon after the release of the 1964 Surgeon General's Report on Smoking and Health, USDA scientists initiated an examination on the presence, source, and possible risk of alpha particles in the plant; of mycotoxins in its leaf; and of pollutants in the air. They also isolated and purified fraction-1 protein and fraction-2 protein from tobacco, and they conducted animal tests identifying the proteins' high nutritional and medicinal value. The removal of those proteins also resulted in removing the precursors of certain hazardous smoke materials. And USDA scientists observed that interspecific hybridization between certain Nicotiana species can develop plant genetic tumors, which is associated with the presence of abnormally high level of polyphenols. As a result of those findings, USDA scientists initiated collaborative studies with several health institutions for in-depth evaluation of the possible risks of this group of compounds.

With authorization from the U.S. Congress and support from the administration beginning in 1968, USDA scientists intensified tobacco plant research in collaboration with other federal agencies, land-grant universities, health research institutions, and industry in and out of the United States. Those projects included intramural, extramural, and cooperative projects aimed at identifying and removing the specific hazardous substances in tobacco plants, either during field production or during postharvest handling. As a result, a theoretical model of "safer" tobacco was proposed.

It is widely recognized that tobacco is an excellent research tool, similar to that of Escherichia coli in biological science. Even as early as the 1940s, geneticists, using tobacco, developed monosomics in studies of gene inheritance—a decade ahead of DNA's discovery. The success with tobacco on parasexual hybridization and the benefit of using tobacco in biotechnology research are well known. Furthermore, there is great potential for using tobacco to produce food, chemicals, medicines, and biomass.

The purpose of this monograph is to encourage scientists to continue using tobacco as a research tool, because of the wealth of existing scientific information about it and the great potential of its future. There is no need to justify tobacco research in view of the changing political climate. As an experienced scientist, I envision that the use of tobacco is only at its beginning.

The Dawn of Plant Sciences

1. Plants and Light

Near Washington, DC, where the Pentagon is currently located, there was a farm plot in Arlington, VA, where USDA scientists conducted research. In 1918, two scientists were waiting for tobacco plants to flower in order to collect seeds. However, one special tobacco plant failed to blossom while others did. In late autumn, they moved that particular plant into a greenhouse. That plant finally flowered at Christmastime and produced seeds. While others paid little attention to this event, W.W. Garner and H.A. Allard knew they had discovered something of great significance: that the relative length of day and night controls flowering. They called it "photoperiodism." In further observations in 1920, the two found that within Nicotiana species, there are day-neutral, day-short, and day-long plants. They extended their tests on many other plant species and observed similar phenomena. Their discovery of photoperiodism revolutionized agriculture and basic science, as well as industry. It led to the essential knowledge on which the year-round, multibillion-dollar horticultural crops industry depends—especially ornamental crops. Most important, it provides plant scientists with a tool for multiple breeding frequencies, resulting in many other beneficial and practical applications. Even in the animal area, photoperiodism is known to affect growth and development—even the human phenomenon of "jet lag."

That early tobacco day-length study led to more complicated examinations on the basic science of light and darkness as it applied to plants and other organisms. For example, did the short days make chrysanthemums flower, or long nights? What about a short period of darkness in the middle of a long day? What about a short exposure to light during the long night? How can we save energy and at the same time make plants more productive?

How about the quality of light or wavelength or what kind of lamp to use? It was discovered that in photoperiodism, red light is more effective than that of any other color when used as a dark-period interruption to control flowering. A later study led to another major understanding that the action of red light on flowering is nullified by light having somewhat longer wavelengths in the near-infrared or far-red range.

The occurrence of reversibility in the ability of seed to germinate and of plants to flower suggested that it may also affect other expressions in biological development. Plant system, which prefers red to other colors, must have a system in absorbing the energy of red light, a pigment that is blue. Scientists in USDA again discovered the presence of phytochrome, which is another milestone in the advancement of biological science. All this began from studies on tobacco!

2. Nutrition and Hunger Signs

Chemical fertilizer was one of the most important factors in the success of the "Green Revolution." Years ago, people knew that plants had to be fed to make them grow—and to grow better. Little understanding was available on when, how, where, and what to feed them. There were little concepts of soil testing, plant analysis, or physiological studies, not to mention the concept of precision agriculture.

When we are hungry, we can speak and ask to be fed. Plants can also do so through their "sign language." Those signs were not fully understood until scientists conducted precise studies and detailed observations with tobacco plants. In conducting the studies for each single element, tobacco scientists had to be sure that there was no contamination from any other minor and rare elements, or from the equipment used, or from the environment. In 1933, McMurtrey led such a study on tobacco plants under specially designed greenhouse conditions with filtered airflow and precise temperature control. Any possible factor which might affect plant growth and development was carefully evaluated, monitored, and tightly controlled to avoid any possible error. McMurtrey used a calculated amount of chemically pure elements dissolved in doubly-distilled water. The nutrient solution was then placed into specially made quartz glass tanks. Each tank was kept in a closed, wooden box to maintain darkness. Plant tops were supported by frames, and their roots were immersed in the test solution. During the whole period of growth, constant air supply was provided to the root system. That way, scientist could be assured that the plants were free from any possible contamination by other known factors. In addition, both plant tops, as well as the root systems, could be observed in detail during the whole growth period. Based on several years of repeated study, McMurtrey reported the hunger signs of tobacco plants in a USDA special bulletin. That classical examination was widely recognized as a pioneering achievement in plant science that led to many other similar studies on various crops. It also provided the means for diagnosing any nutrition deficiency in the field. It was one of the most important pioneering research projects in plant science.

It is unfortunate that a recent major agricultural journal which printed hunger signs of six crops on its cover, did not include—or even mention—tobacco. It is indeed regrettable that today's concern for political correctness could blind the scientists—or even worse, that the writer didn't know about those milestone studies.

The early 1930s was the most active era for examining plant nutrition needs and the mechanism of nutrient usage by plants, using tobacco as research tool. For example, nitrogen assimilation was reported in 1931, 1934; light as a factor for nitrogen utilization in 1933; various weather conditions affecting nutrient absorption and, thus, the chemical composition of plants in 1936. The presence of some micro-elements was reported as early as 1921. Those scientific findings all seem "common sense" today, but they were initially derived from tobacco research.

In 1940, isotope nitrogen, N15, was first used to establish the absorption and utilization of nitrogen in tobacco plants. It was reported that from root absorption to protein incorporation took 72 hours. This led to a series of research projects on organic metabolism among amino acids, protein, organic acids, and carbohydrates in tobacco and extended to other plants. In the middle 1950s, research studies with triple labeling of H3, N15, and C14 isotopes in tobacco plants opened the door for intensive studies of alkaloid biogenesis, loci of biosynthesis, and organic metabolism in tobacco, which led the way to other plants.

Calcium, commonly known to be essential to cell wall structure, is the most reliable element for calculating dry matter changes on weight basis. Most scientists use calcium as the bench mark, as it is the only element which does not "lose." This was first observed during leaf tobacco fermentation but was used by most scientists studying the postharvest loss of dry matter in crops.

Almost all heavy metals and rare elements are reported to be present in tobacco, including Al, As, Ba, B, Cs, Cr, Co, Cu, F, Au, I, Pb, Li, Mn, Hg, Mo, Ni, Pt, Po, Ra, Rb, Se, Si, Ag, Sr, S, Tl, Sn, U, V, and Zn. The presence of those elements may be accidental, acquired from soil or other sources. However, it led to studies on the elements' respective roles in plant growth and development. For example, the effect of B on plant growth was first noted in 1929, followed by reports on detailed progressive symptoms during various stages of plant growth under B deficiency in 1933. Later studies also reported that B, as well as Ca, plays a major role in organic metabolism. Our knowledge on the effects of B to the protein and other organic metabolic changes in general—and of alkaloid formation, transformation, and translocation of tobacco in particular—is built on the basis of that pioneering research.

Another notable example is Zn, the importance of which on plant growth and development was reported from early tobacco research in 1942. Now we understand that Zn plays a vital role in our own life and health. We need Zn to help decode DNA, to make proteins. In recent USDA research, Zn was found to play an important role in the health of the prostate. By the same token, Cu was found to be an important catalyst in leaf tobacco fermentation. That observation not only advanced catalytic chemistry, it also elevated industrial progress involving fermentation. The importance of Mn was first observed in 1922 in tobacco and extended to other crops later.

3. Genetics

The tobacco plant provides beneficial material for genetic studies because of the availability of many Nicotiana species, their abundant seed production, and easy crossing. In addition, there are many distinctive chemical, physical, and botanical characteristics that provide numerous markers for scientific studies. The occurrence of natural mutations in tobacco was observed as far back as 1864.

In 1905, Comes classified existing forms of tobacco into six primary varieties. In 1933, Goodspeed reported the number of chromosome pairs in 40 species of Nicotiana to range from 9 to 32. A plant with variations in its number of whole chromosomes is known as an aneuploid. For example, 2N-1 is a monosomic and 2N+1 is a trisomic. The number of chromosomes in commercial tobacco is 24. By genetic manipulation, tobacco scientists in the early 1940s developed 24 monosomics in N. tabacum, or, missing one of the 24 chromosomes in a special plant. In doing so, scientists identified which chromosome is responsible for which specific characters. Those studies were conducted long before we knew about DNA, or biotechnology, for plant research.

There are many different botanical classifications for tobacco plants.

Commercial tobacco, or N. tabacum, is one of the 64 established species in the genus Nicotiana. This commercial tobacco does not occur naturally in the wild state. To establish the origin of commercial tobacco has been a challenging problem for generations of plant scientists. There were many hypotheses prior to a final conclusion through genetic findings that N. tabacum (N=24) is a result of hybridization between two wild species (N=12) after chromosome doubling. This conclusion was later confirmed by taxonomical, morphological, and biochemical examinations.

Tobacco fraction-1protein is a unique genetic marker. Synthesis of this photosynthetic enzyme is regulated by both the nuclear and chloroplast genomes. Fraction-1 protein is identical to ribulose-1, 5-diphosphate (RuDP) carboxylase-oxygenase. From an analysis by electro-focusing of F-1 protein from N. tabacum and the putative progenitor species, it reconfirms the origin of this commercial tobacco. Those findings also paved the way for the progress of future plant science.

Nicotine, the unique product of tobacco plants, provides another challenge to plant scientists searching for its biogenesis and biosynthesis, including why, how, and where it is produced and what happens after its formation. This search began as early as 1934 and started with tobacco-tomato grafting, which led to broad applications in biochemistry and organic metabolism. Plant-grafting technology is now widely used for scientific studies. A recent application by USDA scientists is for grafting watermelon onto squash or gourd rootstock to make firmer and healthier fruit. Nicotine is the most important alkaloid produced in tobacco and has been investigated since the use of tobacco as smoking material. USDA research scientists examined the nicotine level within Nicotiana species and developed plants with various levels of nicotine for health-related studies. In addition, the history of various "family members" of the tobacco alkaloids—the pyridal-3 relatives including nicotine, nornicotine, and many others—was conducted to understand the biochemical pathway and genetic pattern. Such research did much to increase our scientific understanding, as well as contribute to health-related research.

Through advances of plant genetics in tobacco research, breeding tobacco plants for disease resistance became a routine process. For example, tobacco mosaic virus was first observed in 1886, described then as a "contagious living fluid." The pioneering study on tobacco virus initiated in 1916 by Allard led to the virus' isolation by Stanly in 1937 as a crystalline protein. Those basic studies on tobacco led to the development of modern virology. Because of the crop's high economic value, many other tobacco diseases were reported as early as 1892, and breeding for resistant varieties started in the middle 1920s. Many distinguished scientists paved the way using tobacco for advancement of our knowledge. Now we are able to make further progress in science and technology because we are standing on the shoulders of those giants.

4. Chemical Growth Control

Tobacco is one of the most labor-intensive and end-use-sensitive crop. From seed germination to commercial products, there are hundreds of processing steps. Each step, acted as a single link in a long chain, may affect the more than 5,000-plus chemical components known to be present in tobacco leaf and in smoke—in addition to influencing many critical physical characteristics essential for leaf quality, or even usability. Many chemicals have been developed to control growth and pests and to save labor, but all of them have to be free from any negative effects on leaf usability.

In 1979, research scientists examined 53 chemicals for pest control. Those chemicals included insecticides, acaricides, miticides, and nematiceds. All of them were approved for tobacco use. Researchers made specific guidelines on when, how, how much, and where to apply them so as to meet quality and safety requirements. In addition, they also examined 16 others chemicals which were not approved for use on tobacco in the United States, but were used in other countries. All those chemicals were studied extensively for their disappearance and fate in tobacco, but the research findings had broad application on other crops when those chemicals happened to be used.

In the 1970s and 1980s, alternative approaches for pest control were first applied to tobacco. One was inoculation to induce plant immunity; another took a biotechnological approach by inserting the Bacillus thuringiensus (Bt) gene through genetic engineering. The inoculation approach did introduce plant resistance to blue mold and several other diseases, under controlled conditions. Even aspirin was among the groups of compounds being tested, but it was discontinued because it required excessive labor and caused some side effects on tobacco. That experience should not prevent scientists testing and applying the same approach to other crops. Insertion of the Bt gene is now commonly used for many other crops, especially cotton, and rice will, hopefully, be soon after. Many regulators from different countries are using an "absolute safety" requirement as an excuse for delaying releasing many other Bt crops, including tobacco. Viewed academically, an absolute "zero risk" of any new form of life or any new development is not possible.

Chemicals used for growth control usually can be classified into three groups: herbicides; compounds promoting certain physiological or biochemical actions; and compounds inhibiting specific growth at specific times. The most important in tobacco is inhibition of axillary bud growth after "topping." During tobacco growth, it is necessary to remove the terminal inflorescence, or topping, in order to redirect the energy for leaf development to desired physical and chemical properties. However, because of this removal of apical dominance, axillary buds will grow and develop into branches (suckers) which would defeat the topping purpose unless they're removed. This procedure, called suckering, is usually carried out repeatedly by hand on each tobacco plant. Chemicals used to replace this laborious hand-suckering are called sucker-control agents.

The chemical maleic hydrazine, or MH, was once widely used in the United States and around the world as a sucker-control agent. MH's function is the inhibition of cell division, or mitosis, and layered organization in the tunica-corpus of the apical shoot meristem, as well as DNA and RNA synthesis. However, when MH is applied to tobacco plants, it results in several undesirable effects on leaf quality and, thus, usability. Those effects include changing specific volume (filling power), total ash, and alkalinity of ash, sugar content, and equilibrium moisture content. With special authorization from the U.S. Congress, USDA scientists were requested to find a substitute for MH within a limited time. With more than 3,000 compounds on hand, scientists believed it should be easy to screen and select one from them for use on tobacco. However, after repeated laboratory, field, and industry evaluations, none of those known compounds could meet the farmers' production requirement, industry's usability requirement, and safety regulations. UDSA scientists initiated an intensive search for naturally occurring plant compounds that could serve this special purpose. They finally discovered a new group of compounds that could inhibit axillary growth without causing undesirable side effects: the fatty compounds, including fatty acids, alcohols, esters, and some of their derivatives. This group of compounds is very specific. Even a change of one carbon chain length may change its function. The significance of this finding was of great importance from academic, as well as practical application, points of view. It has been used for fruit thinning and other horticultural practices, and it also has great potential for grass growth control, which is labor-intensive.

Scientific knowledge obtained from tobacco plants has wide application to other areas. For example, certain natural sugar esters, secreted by the leaf hairs of wild tobacco plants to protect themselves against insect predators, kill certain insects when they rub against or chew the leaf. Based on this knowledge, analogs, or look-alikes, of the natural sugar esters are being developed as a new class of insecticidal compounds developed by ARS scientists.

5. Physiological Disorders

Physiological disorders may result from many factors. In tobacco, other than those disorders induced by nutrition, disease, pesticides, etc. and commonly known in many other crops, there are certain characteristic disorders that are of importance in plant science. They are physiological disorders generated from genetic and environmental factors. Here three kinds of disorders are reported: frenching, tumors, and pollutants.

Frenching

Frenching is a noninfectious physiological disorder of tobacco. It usually appears as a network chlorosis of apical leaves, followed by formation of progressively narrowing leaves. In extreme cases there is no stalk elongation or expansion of lamina in younger leaves, which is known as frenching.

Extensive studies were conducted on the cause of frenching, including pathogenic organisms, soil pH, moisture, temperature, fertilizer elements (thallium, manganese), and chemicals (2,4-D), which can induce certain similar symptoms in greenhouses but not exactly the same as those in the field. Frenching occurs only in certain plots of the field. It cannot be transmitted from plant to plant by grafting, mechanical means, or dodder, but it can be readily transmitted from active to inactive media by inoculation. Heat and chemical sterilization of active media (leachates, soils, sand, and vermiculite) eliminated their ability to induce frenching in plants.

Organic toxin produced by Bacillus cereus produced symptom patterns in seedlings' gross morphology that closely approximated those of frenching. Marginal inoculations of the medium were quite effective and demonstrated that the roots and bacteria need not be in contact to produce the symptoms. It is suggested that diffusates from B. cereus, and possibly other soil bacteria, may be the cause of frenching of tobacco in the field. Increased populations of the bacillus have been found in adjacent soil and rhizospheres of frenched plants. Diffusion products of this bacterium and the dead bacteria caused symptoms in aseptically grown tobacco seedlings.

Leaves of frenched plants are high in L-isoleucine, a component of actomycin C. Free L-isoleucine causes frenching in aseptic culture. The effectiveness of various isomers of leucine and isoleucine in producing yellow strap-leaf was evaluated. Listed in order of decreasing effectiveness by soil application, they are: DL-alloleucine, D-isoleucine, L-isoleucine, and D-isoleucine. Although the absolute nature of the toxin has not yet been ascertained, it has demonstrated the complexity of this physiological disorder, as many factors may mask each other.

Genetic Tumors

Certain Nicotiana hybrids produce teratoid proliferations of genetic origin. Nicotiana tumors may grow spontaneously on stems, roots, leaves, or flower systems on tumorous F1 progeny or only on part of the tissue. The species involved in the production of tumorous interspecific Nicotiana hybrids can be separated into two groups--plus group, and minus group. Hybrids among the plus group, or among the minus group, are free from tumors, suggesting that the critical contribution of the plus-parent to tumor production in the hybrid differs from the critical contribution of the minus-parents.

This phenomenon of tumor formation may have similarities in other biological systems. Considerable studies in detailed observation of its genetics, formation, and chemical changes were conducted. Evidence was provided that tumor formation is controlled by "conventional" genes that show segregation, linkage, and mutation, such as: a) tumor-forming Nicotiana species hybrids compromise genetic systems that control a precarious balance between normal and tumorous, b) the base factors controlling transformation in the hybrids are genes located in the chromosomes, and c) tumor induction depends on the accumulation of greater than regular amounts of growth-promoting substances.

Various morphological types of tumors were observed by induction by radiation on an interspecific hybrid, N. glauca x N. langsdorffii. Wounding of leaves of the same hybrid caused tumor formation at the site of the wound where metabolites would have collected under transport conditions.

The interaction of IAA, kinetin, and GA on tumor induction in seedlings of amphidiploids N. suaveolens x N. langsdorffii was observed. Kinetin does induce tumor formation, but IAA does not. However, IAA plus kinetin combined together was the most effective inducer.

Changes in chemical composition of tumorous Nicotiana plants are of great interest to scientists. Newly formed tumors accumulated high levels of free amino acids, along with variations in levels of principal alkaloids. Most important, a sharp increase of scopolin and the new formation of scopoletin in the tumor tissue of Nicotiana hybrids was observed, as compared with the non-tumorous parent material. Observations of an association between the sudden increase of polyphenols and tumor formation was also very important for health scientists, as it is not an isolated case in Nicotiana hybrids.

6. Organic Metabolism

Extensive studies on organic metabolism were conducted in Nicotiana plants because the change of each compound may affect its quality and thus usability. Tobacco scientists closely observed the formation, transformation, and interaction of those organic compounds—not only during the plant growth in the field, but also during the postharvest handling processes of curing, aging, and fermentation, as well as during manufacturing, including additives and blending. Those studies involved all phases of biological and physical sciences, and in turn the knowledge generated is broadly beneficial to all. For example, the tea industry, food industry, ornamental horticultural industry, and poultry industry all share the fruits of research using tobacco as a tool. The use of isotopes in tobacco research—such as triple labeling with N15, H3, and C14 in the early 1950s in USDA—was indeed a pioneering breakthrough in the early stage of plant science. With this new approach and the science of organic metabolism moving speedily forward, we learned that all organic components are dynamic in nature in any biological system.

Following are a few illustrations conducted on organic metabolism with tobacco.

Alkaloids

Alkaloids, especially in the nicotine family, have been the main focus of tobacco research because of their special natural characteristics. Scientists always wish to know how they are formed, where they are formed, their function in the plant, what they do after their formation, and their role in the plant's organic metabolism. In other words, do alkaloids take an active part in the general organic metabolism among major plant compounds, such as carbohydrates, proteins, etc.?

Alkaloids are a group of basic substances which contain a cyclic nitrogenous nucleus and are present in plants as well in animals. For example, anabasine, a tobacco alkaloid, is identified as a poison gland product in Aphaenogaster ants, in which it functions as an attractant.

Most alkaloids in Nicotiana plants are 3-pyridyl derivatives, with nicotine the principal alkaloid in commercial tobaccos. The early studies on the loci of alkaloid formation were mostly dependent on tobacco-tomato, or tomato-tobacco grafting, and they showed that tobacco roots were the loci of alkaloid formation, later translocated to the top via xylem. Later studies using isotopes showed that most of the precursors of tobacco alkaloids are formed in the root, but that both the roots and tops of tobacco plants can form alkaloids independently. Although each Nicotiana species may have specific alkaloids, it can metabolize foreign ones into its own system. Certain species and varieties are genetically oriented to have high or low levels of various alkaloids. However, the alkaloid content in tumors of interspecific Nicotiana hybrids may accumulate 3-15 times higher than in respective healthy host tissue.

Alkaloids, once formed, are subject to interconversion and degradation, or they take an active part in the plant's organic metabolism. Observations of such degradation were most detailed during leaf fermentation, whether microbial or enzymatic.

Tobacco-specific N-nitrosamines have received great attention in laboratory tobacco studies, as well as in the production field, to gain insight on the formation of a potentially carcinogenic group of compounds. Various tobacco alkaloids, tobacco types, cultural practices, stalk positions, curing methods, processing, and additives all have important roles in the formation and level of various nitrosamines.

The presence of high concentrations of alkaloids in plant cells—which would be toxic to animals, but has no similar effect on tobacco leaf—is of great interest to biological scientists. There are many hypotheses regarding their functions, such as that they serve as a) protection against insects and herbivores, b) detoxification products, c) reserves, d) regulatory agents, such as nicotinic acid, or e) waste products of metabolism.

Free nicotine is well known to be very toxic. It appears generally in the salt form when used as a pesticide. Spreading tobacco powder around the poultry house or bathing quarantined animals in a solution of "black leaf 40°®" are some old examples of using nicotine. It is of scientific interest why so many insects that attack tobacco can survive. The adaptation of insects to tobacco alkaloids is a fascinating problem. Green peach aphid is able to subsist on tobacco because it feeds in the phloem of the plant and avoids the nicotine-containing xylem. Tobacco hornworm may excrete and egest nicotine without degradation. Several other insects, including flies, grasshoppers, tobacco flee beetles, and southern armyworm have been found to metabolize nornicotine. The mechanism is not analogous to the production of cotinine when insects were treated with nicotine, nor it is similar to the metabolizing of nornicotine in mammals.

Proteins

Leaf protein is the most important and abundant protein in nature. Tobacco leaf, as well as the leaves of other higher plants, contains two classes of proteins: soluble and insoluble. Of the total tobacco leaf proteins, approximately half are soluble and half insoluble. Fraction-1 protein (F-1 protein) can be as much as 50 percent of the total soluble leaf protein. Soluble leaf protein other than F-1 protein, both chloroplastic and cytoplasmic, is called unfractionated protein. In tobacco, soluble protein can be further divided into two major categories on the basis of molecular size. One with a sedimentation value of 18S, representing a single protein, is fraction-1 protein; all the remaining smaller (4 to 6S) soluble proteins combine together to form the unfractionated, or fraction-2 protein. Generally, there are equal amounts of F-1 and F-2 proteins during earlier stages of plant development. Approaching maturation, however, this proportion is altered due mainly to the degradation of F-1 protein. F-1 protein has a molecular weight of 550, 000 and consists of eight large and eight small subunits (LS and SS) arranged in two layered structures, each layer consisting of four large and four small subunits.

This F-1 protein is found in all organisms containing chlorophyll a, including the prokaryotic blue-green algae. F-1 protein is ribulose-1,5 biphosphate (RUBP) carboxylase-oxygenase (Rubisco) in higher plants. This enzyme has a dual function in that it catalyzes both the carboxylation and oxygenation of RUBP. Therefore, it catalyzes the crucial reactions of both photosynthesis and photorespiration, the ratio of these two processes determining plant productivity.

Tobacco leaf proteins contribute little to smoking quality, but they serve as precursors of several harmful smoke components, including quinoline, HCN, and several other undesirable nitrogenous compounds. In addition, several amino acids—especially tryptophan, glumatic acid, and lysine—had been reported to form mutagens when subjected to the high temperature of tobacco combustion. Therefore, removal of proteins from green tobacco leaf prior to the leaf curing processes may result in a better tobacco smoking product.

Through our research, a process was developed for extraction and separation of soluble proteins from green leaf tobacco before curing. Either whole young tobacco plants including stalks, or regular field plant tobacco leaves including midribs were harvested before reaching full maturity and homogenized into slurry that was filtered to collect the liquid portion. The green liquid suspension was centrifuged, and the supernatant was passed through a special column. Crystals obtained were purified and recrystalizd to remove any possible bacterial contamination. After the crude F-1 protein had been collected, the mother liquid was processed to precipitate the remaining soluble protein, or the F-2 protein. It was observed that the ratio of F-1 protein to chlorophyll varied with species, stage of growth, and conditions of development, within the range of 8-10 mg of F-1 protein per mg of chlorophyll. An approximately equal amount of F-2 protein was also present in these leaves. Removing the F-1 and F-2 proteins resulted in reducing the precursors of many undesirable smoke products. The remaining solid leaf materials from the slurry were subjected to a newly developed homogenized leaf curing (HLC) process to achieve the required chemical and physical changes desired. The "cured" mess was then reconstituted into a sheet of favorable physical character needed for the making of smoking materials.

The amino acid compositions of the F-1 and F-2 proteins were nearly identical, with their relative amounts suggestive that both F-1 and F-2 proteins had high nutritional value. F-1 could be crystallized, while F-2 protein couldn't be crystallized but could easily be purified from any contaminants. The essential amino acid composition of tobacco F-1 protein was similar to that of egg and milk proteins. In rat feeding studies, we found that the average weight increment expressed as protein efficiency ratio (PER) from tobacco F-1 protein was significantly higher than that of rats fed a diet containing casein. The PER for F-2 protein was similar to that of F-1 protein. Those results showed that tobacco leaf proteins, F-1 and F-2, are at the top of the plant protein range in nutritive quality and thus could provide viable food as a by-product. In addition, soluble tobacco leaf proteins are of high nutritional value for medical use.

Metabolism of Other Organic Compounds

Aside from alkaloids and soluble proteins that are of special importance in tobacco, other major components which are common in plants—including carbohydrates, organic acids, pigments, polyphenols, fatty compounds,

267

phytosterols, and many other primary or secondary compounds—were examined in detail. Many findings are of significance in plant science and biological science, such as phenol and fatty compounds as mentioned in above sections.

However, curing, aging, and fermentation are special processes in tobacco postharvest treatment. Knowledge developed from tobacco research is widely valued in enzymatic science, catalytic chemistry, microbiology, as well as in the tea and wine industries.

In tobacco technology, curing refers to the changes undergone by harvested fresh leaves under regulated conditions of temperature and humidity. It is a vital process and falls into the category of starvation phenomena, or inanition, of excised plant parts. The purpose of curing is to produce dried leaf of suitable physical properties and chemical composition. Respiratory losses involving hydrolysis and oxidative deamination may lead to a 20% decrease in dry matter with the slow stem curing method. Various regimes of ventilation, temperature, and humidity control are employed to achieve results considered desirable for different types of tobacco. For example, it takes several weeks for stalk-cured tobacco to become dry, but the primed, or picked, leaves of flue-cured tobacco become bone-dry in four or five days at elevated temperatures.

The most conspicuous chemical conversions during curing involve several phases. The first phase is dominated by activities of hydrolytic enzymes and occurs in either flue curing or stalk curing. In this phase, disaccharides and polysaccharides hydrolyze to simple sugars; proteins hydrolyze to amino acids that undergo oxidative deamination; pectins and pentosans are partially hydrolyzed to pectic acid, uronic acid, and methyl alcohol; and there is little or no loss of dry weight. The second phase of conversion is dominated by oxidative reactions and takes place primarily in stalk-cured tobaccos. These conversions include the oxidation of simple sugars to acids, CO_2, and H_2O; increased oxidative deamination of amino acids to form ammonia and amides, particularly asparagines; the changes in organic acids, including the conversion of malic to citric acid and decarboxylations;

and oxidation and polymerization of phenols to brown products and a small decrease of alkaloids. An appreciable loss of dry weight occurs, particularly in those leaves cured on the stalk, some of which may be due to translocation between leaf and stalk.

The changes in leaf tobacco during curing, aging, and fermentation are results of complicated physical, chemical, and biological processes. Chemical, catalytic, enzymatic, and bacteriological activities may all be involved during the changes from green vegetable materials to aromatic products. According to their relative stability or potential for change, the main components of freshly harvested green leaf may be classified into three groups. The static group are more inert toward changes--crude fiber; pentosans; inorganic substances; ether-soluble components; and pectins, tannins, and oxalic acid. The nitrogen group may undertake limited changes— insoluble N, or protein; soluble N including ammonia, amino compounds, nitrates, amides, alkaloids, etc. The dynamic group is the least stable— carbohydrates, ether-soluble organic acids, and some yet-to-be-identified compounds.

Freshly cured tobacco leaf is unfit for use because of its pungent and irritating smoke. By the process of aging and fermentation, the leaf delivers mild and aromatic smoke. Aging is generally applied to cigarette tobacco, allowing a mild fermentation. Fermentation, or sweating, is usually applied to cigar tobacco and is characterized by high initial moisture content (may reach 50 percent), by generation or heat, and by 10- to 20-percent loss of dry weight. During the fermentation process there is evolution of CO_2, ammonia and other nitrogenous compounds, and methyl alcohol; an uptake of O_2; a change of pH; a change in water retention; and an improvement of fire-holding capacity.

The aging of tobacco is comparatively a much milder process than fermentation. The first aging process is to redry the cured leaf and bring it to uniform moisture content (9-10 percent). During aging, little self-heating is taking place. Small amounts of CO_2, acetic acid, formic acid, and ammonia are evolved during aging. There is an increase in moisture and a decrease in sugar, total nitrogen, water-soluble nitrogen, amino nitrogen, nicotine, total acids, and pH. It is essentially a chemical process, the main reaction being that between sugars and amino compounds with the formation of melanoidins and CO_2.

Toward Public Health

1. Radioactive Elements

The presence of radioactive elements, such as beta and alpha, in leaf tobacco and tobacco smoke has been reported in many publications. Naturally occurring beta activities, such as $K40$ and isotopes of rubidium, strontium, and cesium were negligible and believed to be of no significance.

However, the alpha-emitting radioactive isotopes were suggested to be of significance in that they may tend to be localized and accumulate in bronchial epithelium. The total activity varies with tobacco types and products. For example, in cigarette tobacco there was reported 0.61-1.88 pc/g , including 0.08-0.22 from $Ra226$ and 0.06-0.19 from $Ra228$; in cigar tobacco, it was 0. 9 -9.75 pc/g, including 0.18-0.74 from $Ra226$ and 0.0 4-1.35 from $Ra228$. The alpha activity also varied widely in tobacco grown in soils with different levels of radioactivity.

Most research efforts by plant scientists in this area are aimed toward identifying the source of radiation and finding the means to reduce or remove it. In addition to $Po210$, the associated radionuclides $Ra226$, $Pb210$, and $Bi210$ are found in leaf tobacco. It was believed that the source of $Pb210$ in tobacco is independent of that of $Ra226$ or its daughter $Bi210$. A series of studies was conducted to examine the source of $Po210$ and $Pb210$ in leaf tobacco. Scientists grew plants under various experimental conditions, including an environmental chamber enriched with $Rn222$ in the atmosphere, or in field and greenhouses with different sources of phosphate-containing fertilizer, and also in nutrient culture containing $Pb210$. They concluded that the major portion of the $Pb210$ in tobacco plants was absorbed through the root. The polonium seems not to be derived entirely from the radium within plants;

plants may take it directly from soil. In one study, the Rn222 concentration in the chamber was maintained to approximately 50 pc/liter, which is about 500 times the level that occurs in the normal atmosphere. This result showed that Rn222 —and increased concentration of Pb210 in the air—is not a major source of Po210 in tobacco.

Many agronomic factors were observed to affect the Po210 and Pb210 levels in tobacco. The amount of phosphate fertilizer applied and the cropping system used contribute to the wide variation of Ra226, Po210, and Pb210 activities in the soil. Phosphate is the main source of Ra226, Po210, and Pb210 in fertilizer. The amount of radiation carried by fertilization to the field may not be reflected in the radiation level of the immediate crop. The continued addition of fertilizers with high levels of radioelements would certainly build up these elements in the soil, which would be available to subsequent crops. In addition, the distribution, translocation, and accumulation of radioelements may be of significance. Tobacco seedlings were found to accumulate Pb210 and Po210 to a concentration much higher than that in the soil in which they grew. Direct absorption of Po210 is considered a major source of Po210 supply, in addition to that from ingrowths of Pb210 in leaf tobacco.

In bioassays of tobacco smoke condensate with small animals, some alpha-emitting particles were observed in the lungs. The possible continuous exposure to radiation in a fixed location is of concern to health scientists. However, tobacco crops are different from other crops, as tobacco is used mainly for combustion. If necessary, phosphate fertilizers can be purified to be free from Ra210 and its daughters—but at a rather high cost. On the other hand, food crops grown all around the world in contaminated soils under cultivation for years with phosphate are almost impossible to be clean and free from radioactive elements.

2. Mycotoxins

Many microorganisms were found on tobacco plants and leaves during all stages of field production and postharvest processing, including curing and fermentation. It is, therefore, a reasonable concern whether any of the toxins produced by those microorganisms would contribute to consumer health problems.

Generally, tobacco and many other plant systems may automatically respond by a mechanism to produce phenolic compounds as a regulatory measure upon unfavorable conditions. The regulatory system governs formation of a particular enzyme in plant tissues. The enzyme, phenylalanine ammonia lyase (PAL), initiates the chemical activities that lead to formation of phenolic compounds. This regulatory system also provides a feedback capacity by the formation of another protein capable of destroying the PAL enzyme as soon as sufficient phenolic compounds are produced.

When N. tabacum or N. glutinosa plants were infected with tobacco spotted wilt virus, a fluorescent substance was present in a halo ring around the necrotic lesions. This substance was identified as scopoletin. The accumulation of scopoletin and scopolin in tobacco plants was observed as a response to injury by bacterial, viral, fungal, chemical, or mechanical agents, or even as a consequence of aging or lack of growth. In the tumorous tissue of Nicotiana hybrids F1 (N . glauca x N. longidorffii), a sharp increase of scopolin and the new formation of scopoletin was found. This response appears to be associated with tumor formation, which did not occur in either of the parents.

In tissues adjoining infected xylem vessels of tobacco plants infected by the wilt-inducing bacterium Pseudomonas solanacearum, an increase of scopolin and scopoletin was found. In stem tissues, a threefold increase of scopolin was found 48 hours after inoculation, and an eightfold increase after 120 hours. Such a rapid increase of scopolin appeared to be associated with rapid multiplication of bacteria in the stem. An increase in scopoletin followed a similar pattern, but it occurred a few hours later with more rapid speed than that of scopolin.

Aspergillus flavus was found in various types of tobacco leaf. The organism is known to produce aflatoxins that are extremely toxic and carcinogenic. In defined medium, A. flavus may use aromatic amino acids as precursors for the formation of aflotoxin B and aflotoxin G. In addition, phenylalanine and tyrosine have also been found to be incorporated into aflotoxin B1 by A. flavus. Although tobacco plants are rich in these two aromatic amino acids, there is no evidence that aflatoxins may be synthesized per se in tobacco. In examination of various types of cured tobacco leaves, scientists failed to find the presence of either aflatoxin. Furthermore, researchers injected a high amount of aflotoxin B1 into manufactured cigarettes and found it was destroyed or transformed by elevated temperatures during combustion.

3. Air Pollutants

Plants are sensitive to air pollutants the same as animals—or even more sensitive—and can serve as an advance warning system. For example, tobacco is known to be very sensitive to air pollutants, and in particular, to ozone which induces the widely recognizable "tobacco weather fleck" in the open field.

Air pollutants are collectively called "smog," which is a mixture of gaseous oxidants in the atmosphere resulting from phytochemical reactions of which ozone is the major component. Under normal situations, the concentration of ozone, or $O3$, is low by its continuous reaction with NO to form NO2 and O2. On the other hand, if gaseous hydrocarbons (exhaust gases) are present in the atmosphere, they become oxidized, which in turn oxidizes NO from NO2 without destroying ozone. The consequence is that ozone accumulates and thus becomes a major component of smog.

Many factors contribute to air pollutants, but energy conversion is the most significant source. The conversion products include water, carbon dioxide, carbon monoxide, sulfur dioxide, sulfuric acid, hydrogen sulfide, nitric oxide, nitrogen dioxides, hydrogen fluoroxide, ethylene, ozone, aldehydes, soot, and hydrocarbons. Those pollutants not only damage plant quality and reduce crop yield, they also are a serious health problem.

Symptoms begin to appear on tobacco with a low level of pollutants, which may serve as a warning for factory construction, air movement, and other corrective measures.

Weather fleck is one of the early findings about plants' sensitivity to pollutants. In general, air pollution causes injuries that are visible either as small patches of brown necrotic areas covering the upper surface of leaves or the margins of leaf tips. Those visible injuries are the result of the localized death of previously living tissues that starts to occur about 24 hours after exposure to air pollutants. "Invisible" injuries, on the other hand, may involve impairments of the photosynthetic system in the messophyll cells, a change in the stomata control of gas exchange, or changes in enzymatic activities, such as peroxidases.

Policy Sensitivity and Academic Research

In 1492, Columbus introduced tobacco to the civilized world. In 1558, Portugal began to grow tobacco. Commercial production of tobacco soon extended to every corner of the world. Even at the very beginning, tobacco was—and still is— a controversial commodity politically, socially, and economically. On the other hand, almost every country which consumes tobacco products grows tobacco if its soil and climate conditions allow it. In the course of history, tobacco usage has experienced frequent ups and downs, reflecting a changing political climate. This down climate was particularly true in the European countries of the past, and lately it is very strong in the United States.

1. The U.S. Mandate on Tobacco Research; policies change with time

Tobacco is a highly valued cash crop around the world, especially in the United States because of its ideal soil and climatic conditions, plus advanced technology which produces an excellent quality tobacco leaf. In fact, tobacco-producing states and farmers enjoy abundant revenue and returns, as quality tobacco is a domestic and international commodity in high demand.

In the United States, public support of funding for tobacco research at federal and state agencies, land-grant universities, as well as independent institutes, has been made available from various levels of government. Tobacco-related taxes, even today, are a major source of national and local revenue, and the crop provides increased opportunities for employment.

The association between tobacco use and health hazard was first suggested and reported in the press many years ago, but it wasn't seriously considered by the general public or government. One of the earliest suggestions of risk was that tobacco smoking may cause tuberculosis, not lung cancer.

In early 1964, the U.S. Surgeon General's Committee on Smoking and Health indicted that cigarette smoking contributes significantly to ill health and early death, particularly in connection with cancer of the upper alimentary and respiratory tracts; chronic bronchitis and emphysema; and also cardiovascular disease. The committee summarized its findings in a statement that said: "Cigarette smoking is a health hazard of sufficient importance in the United States to warrant appropriate remedial action." However, following this report, the U.S. Government did not initiate any immediate action or provide special funding for identification, reduction, or elimination of the possible "hazardous" materials in tobacco or in smoke.

On January 30, 1964, USDA's Agricultural Research Service (ARS) administrator led a team of six scientists to a meeting at the National Cancer Institute (NCI) to discuss possible research approaches and cooperation between USDA and the U.S. Department of Health, Education, and Welfare (HEW) on what USDA might do to promote a less hazardous tobacco. Among the major research areas suggested were: examining the mechanism of smoke formation; identifying hazardous smoke compounds and their respective precursors; removing or reducing those precursors in tobacco plant via selecting germplasm, breeding, or cultural practices; controlling the formation of undesirable components during production and postharvest periods; and developing new curing methods. At that time, ARS plant scientists initiated several important studies with existing funding. Those studies, for example, included using isotope labeling technology to search for mycotoxins, for the source of alpha-emitting particles, and for possible components in tobacco leaf which may serve as precursors of harmful smoke components. Information generated from those early studies in plant science provided important basic information for developing the total U.S. national program on smoking and health.

In 1965, the U.S. Congress reviewed the Surgeon General's report on smoking, heard testimony from medical witnesses, determined that cigarette smoking was a significant health hazard, and required a cautionary label to be put on cigarette packages. In addition, in August 1965, the Surgeon General's 1964 report on smoking and health was officially released to the general public. Later, the 1967 Surgeon General's report on the health consequence of smoking substantiated and expanded on the basic conclusions of the 1964 report.

Two years after the 1964 Surgeon General's report, the U.S. Congress began to authorize additional funding through USDA that was earmarked for tobacco research at land-grant universities, especially to the University of Kentucky. However, there was no significant funding increase for the USDA's in-house tobacco research program.

In 1967, three years after the 1964 Surgeon General's report on tobacco smoking, President Johnson asked that a Lung Cancer Task Force (LCTF) be established in his annual Health Message to Congress. That mission fell to the National Cancer Institute (NCI), and the LCTF was established in July 1967. That task force and its subgroups were only concerned with research on various aspects of lung cancer. A separate group, the Committee on Smoking and Health established by the Surgeon General, was concerned with conducting educational and motivational studies related to smoking, plus collecting and disseminating information on smoking and health.

Soon after establishment of the LCTF, a group of leading NCI scientists visited the USDA Beltsville tobacco research site and was briefed on the progress of projects involving alpha-emitting particles, mycotoxins, and other plant-phase research that could serve as a basis for promoting the tobacco group functions of the task force. In addition, USDA scientists discussed with NCI leaders the drafting of a master plan for developing a less hazardous cigarette, from the point of view of plant science, in a programmatic scheme. It was finalized September 30, 1967, and met with support from all tobacco-interested institutions, including NCI, industry, and academic institutions.

In the same year, the Committee of Commerce, Consumer Subcommittee, of the U.S. Senate, held a two-day hearing to review progress toward development and marketing of a less hazardous cigarette, heard the testimonies of several expert witnesses, but not involving any funding or project authorization.

In late 1967, the National Advisory Council of the NCI concurred that there would be three working groups within the LCTF: one on a less-hazardous cigarette; one on atmospheric-industrial-occupational hazards; and one on clinical management, with emphasis on early detection and diagnosis. The council also recommended that monies be made available for task force activities. This author was invited by the chair of LCTF, and authorized by USDA, to serve as a member of this group in February 1968. The less-hazardous cigarette group, at its initial meeting on March 11, 1968, was initially composed of 10 members, all from government and known health experts. Leading scientists from the tobacco industry were invited to join as members at the first formal group meeting, as this project definitely needed their expertise, as well as the active participation of the tobacco industry. The first meeting also strongly recommended that special federal funding be made available for the recommended program.

Many experimental tobacco samples generated by USDA had to be evaluated through the mechanism and funding of the NCI program, such as the studies of smoke chemistry and various forms of bioassay. In 1972, at the recommendation of the Tobacco Working Group (TWG, originally the less-hazardous cigarette group), the Secretary of HEW wrote to the Secretary of USDA to request more support for the development of less-hazardous

277

cigarettes by supporting tobacco plant research, in addition to projects that were associated with the TWG. Those projects were mostly bioassays of smoke from plant samples originating from USDA and extremely expensive bioassays using animal inhalation.

The various projects under TWG were proposed and approved by members of this group of experts and health scientists representing the best minds in this area and were funded by the U.S. Congress to the NCI, from 1968 to 1978. During this period, much progress was made toward developing less-hazardous tobacco. However, the political climate changed in 1978 in favor of abolition of smoking, leading to the termination of TWG and all the projects it funded.

In the 14th annual report on the health consequences of smoking from HEW to the Congress in 1981—or 3 years after termination of TWG—the Surgeon General concluded that "the single most effective way to reduce the hazards associated with smoking is to quit." While the TWG projects generated abundant new information, they also generated many additional questions needing answers. Take bioassays, for example. There are different systems using different subjects with different smoke products. One can always question where the end point is, and which system is the best model. In addition, animal inhalation takes time and is extremely expensive, in part because there are too many variables in plant samples, as well as too many variables in commercial products—not even considering smoker variables.

At the termination of TWG, there was a need for a new mechanism for communication, especially to exchange information around the world, updating progress on various smoking and health projects still active in different institutes, identifying highest research priorities, developing a list of prospective investigators, and most important, considering which agency might best meet these needs. For this propose, an Interagency Meeting on Smoking-Related Research was initiated and coordinated by the American Cancer Society (ACS), chaired by the former Surgeon General, with only 10 expert members including two from HEW and one from USDA, this author. The first meeting was conducted in September 1978 at Washington, DC; other meetings were held during American Chemical Society meetings in New York City. This effort lasted only for four years, due to lack of funding.

Another Interagency Forum on Health-Related Tobacco Research was organized by USDA, mainly for information exchange began in 1978. It included federal and state agencies, universities active in tobacco plant research, tobacco-health research institutes, and industry-related research institutes. It lasted until 1985, not long before the termination of all federal tobacco research programs, including USDA's.

2. Tobacco Research in Land-Grant Universities and Other Institutions

Various tobacco research projects were conducted at federal research laboratories, land grant universities, and independent institutes of an academic or health-related nature. Most of them were production-oriented, some of them health-related, and others totally academic in nature using tobacco as a research tool. Funding sources included Congressional authorization, state or local governments, industry, or independent foundations. Among them, Kentucky was the most active and productive in both production and health-related studies, basic and applied research. Most of the research findings were published as scientific reports.

Generally speaking, all tobacco research supported by public funding has been of benefit to the progress of plant science—not limited just to tobacco as a single crop. Research facilities of different scales are still available in several tobacco-producing states even since termination of federal funding. Many brilliant scientists from excellent academic institutions have frequently used tobacco as a research tool and, with it, have made breakthrough findings in life sciences. Use of tobacco as a research tool has been essential to the advancement of science, both past, as well as future.

The Benefits of Using Tobacco as a Research Tool

1. One of the Most Valuable

As is well known, tobacco research has contributed greatly toward the advancement of plant and biological sciences. Examples mentioned above included work on photoperiodism; genetics and breeding, including parasexual hybridization and molecular genetics; growth regulators; pollutants; viruses; nutrition "hunger" signs; photosynthesis and photorespiration; organic metabolism and postharvest physiology; and many other natural processes. Furthermore, since we are still in the dawn of science, the use of tobacco as a research tool is only at its beginning.

Tobacco plants are easy to grow and have a short growing period. Each tobacco plant may produce one-half an ounce—or about 150,000—seeds which may provide seedlings for 2 to 5 acres of field tobacco, depending on the type. In addition, cell culture or tissue culture technology is well developed for both research and commercial proposes.

Within the genus Nicotiana are 64 known species—some of them known as ornamentals—each one well examined as to its genetic, physiological, botanical, and chemical characteristics. The somatic chromosome numbers vary between 18 to 48; the commercial, smoking product species, N. tabacum, has 24.

In almost every phase of plant or biological sciences, tobacco can serve as a valuable tool, in the dawn of science as well as in the frontier of science.

2. Most Abundant Scientific Information

Tobacco research has generated abundant scientific publications and a wealth of valuable knowledge. In 1970, when this author was preparing the monograph " Physiology and Biochemistry of Tobacco Plants," only about 9,000 total tobacco publications were available. From 1971 to 1989, when this author was preparing the second monograph "Production, Physiology,

280

and Biochemistry of Tobacco Plants," almost 60,000 new publications were generated on tobacco and tobacco related subjects. At its height, 60 or more scientific publications on tobacco were published each week. The surge of strong interest in tobacco research during that period may be attributed to many causes, but it mainly falls into the areas of chemistry, genetics, plant physiology, organic metabolism, plus some biological evaluation of specially-produced plant material. Significant progress was made in pioneering research, especially in the fields of biotechnology, molecular biology, biotic and abiotic stress physiology, and others.

The change of political climate beginning at 1989 has led to less funding support for tobacco research, and thus reduced the frequencyand numbers of publications on tobacco. In the peak period of tobacco research, about 3,000 active research scientists were working on tobacco in public and industrial laboratories, not including those at independent academic institutions. Currently, the total number of tobacco scientists is greatly reduced, especially in U.S. public institutions. Many plant scientists in academic institutions cannot obtain grant support for projects using tobacco as a research tool. Some even have to avoid tobacco because of the policy sensitivity, or by following "political correctness" to academic research.

The tobacco plant has served as a valuable tool since the dawn of plant and biological sciences, so it is indeed a great loss to scientific progress that a research tool already invested with so many resources and about which there is such abundant knowledge—and such great potential for new advancement—is now being wasted.

Beyond the Frontiers of Science

Contrary to general public opinion, tobacco has many valuable uses of high economic value other than smoking. As we face the health hazards of smoking, we need to realize the benefits of using tobacco for many other purposes—not only as a tool for pioneering science, but also for uses such as food, medicine, and many others. Following are merely a few illustrations.

1. Tool of Pioneering Science

Molecular biology and genetic engineering offer new and additional tools to meet agricultural needs. Working with single genes rather than a whole plant or animal provides a great advantage in biological science. The most noted advantage is specificity. For example, the insertion of Bt genes began with trials on tobacco. Schell et al, in the late 1970s and early 1980s suggested three far-reaching major possibilities using tobacco: a) using tobacco cell cultures to produce valuable drugs, exploiting both the available synthetic capacity of tobacco cells and specific activities resulting from the introduction of new genes; b) modifying tobacco cultivars through genetic engineering to obtain plants with improved resistance towards various viral, bacterial, fungal, or nematode pathogens; tolerance to biotic or abiotic stresses; or with modified chemical or physical characteristics; and c) breeding of tobacco for production of food.

Of course, there are many other potential applications common to all plants, including tobacco, such as nitrogen fixation, pesticide and herbicide resistance, and tolerance to environmental and physiological stress. The best approach is to use tobacco as a research tool, based on its abundant knowledge and rich resources to develop new information for all biological sciences.

The extent of the potential benefit of this new technology with tobacco is only limited by the availability of basic knowledge and further development. Once available, it should be easy to extend to other crops. For example, within Nicotiana species, there are short-day, neutral-day, and long-day plants of different photoperiods as in many other plant or biological systems. These are represented by Maryland Mammoth type, regular cultivated tobacco type, and N. gossei, respectively. If the light-inducible genes can be identified and constructed, it would be possible to construct light-inhibiting genes in order to combine those three plant types and create a high-yield, high-quality, and low-labor-intensive plant.

2. Food

Soluble fraction-1 and fraction-2 proteins isolated from tobacco leaf are of high nutritional value, as well as clinically useful. Those edible proteins, ribulose-1,5-biphosphate-carboxylase-oxygenase (RUBP), which is an enzyme itself, catalyze photosynthesis and photorespiration.

The biological efficiency of fraction-1 as a mammalian nutrient is very high. Its amino acid breakdown is very similar to that of human or cow milk—far superior in this respect to soybean protein. Fraction-1 protein cannot be crystallized out from soybean, or indeed from other crops. In addition, there are indications that fraction-1 protein can be used in clinical or medical purposes. Fraction-2 protein also has high nutritional value as human food—only a little below that of fraction-1—but is superior to soybean protein. Both fraction-1 and fraction-2 are colorless crystals, although in bulk they appear as white powders. They are tasteless and consist entirely of amino acids.

The insoluble proteins and some other valuable materials (e.g. xanthophylls) could also be removed in a subsequent solvent extraction and purification process, but further research is needed.

To increase protein yield, the desirable direction is a plant with increased photosynthesis and decreased photorespiration. In addition, there is also a need to increase the efficiency of solar energy utilization. The key is to find how to maintain the balance of essential biochemical processes to achieve this goal, since some essential building blocks for protein formation are products of photorespiration.

Searching for edible protein from plant sources is nothing new. Many problems observed in other crops are also found in tobacco during the process of protein recovery. Take tobacco seed for example: Certain phenolic compounds have to be removed in order to obtain the final protein products suitable for food or feed.

3. Medicine

Tobacco plants have long been selected to produce plant-made vaccines. A recent survey from Arizona State University demonstrated strong potential public support for plant-made vaccines. The use of transgenic plants for production and oral delivery of vaccines has been shown effective in animal trials and phase-I human clinical testing, although it is known that public acceptance of genetically-modified (GM) foods is variable on a global scale.

Some of the most recent research conducted by Daniell at the University of Central Florida, partially funded by USDA and NIH, demonstrated the benefit of using tobacco as a vehicle for saving lives. One acre of GM tobacco plants was shown capable of producing enough anthrax vaccine to inoculate the entire U.S. population safely and inexpensively. To create the anthrax vaccine, the vaccine gene was injected into the chloroplast genome of tobacco cells. Testing of the vaccine so produced with mice showed it to be very effective, and Daniell is expanding his research, working with tobacco-grown treatments for type-1 diabetes, hepatitis C, plague, and cholera. Approaches using genetically engineered tobacco plants will greatly reduce the cost of plant-based vaccines.

Afterswords: Treat Tobacco With Respect

In this monograph, this author has noted numerous academic contributions using tobacco as a research tool since the dawn of plant science development and has reported the changing political climate leading to reduction—even to the near extinguishing—of research using tobacco tissue or tobacco plants. Some anti-tobacco activists, including a few officers from other branches of the U.S. government, ignoring the scientific value of the tobacco plant, have condemned all research related to it.

Knowing that tobacco is a valuable research tool and has great potential for the future, this author recognizes that the use of tobacco is only at its beginning, and that we need to treat tobacco with respect. As we face the challenges of environmental damage, disease, hunger, and energy shortages in the very near future, we will need to have available every means to meet those challenges. Tobacco can, and will, help solve some of these problems. The basic knowledge built on past tobacco research is already in hand. What we need now is intensive work on transferring this basic knowledge to industrial applications. In addition, we need to formulate a complete infrastructure to make new tobacco-oriented industries economical and beneficial for all concerned.

Conventional tobacco crops are estimated to be capable of producing 2-4 percent of leaf yield as fraction-1 and fraction-2 proteins, which is only 40-80 pounds per acre (lb/A), or 45-90 kilograms per hectare (kg/ha). Plant protein content is at a maximum before the onset of leaf senescence. Preliminary indications suggest that cutting the whole plant when it reaches a height of 12-18 inches (30-45 cm) would optimize protein yields. Condensed planting population, plus multiple harvesting of second or even third growth of tobacco leaf, would certainly increase the protein harvest. A reasonable expectation of total soluble protein yields would be in the range of 750-1, 200 lb/A, or 840-1,344 kg/ha. Considering the high nutritional and clinical value of soluble proteins and the use of plant residues for energy biomass, further in-depth research on tobacco protein production is highly desirable.

The world is searching for sources of renewable energy, with most attention concentrated on new methods of making ethanol—not just from corn, but from wood chips, plant stalks, or grasses. We need to make this biomass-based ethanol practical and competitive. Obviously corn is needed for food and feed, especially in nations short of arable land or with huge populations. Different countries may use to their advantage whatever native resources are available. For example, Brazil can use sugarcane-derived sucrose and directly ferment it with yeast to make ethanol. In Europe, wheat, barley, and rye are being used as starch sources. In the United States, we generally use cornstarch broken down into glucose by amylase and amyloglucosidase enzymes and then ferment into ethanol.

The most practical way is to use "waste" agricultural materials of little or no commercial value, such as residues from tobacco as mentioned above. Those materials are mostly cellulose and would have to be broken down by certain "digestive" processes followed by degradation with cellulose enzymes to obtain glucose and other five- or six-carbon sugars.

Past experience has taught us many other uses for tobacco-derived materials, although they are currently not in practice or are being replaced by newer materials and technology. Some of those applications, however, might show us how we got where we are and also may serve as references for future applications. For example, in the not too distant past, tobacco waste—leaves and stems in powder form—were used effectively by the poultry industry for pest control. Tobacco "water", a watery solution containing small amounts of nicotine ("black leaf 40"), was used to quarantine imported animals and for controlling aphids in orchards and on other plants. This naturally-occurring organic compound can easily be decomposed, unlike some synthetic chemicals that may pollute the environment. In addition, growing tobacco plants to remove heavy metals in polluted areas could be an effective and economic approach to bioremediation.

In addition to the need for intensive research, there is a need for a systematic approach to better production of potential tobacco products into commercial and competitive industries, combining all the possibilities mentioned above. A solid infrastructure is, therefore, needed to make tobacco production economically profitable as a commodity, and scientifically respectable as a research tool.

Appendix B. China Agricultural University and Einstein
(Keynote Address by T.C. Tso on the Occasion of the One-Hundredth Year
Anniversary of the China Agricultural University, 2005)

The year 1905 was indeed a miraculous year. The China Agricultural
University was established with a humble beginning. CAU initiated the
Chinese agricultural revolution of agricultural technology, of agricultural
research, and of agricultural education. In the same year 1905, Einstein, a
so-called "dumb" and "shabby" patent clerk, published a series of papers
which changed the world of physics, including our conceptions of time, of
space, of matter, of energy, of gravity, and of light.

Now in the year of 2005, we celebrate CAU on its 100 years of splendid
achievements, we also celebrate the genius of Einstein. We are inspired by
the similarities that CAU and Einstein have in common. However, in 2005,
Einstein passed us without leaving a unified law of physics, but CAU is
moving toward discovery.

Not being an educator, but as an experienced scientist, I dare to say
what education can do, and what education can not do. The key is to inspire
students to think, to dream; to allow them space to envision, to fly; and to
provide them environment to achieve their full potential. Today, in the
presence of leading authorities and young friends, I ask you let not education
prevent you from learning and from full development.

In particular, I wish to share with many young student friends of my
thoughts on how to build yourself in addition to, and in spite of, classroom
education. Emerson once said: "The things taught in schools and colleges
are not an education, but the means of education". Wilde also noted that
nothing that is worth knowing can be taught.

Not every student can be, or need to be an Einstein; neither can every
school be among the top of the world. The key is how to develop the young
minds without the limitation of classroom, and free from the fixed agenda!
In high education, there are many excellent talents being developed; but on

287

the other hand, there are many top talents who failed to reach their full potential. A brilliant mind is a terrible thing to waste!

The main objective of my presentation today is to share my views with young friends, especially students and those who are young at heart. In developing own potential, students must exercise initiative and self-confidence; be open-minded; be able to challenge yourself on what you think you know; be able to challenge those giants on what they think they know. It does not matter if you are standing on the shoulder of those giants. More important, questions are more important than answers. I am talking about your vision. To envision is not to seek an impossible dream; it is to guide your wisdom to see something which is actually there, your vision makes it possible to visualize the visible.

We are used to talking about what we do know, but why not about what we don't know? In the July 1st, 2005 issue of Science, on the occasion of celebrating its 125th anniversary, one hundred twenty five hard questions were raised on "WHAT WE DON'T KNOW?"

Now, on the occasion of celebrating the 100th anniversary of CAU, why not challenge ourselves and world agricultural community in raising one hundred hard questions on what we do not know? Can those questions be answered at the CAU 200th celebration in 2105? I hope that some one of you would be here to provide the answer. For example, why not bring the seasonal rain from the Indian Ocean to China West? Why not plant and harvest food in the Gobi desert? Why not make use of that microorganism which can grow in sulfuric acid? Why not harvest the energy from open seas? Why not harvest energy from the sun to meet our need of 13 trillion watts by year 2050? Yes, we can chase the moon, and Mars, but why not penetrate the deep interiors of our mountain, our land, and our sea? We must soar above the trees of tradition, so that we can glimpse the fresh field beyond our imagination. Your future is indeed unlimited only if you dare to envision.

I recall that last year, there was a lecture session in the Great Hall of the People featuring four Nobel Laureates. Throughout the whole four-hour program, not one of the twelve hundred students present asked one single question. They either doubted their ability on English communication, or were afraid of asking a wrong question. I can tell you that I know no one of those four Laureates could speak a word of Chinese, so they have to use English for lecture. Your English is much better than their Chinese, and making mistakes is the only way to learn. Furthermore, in any academic discussion, there are no wrong questions, only wrong answers.

My young friends, you must have confidence in your own talent. Each one of us has special talent different from any others only if we dare to express it. Here I would like to share with you a story. Once I was in New York for a meeting, and my friend John, a scholar and successful businessman invited me for dinner. John told me that he had scheduled three interviews in the next thirty minutes and asked me to join them at his office. As soon as the three candidates arrived, John opened his desk drawer, and took out three magic blocks. The solid cube had six equal square sides and each side was already changed from Its original solid color to a mosaic color. John gave each candidate a cube and asked each of them to return the next morning with one single color on each side. I was so attracted by this kind of interview that I invited myself to be with them early the next morning. Right on time, the three candidates reported to John's office and all had completed their assignments. Mr. Wang said it took him more than six hours, with the help of family members to get the solid color back to each side. Mr. Li said it took him one hour; he bought fresh paints and colored each side. Mr. Zhang said it took him ten minutes; he went next door and bought a magic block. Now, John announced his decision: all you three are hired, Mr. Wang to the accounting office, Mr. Li to the sales department, and Mr. Zhang to the public relations department. Yes, each one of you has your own talent; that special talent will lead you to success only if you dare to use it.

Later That morning when I arrived to the airport, it was 5 minutes too late to catch my shuttle flight from New York to Washington. There was 55 minutes to wait for the next flight. So, I bought a pack containing six cheese crackers from the coin machine, left my briefcase on an empty seat and went for a cup of coffee. When I returned to my seat with coffee, I was surprised to see that the lady in the next seat was holding my crackers in her hands and trying to open the pack. To be polite, I said to her that the coin machine sells many kinds of goodies. She gave me a half smiling look and continued her examination. I took the pack from her hands and opened the package with ease. Before I knew it, she started to eat the first cracker. It was very unusual under such circumstances. However, I did not say anything but quickly took the second cracker for myself. Surprisingly, she soon took the third, and the fourth, and I rushed to get the last two crackers into my mouth. Before long, she went to board her plane without a word of thanks. I was surprised about the happenings and got on board myself. When I arrived in Washington and returned to my office, my secretary was waiting and ready to type the meeting notes. As I opened my briefcase to get the material, I was so shocked and stood there speechless. I found a pack of cheese crackers in my own briefcase! All the time in the airport it never occurred to my mind that the pack of crackers she held in her hands might not be mine! It irritated me that she took my crackers, and that I fought to eat the crackers which belonged to her! This experience taught me a valuable lesson, which I now pass on to you: Do not under any circumstances insist that you are 100 percent correct and others are wrong. Challenge yourself all the time.

Since we started with CAU and Einstein, let me complete my story with CAU and Einstein. On the occasion of Einstein's seventy's birthday many scholars and friends at Princeton University planned to give him a big celebration party, but thay had difficulty in selecting a suitable gift that would please him. Einstein's secretary suggested that it would be best to select something the professor could talk to, or even better, debate with. They searched all over the world and found an intelligent parrot that could speak English, and when in good mood, even speak German. Every one was so pleased with this parrot, especially the professor himself. At the end of the party, Einstein carried the caged parrot home while walking and dancing all the way, but the bird seemed to pay little attention. As soon as they arrived into his study, Einstein immediately tried to interest the bird by telling old German jokes and singing old German songs. But the bird was obviously not impressed and did not speak or do anything. Einstein then got out his treasured violin and played for the bird, but the bird only looked at him, silently. By now Einstein was frustrated and tired. He took a chair and sat himself down, ready to rest a few minutes. As Einstein was almost closing his eyes, suddenly the parrot said, in English: "Professor, is that all you can do?" That bird brought Einstein down to reality!

I challenge you, young friends, if a bird can challenge a giant like Einstein, why can not you challenge any academic giant? This year, 2005, Einstein had passed us, but not his wisdom. Some scholars even considered Einstein a 'relic' by the time he moved to Princeton in the 1930s. However, the laws of physics, even today, have yet to be unified.

Here the similarity ends between China Agricultural University and Einstein. Einstein is an absolute immortal; he was the greatest genius in the history of the world for science, but only for a while. For China Agricultural University, one hundred years is only its beginning. CAU can, and CAU must continue to grow, to elevate, to face the challenge, and to achieve the excellence of science by answering hard questions.

Yes, CAU is to spread the seeds of wisdom for generations to come. You, and only you, have to pass the torch to others.

Appendix C. Xinjiang: The California of China
(From Chapter 7 by T.C. Tso, "Dare to Dream: Vision of 2050 Agriculture in China", edited by T.C. Tso and He Kang, published by the China Agricultural University Press, Beijing, China, 2004.)

Xinjiang: The California of China

Geographically, Xinjiang holds a strategic location. It connects eight countries and is the center of the Central Asia and Asia-Pacific economic zone. It is a bridge between Europe and Asia. It is China's gateway to western Asia, a trading harbor without an ocean. Because Xinjiang is the farthest border region and is inhabited by multiple ethnic groups, it requires special strategic commitment for fast economic growth and social stability. With the proper incentives, its rich resources and vitality, it could easily attract talent and investment.

There are four keys for Xinjiang development, with water being the utmost important of all:

Water (both conservation and exploitation of new resources);

Science and technology, including investments in cultivating and maintaining human talent;

Policies that create favorable conditions to attract mass migration, land development and investment for industrial development;

Infrastructure.

Water

Water is life in Xinjiang. With water, Xinjiang will become the treasure of China. Without water, Xinjiang will be the sorrow of China. An example of a successful water development project in China West is the so-called 'one Jiang and two rivers' project in Tibet. This is an engineering effort to tame and manage the waters of the Yarloungzungbo (YLZB) Jiang, Lassa He and Lianchu He rivers. It has resulted in flourishing agriculture and animal populations, economic growth, areas reclaimed from desertification, reforestation and in turn improved social stability.

Following on this success, three immediate water-related tasks can be envisioned:

* improve water-use efficiency, by adopting new water-saving technologies and developing locally suitable systems;
* complete four existing major water engineering projects to meet urgent needs of conservation and diversion;
* release Bosten Reservoir water for the lower reaches of the Tarim River.

For the longer term, there are also three tasks:

* develop a master plan to retain runoff waters and to avoid seasonal supply and demand imbalances;
* develop a comprehensive scientific management system for land and water usage, soil conservation, forestry, ecosystem and environment;
* vigorously promote water diversion plans, within Xinjiang as well as beyond its borders using southwest water resources (the Great West water diversion plan).

Human Talent, Science and Technology

Xinjiang, because of its local characteristics and special needs, must cultivate and retain human talent for its own development and maintain front-line science and technology capacity. Building this will be a time-consuming process however, starting with education. National and international cooperation are needed to achieve several goals:

* establish a national scientific center of excellence;
* build consortiums of higher education in science and technology (foreign and domestic);

* create and perfect educational systems, especially in higher agricultural and mechanical sciences, promoting distance education (foreign and domestic).

Policy

Policies must aim at creating favorable conditions to attract international talent, investment and cooperation. Learning from experiences in the development of the American West, it was the Homestead Act that provided favorable conditions for mass migration. Xinjiang has great potential for water resources development alongside 8 million hectares of arable land and 47 million hectares of pasture not in use. These resources could attract pioneers to Xinjiang for permanent residence and entrepreneurship if the conditions are right. The region has the capacity to house 8 to 10 million people working in agriculture and animal husbandry. It could also provide job opportunities for industrial and service development.

Spurring such a large-scale migration, admittedly, is a sensitive issue among many scholars and some international organizations. They either blindly oppose such undertakings or hesitate to touch on the true issue. Their concerns are justified if migration could result in destruction of peoples' cultures or livelihoods, in which case it would be construed as a form of invasion or occupation, or an act of displacement of a region's native inhabitants. In the case of developing the American West-and of Xinjiang-the aim of large-scale migration was to develop natural resources and make use of lands that otherwise would be lost. Such migration should be encouraged. However, any migration should be in harmony with the environment and in concert with local residents and minorities. This can be achieved by involving the native inhabitants in shaping the master plan, as well as by offering them a first refusal right of relocation.

Favorable conditions could also stimulate financial inputs, from within as well as outside of China, public and private. For example, it is not wise to further develop industry in the east, as it would occupy China's most fertile lands. There is plenty of non-arable land in the vast China West. Favorable policy can bring industry to the West, also bringing jobs and better use (higher value) of agricultural products, resulting in stronger economic growth. Long-term policy must consider the sustainability of growth and continued financial returns. In addition, it must clarify rules. For example,

* do not bring land into production under irrigation without measures to control salinity and related problems;
* do launch a long-term collaborative effort to establish an integrated plan;
* do build the infrastructure to support the implementation of the plan before initiating any specific projects.

Infrastructure

Infrastructure is not only airports, railroads, highways and information. It also encompasses means for development of human and natural resource potentials:

* development and management of water resources;
* inventory and characterization of soil resources;
* monitoring and assessment of potential environmental impacts;
* establishing appropriate and sustainable agricultural enterprises;
* education, research and outreach/extension programs in support of production, processing and marketing.

Appendix D. Map of China